CONFLICT IN EARLY STUART ENGLAND

Conflict in Early Stuart England

Studies in Religion and Politics 1603–1642

Edited by Richard Cust and Ann Hughes

Longman
London and New York

Longman Group UK Limited,
Longman House, Burnt Mill, Harlow,
Essex CM20 2JE, England
and Associated Companies throughout the world;

Published in the United States of America
by Longman Inc., New York

First published 1989

British Library Cataloguing in Publication Data

Conflict in early Stuart England: Studies
   in religion and politics 1603–1642.
   1. England, Political events, 1603–1649
   I. Cust, Richard   II. Hughes, Ann
   942.06'1
ISBN 0-582-03450-7 CSD
ISBN 0-582-30173-4 PPR

Library of Congress Cataloging-in-Publication Data

Conflict in early Stuart England: studies in religion and politics,
1603–1642/edited by Richard Cust and Ann Hughes.
      p.   cm.
   Bibliography: p.
   Includes index.
   ISBN 0-582-03450-7. ISBN 0-582-30173-4 (U.S.: pbk.)
   1. Great Britain——History——Early Stuarts, 1603–1649   I. Cust,
Richard.   II. Hughes, Ann.
DA390.C66 1989
941.06——dc19

Set in Linotron 202 10/12 Baskerville
Produced by Longman Singapore Publishers (Pte) Ltd.
Printed in Singapore

Contents

List of Abbreviations

Place of publication is London unless otherwise stated.

Add.MS	Additional Manuscript, British Library
APC	*Acts of the Privy Council*
BL	British Library
BRO	Berkshire Record Office
Bodl.L	Bodleian Library, Oxford
BIHR	*Bulletin of the Institute of Historical Research*
Chamberlain	*The Letters of John Chamberlain*, N. E. McLure (ed.), 2 vols (Philadelphia, 1939)
CD 1621	*Commons Debates in 1621*, 7 vols, W. Notestein, F. H. Relf and H. Simpson (eds), (New Haven, 1935)
CD 1625	*Debates in the House of Commons in 1625*, S. R. Gardiner (ed.) (Camden Soc., new ser., vi, 1873)
CD 1629	*Commons Debates for 1629*, W. Notestein and F. H. Relf (eds) (Minneapolis, 1921)
CJ	*Commons' Journals*
CSPD	*Calendar of State Papers Domestic*
CSP Ven.	*Calendar of State Papers Venetian*
C and T, Jas 1	*Court and Times of James 1*, T. Birch (ed.), 2 vols (1848)
C and T, Chas 1	*Court and Times of Charles 1*, T. Birch (ed.), 2 vols (1848)
DNB	*Dictionary of National Biography*
Ec.HR	*Economic History Review*
Eg.MS	Egerton Manuscript, British Library

EHR	*English Historical Review*
FSL	Folger Shakespeare Library, Washington
Gardiner, *History*	S. R. Gardiner, *The History of England 1603–42*, 10 vols (1883–84)
HLRO	House of Lords Record Office
Harl.MS	Harleian Manuscript, British Library
Hist.	*History*
HJ	*Historical Journal*
HMC	Historical Manuscripts Commission
Holles	*The Letters of John Holles 1587–1637*, P. R. Seddon (ed.), (Thoroton Soc. Rec. Ser., xxxi, xxxv, xxxvi, 1975–87)
HR	*Historical Research*
JBS	*Journal of British Studies*
JEH	*Journal of Ecclesiastical History*
JMH	*Journal of Modern History*
KAO	Kent Archives Office
Laud	W. Laud, *The Works*, 6 vols (Oxford, 1853)
MH	*Midland History*
Neg.Post.	*An Apology for Socrates and Negotium Posterorum by Sir John Eliot*, A. B. Grosart (ed.) (1881)
NH	*Northern History*
NLW	National Library of Wales
NRO	Northamptonshire Record Office
P&P	*Past and Present*
PD 1610	*Parliamentary Debates in 1610*, S. R. Gardiner (ed.) (Camden Soc., old ser., lxxxi, 1862)
P in P 1610	*Proceedings in Parliament 1610*, E. R. Foster (ed.), 2 vols (New Haven, 1966)
P in P 1628	*Proceedings in Parliament 1628*, R. C. Johnson, M. F. Keeler *et al.* (eds), 6 vols (New Haven, 1977–83)
Proclamations	*Stuart Royal Proclamations*, P. L. Hughes and J. F. Larkin (eds), 2 vols (Oxford, 1973–83)
PRO	Public Record Office
Rushworth	J. Rushworth, *Historical Collections*, 7 vols (1659–1701)
Rymer	T. Rymer, *Foedera*, 20 vols (1704–35)
SRO	Somerset Record Office
Scrin.Res.	*Scrinia Reserata: A Memorial offr'd to the great deservings of John Williams D.D.*, John Hacket, 2 parts (1692–93)

SP	State Papers
ST	*State Trials*, W. Cobbett and T. B. Howell (eds), 33 vols (1809–26). References are to column numbers.
Strafforde Letters	*The Earl of Strafforde's Letters and Dispatches*, W. Knowler (ed.), 2 vols (1729)
THES	*Times Higher Education Supplement*
TLS	*Times Literary Supplement*
TRHS	*Transactions of the Royal Historical Society*
Wentworth Papers	*The Wentworth Papers 1597–1628*, J. P. Cooper (ed.) (Camden Soc., 4th ser., xii, 1973)
VCH	*Victoria County History*
Yale Univ.	Yale University, Beinecke Collection

Dates are old style unless otherwise stated, except that the year is taken to begin on 1 January.

Preface

The editors are grateful to Christopher Hill and Conrad Russell whose work has always convinced us that this period is worth studying and who have both helped practically in the completion of this volume. Christopher Hill helped persuade us that such a collection would be useful, and Conrad Russell invited many of the contributors to read drafts of their papers at the seminar he runs with his colleagues at London University's Institute of Historical Research. We all gained immensely from the stimulating and open-minded criticisms of our papers, not least those of Professor Russell himself.

We take full responsibility for the views contained in the Introduction, although the volume as a whole was designed and executed as a co-operative enterprise; it has developed from discussions amongst friends over several years. The Introduction and the essays have been subject to criticism and suggestion by all the contributors and we have all benefited from this. The editors are grateful to the other authors for their cheerful co-operation in a sometimes lengthy process of discussion and revision. The contributors are not, of course, in complete agreement over the nature of developments in early-seventeenth-century England but in many ways our views and approaches are similar. We hope the collection provides a coherent picture of politics and religion before the Civil War. We have enjoyed producing it.

Richard Cust and Ann Hughes
December 1987

1 Introduction: after Revisionism

Richard Cust and Ann Hughes

I

The English Civil War once had a prime place in an account of Britain's (or rather England's) history as a linear progression towards liberal democracy, religious toleration and world leadership. As recently as the 1960s many historians accepted some version of a 'progressive' interpretation, whether liberal or Marxist in tone. The Civil War was an important event, with long-term causes, social or political, and it had a significant impact on England's later political and economic development. Recently it has been eloquently shown that this framework for the past has crumbled as confidence in Britain's development and in ideas of progress themselves have disappeared.[1] The view of the Civil War as a progressive landmark is particularly vulnerable because it seems an embarrassing exception to the dominant view of England's development whereby change occurs through gradual and consensual mechanisms. Englishmen being engaged in armed struggle over differences of principle was not a phenomenon which fitted easily with this cosy picture. We live now in less hopeful times, when collective social and political action is widely seen as both futile and 'extremist'. It is perhaps unsurprising that many historians now portray the Civil War as a confused and 'accidental' conflict with mainly short-term and 'contingent' causes; and also see it as a largely futile conflict which did little to alter the broad contours of English development. England, it has been alleged, remained an *ancien régime* state, dominated by divine-right monarchy, the established Church and the landed aristocracy until 1832.[2]

1

We do not wish to add to the many comprehensive discussions of the historiography of the Civil War already available, but merely to sketch out the broad lines of recent debate so as to specify the contribution we hope to make in this volume.[3] What follows does not do justice to the subtlety of the debate but is intended as a broad account of the main arguments. For the 'Whig' historians, working within a liberal tradition, the Civil War was a constitutional and political struggle between authoritarian, arbitrary monarchy and the rule of law, the property rights and liberties (or even the 'liberty' in some modern sense) of individuals. An 'opposition' based particularly in the House of Commons stood for laws and liberties, and also for a staunch English Protestantism against the superstitious, unpatriotic, near popish religious tendencies espoused by Charles I. In complex and unintended ways this religious struggle paved the way for the toleration of a diversity of Protestant worship. The reckoning of 1642 was the culmination of a long period of increasing tension from the last years of Elizabeth, when the Queen's political skills deserted her, to the 'eleven years' tyranny' of Charles I.

Classic Marxist accounts of political developments are often similar, if less approving, but this 'superstructure' is given a material base in the nature of economic developments and class relationships in England. The Civil War thus becomes in some sense a 'bourgeois revolution', a crucial step in England's transition from a traditional 'feudal' to a modern 'capitalist' society. It is linked to the emergence of a new class, made up in some versions of new men, in others of transformed sections of earlier élites. This was a capitalist class concerned to maximize its profits from agriculture, and involved in industry and trade. For this group the royal government was a 'feudal' barrier to its economic advance – through its pusillanimous foreign policy, its hamfisted attempts at social regulation of enclosure, and its unpredictable and arbitrary interference in private property. Through the Civil War this emerging capitalist class secured a political system that protected their interests. In recent years, it must be admitted, this bourgeoisie has been less prominent in Marxist-influenced interpretations. An understandable disillusion with the hard-faced men who did well out of the war, and the apparent elusiveness of a future transition from capitalism to socialism in Britain, have prompted an examination of the 'middling sort' – always an important element in the emerging bourgeoisie – and of poorer groups, along with the more dramatic if unsuccessful radical movements of the 1640s and 1650s.[4] For good or ill, however, most Marxists and the mainly American heirs of the Whigs continue to see the Civil War, with its epilogue in 1688–89, as a crucial stage in England's development as a constitutional monarchy and a market economy.

Both versions of the progressive interpretation have been subjected to a formidable 'revisionist' assault in recent years. The origins of this are very diverse. They include the critique of Tawney's thesis on the 'rise of the gentry' by Cooper, Hexter, Trevor-Roper and others; Everitt's work on 'county communities', stressing the importance of local loyalties and the harmony within local society; Ball's and Barnes' work on Sir John Eliot and Sir Robert Phelips showing that such MPs do not fit easily into models of conflict based on 'court' *v.* 'country' or government *v.* opposition; and Elton's challenge to one of the accepted milestones on 'the High Road to Civil War', the Commons' Apology of 1604. Several of these threads were drawn together in Russell's introduction to *The Origins of the English Civil War*, with its argument that this was 'an accidental war', arising out of 'a state of chronic misunderstanding, terror and distrust'.[5] This view has crucially influenced the work of, amongst others, John Morrill, Mark Kishlansky and Kevin Sharpe.[6] These historians do not necessarily accept that they form a 'revisionist' school, and they differ in their positive interpretations of the early seventeenth century. Nevertheless it is possible to trace certain common themes and similarities, particularly in their criticisms of earlier work.

They are generally united in their rejection of Marxist interpretations. In fact these have received relatively little in the way of detailed consideration, but, for reasons which will be discussed below, it has been possible to dismiss attempts to link the political conflict with processes of social change. The developments highlighted by Marxists are regarded as illusory, ambiguous or irrelevant, and at best as unproven assertions. Their efforts to trace long-term causes for the Civil War, rooted in economic and social shifts, have generally been rejected as deterministic or based on hindsight. And the designation of the resistance to the monarchy as 'progressive' by both Whigs and Marxists is also discarded. In some versions it is the monarchy which is innovative as kings, especially Charles I, sought to maximize their resources, evade the limitations of an obstructive Parliament and make an impact on European affairs. It was the Crown's opponents, especially in the House of Commons, who were 'conservative', stubbornly clinging to outmoded customs and rights. In other revisionist writing the progressive-conservative split is meaningless, partly because seventeenth-century ideas did not include a view of progress or willed forward-looking change, but also because the ideological divide implied in such a split did not exist.

This last point is amongst the most fundamental made by the revisionists. In place of the sharp and increasing political and religious divisions perceived by earlier writers, revisionists posit a fundamental ideological consensus: a political consensus which survived to the eve of the Civil War and religious unity which lasted until the accession of Charles I. In political terms, it is argued, there was general agreement that kings ruled with divine approval, should take the advice of leading men through their council and meet with Parliaments whose role was generally subordinate and focused on the provision of finance, advice and information. As well as agreement on the structure of the political system there was a wide degree of unity on how it should function. Division and conflict were almost universally seen as illegitimate and abhorrent. Since only the king could form a government and make decisions on high policy there was no place for the existence of 'an opposition' in the modern sense of the term. Political parties and 'adversary politics' were widely regarded as factious and divisive. The first duty of all participants in the political process was to strive for unity and harmony. Thus debate and procedure in the House of Commons were designed to secure consensus and agreement; and MPs saw themselves as constructive critics rather than opponents of royal policies. Conflicts occurred, but, it is argued, they do not reflect any straightforward division between government and opposition or 'court' and 'country'. For the government itself included those advocating a forward Protestant foreign policy and rule in partnership with Parliament; and clashes in Parliament in the early seventeenth century, as in the late sixteenth, were often a by-product of rivalries and divisions within the council and the court.[7]

In keeping with these views revisionists also reject the Whig notion that conflict arose because Parliament, and in particular the Commons, was becoming stronger and more assertive. The Commons' 'winning of the initiative' over legislation has been shown to have been less significant than Notestein supposed because in this period the Crown had little wish to legislate on matters of major political significance. In general the Commons sought to avoid responsibilities rather than assume them. Parliament, Russell argues, remained an event rather than an institution, dependent on the whim of the monarch for its existence and made up for the most part of MPs who had no wish to see it become a permanent arm of government. These were conservative men, whose local interests took priority over more general concerns and who had no real understanding of the legitimate financial needs of the monarchy. Their refusal to provide kings with an adequate revenue made it increasingly counter-productive for monarchs to work with parliaments. And their inability to use successfully the weapon of supply to obtain concessions brought a very real threat of Parliament's extinction by the late 1620s. In any case, revisionists argue, the Whigs placed too much emphasis on the Commons. The crucial political actors in an hierarchical, deferential society were to be found mainly in the House of Lords, in the council and at court.[8]

The stress on hierarchy and deference has also done much to shape the revisionists' view of local politics. Whigs and Marxists tended to ignore this or to assume that local people shared the concerns and attitudes of those at Westminster. Revisionists have emphasized the divergence of local and national. Following Everitt they see local society as basically settled and harmonious, with vertical links binding together the different social groupings and a general acceptance of the authority and leadership of the gentry. Thus Kishlansky has stressed that parliamentary elections in this period were more akin to selections, with the ordinary freeholders doing little more than give their assent to candidates presented to them by the leading gentry. Most members of local society are seen as having little understanding or knowledge of national issues and events. Their first concern was with local matters and their first loyalty to their locality, often described as their 'county community'. Consequently revisionists place considerable emphasis on what they see as more or less continual friction between the centre and the localities. The central government in this period was forever making demands and imposing burdens which the localities did their best to withstand.[9]

The traditional picture of religious developments from the 1590s to the 1630s has also been challenged. Where earlier historians saw an Anglican establishment challenged by a Puritan opposition, recent work presents a less clear-cut spectrum of Protestant opinion. The dominant trend is to emphasize matters uniting English Protestants rather than the issues on which they were divided. From the Elizabethan settlement to the period of William Laud's ascendancy most educated English Protestants were

5

Calvinist in their theology; after the decisive defeat of the Presbyterian campaign in Elizabeth's reign, most were Episcopalian in
their ecclesiology. They hated popery and supported the preaching
of the word. There were, of course, as in politics, differences of
emphasis over the need for further reformation, for example,
or on the question of conformity to contested ceremonial; but
Puritans, it is argued, did not form an alienated opposition. Rather
they were the most enthusiastic, the 'hotter sort', of Protestants.
Many of their ideas and initiatives were aimed at establishing a
more secure, morally reformed social order; their allies included
central Elizabethan figures like Burghley and Leicester; and there
was sympathy for much of their stance amongst Stuart councillors
and members of the ecclesiastical hierarchy, not least from James'
Archbishop, George Abbot. In this account it is not Puritanism
but the rise of Arminianism under Charles and Laud from the
mid-1620s which caused a decisive split in English Protestantism.
Arminianism was a theologically innovative challenge to Calvinist
certainties; it was aggressively conformist and hierarchical, and in
its concern for the sacraments, for ceremonial, and for the status
of the clergy, was easily seen as the harbinger of a return to
popery.[10]

In many revisionist explanations of the breakdown in England
the 'contingent fact' or accident of Charles' promotion of Arminianism is an important element.[11] However, there are several
variations in these explanations. One recent tendency holds that the
religious developments of the 1630s had much continuity with the
earlier conformist position of the Elizabethan Archbishops Whitgift
and Bancroft. They were concerned mainly with order and good
government in the Church and represented a relatively moderate
'Anglican' mainstream struggling against Puritan radicalism.[12] A
more sweeping and contradictory revisionist account bases its
analysis of early-seventeenth-century developments on the work of
those Reformation historians who stress the vitality of, and popular
support for, the later medieval Church. In this framework, the
bulk of the population was only converted to Protestantism reluctantly and slowly. By the seventeenth century there was popular
adherence to Protestantism, but it was adherence to an easy-going
'prayer book' Protestantism with a regular pattern of worship
through the year, and an element of ceremony and communal
parochial festivity. The Puritans were unpopular, over-demanding
kill-joys who terrified most people with their sermons about sin
and damnation and set neighbour against neighbour with their

moralistic prying. On this view Puritanism was not necessarily subversive of monarchical authority; it was an élitist, minority movement, subversive of ideals of good neighbourhood and of settled social relationships.[13] This casts a different light on the alternatives to Puritanism. Dr Haigh and Dr Sharpe would argue that by comparison Laudianism had considerable popular appeal, with its modification of Calvinist predestinarianism, its emphasis on ceremonial and its promotion of 'lawful recreations'. On the other hand Dr Morrill would see the Laudians as yet another unpopular minority, with an overly intrusive, expensive and divisive programme which was rejected in 1641–42 when it became apparent that a pre-Laudian moderately episcopal, moderately ceremonial church had wide appeal. In this account the Civil War was brought about by small minorities of extremists: the Laudians with their clerical pretensions and near papist practices provoking the Puritans into a godly crusade of reformation.[14] Both groups were alien to the moderate good sense of most English parishioners.

This reference to the way in which some revisionists account for the outbreak of Civil War leads us on to examining their positive contributions to understanding divisions in early Stuart England. Religious conflict in a variety of guises is part of their explanation but other elements are also important. If social change cannot explain political conflict, if there was a broad ideological consensus on what the English government system was, and how it should operate, if Parliament was an ineffective body, how can revisionists explain the conflicts between Crown and subject? For the 1620s especially, Russell has emphasized the long-term structural weaknesses in the bureaucratic and financial resources of the Crown which foreign war brought to the point of 'functional' breakdown. He stresses the effects of inflation which during the early seventeenth century steadily eroded the Crown's traditional sources of revenue: Crown lands, customs, feudal dues and subsidies. One consequence was that it was unable to provide adequate salaries for its leading officials. It therefore had little alternative but to allow them to reward themselves by taking a rake-off from the revenues they received. This further diminished the traditional royal revenues and in the process generated political resentment. At the same time the unpaid local élites on whose co-operation the Crown depended to govern and collect taxes were allowed to underassess themselves and their neighbours with the result that parliamentary subsidies were worth much less than under Elizabeth. So direct taxation could not compensate for the Crown's difficulties elsewhere. These fundamental weaknesses were exacerbated by the growing scale and sophistication of warfare and the reluctance of MPs to meet, or even comprehend, the costs of an aggressive foreign policy. Russell thus argues that by the 1620s the English monarch could fight an effective war only by drastically curtailing the autonomy of the localities and offending traditional constitutional proprieties. External war is seen as a crucial generator of internal tensions. Consequently, it is argued, there is no linear process of steadily increasing division until 1642. The early 1630s, with external peace and no parliaments as arenas for mischief-making, were more tranquil than the 1620s or another war-torn decade, the 1590s.[15]

Russell's work has tended to dominate accounts of the 1620s, but other aspects have also been emphasized. Sharpe, for example, stresses the 'crisis of counsel' which occurred when Buckingham was firmly installed as first minister in Charles' reign; and Tyacke and Collinson have pointed to the political consequences of Charles and Buckingham's support for Arminianism, something which Russell also incorporates into his account.[16] By and large, however, there has been substantial agreement amongst revisionists on how to explain the problems of the 1620s. This has not been the case with accounts of the outbreak of the Civil War.

To some extent similar structural factors are emphasized, particularly Charles' inability to fight the Scots without capitulating to those, including members of his own council, who wanted him to call and co-operate with a Parliament. The structural weaknesses of the English Crown, faced with the consequences of the 'military revolution', were far from unique and so the Civil War can be seen as an example of a European-wide phenomenon of tensions between aggressive monarchs and obstructive subjects. Another aspect of Charles' situation, his rule over multiple kingdoms, can also be assimilated to a general European problem, seen most starkly in the Spanish monarchy. The European comparison serves to undermine further Whig and Marxist views which both stress the 'peculiarity' or 'precosity' of the English. That Charles was a *British* monarch is seen as contributing in a variety of ways to the *English* Civil War. One early version in Russell's 'Parliamentary history in perspective' seems to see the Scots' intervention as a *deus ex machina*, an almost unconnected outside blow, which created a crisis which could not have been generated from within England. In a parallel process it is only Dutch intervention in 1688–89 that can account for a later political upheaval in England. More recently Russell sees the British dimension, combined with the diverse religious affiliations of Charles' three kingdoms, driving the King almost inevitably into conflict with important groups of his subjects and fatally limiting his freedom of action once conflict had occurred. It was his duty to secure religious uniformity which drove Charles into confrontation with the Scots, but it was his role as King of Catholic Ireland which in part prevented him from agreeing to a religious settlement which would satisfy English anti-papists.[17]

We have already touched on the religious explanation of 1642, most forcefully argued by John Morrill who writes that, 'The English Civil War was not the first European revolution: it was the last of the wars of religion', brought about mainly by a small band of Puritan extremists seeking godly reformation.[18] The most elaborate analyses, however, are those of Russell and Anthony Fletcher. Fletcher's monumental narrative of November 1640–August 1642 cannot easily be assimilated into a revisionist or anti-revisionist stance. However it includes some affinities with revisionist interpretations, partly in its very structure which implies that the outbreak of war can be explained through a detailed narrative of a period of less than two years: 'great events', Fletcher writes, 'do not necessarily have great causes'. A settlement was widely expected and hoped for on the meeting of the Long Parliament, and Fletcher argues that the eventual breakdown came about through rising mutual misunderstanding generated by the rival conspiracy theories held by the King and his associates on the one hand, and by Pym and his allies on the other.[19] This view has some similarities with the account of the war as caused by small minorities of extremists, but can be connected also with a wider-ranging and more long-term analysis as we shall indicate below.

Russell's explanations have also concentrated on the period from the meeting of the Long Parliament, and have focused on the high politics of relationships between the King and crucial parliamentary leaders such as Bedford, Saye, Warwick, Pym and St John. Unlike most MPs, this group had positive aspirations to change (or restore) the direction of the government. They wanted to offer the King an adequate financial settlement on a parliamentary foundation, and to secure English Protestantism, while success would be guaranteed by themselves taking office under the Crown. Such a settlement failed in 1641–42 for a variety of short-term reasons: personal mistrust between the King and his opponents, particularly after the death of Bedford, a promising mediator, in May 1641; the reluctance of most of the House of Commons to underwrite the necessary financial settlement; and increasing divisions over how to reform or replace the Laudian church.[20] In his most recent work Russell has looked more precisely at the outbreak of *war* rather than the failure of *settlement* and suggests that it is more fruitful to examine why Charles sought war than to see armed conflict as originating from Parliament. The early seventeenth century was a 'good period for gentry and a bad period for kings' and so Charles had the more reason to fight. In the 1620s Charles had been willing to work with parliaments but he had been disillusioned by their persistent and illegitimate attempts to deprive him of Buckingham, his closest adviser and favourite; and particularly by the approach of the Commons to war and finance.

In 1624 the Commons had enthusiastically endorsed a war to recover the Palatinate and had then refused to pay for it. They consistently denied the King an adequate legal revenue by their reluctance to vote subsidies, their attacks on monopolies and impositions, and their refusal to grant tonnage and poundage; yet the Commons also fanned opposition to the illegal or quasi-legal financial expedients he had to adopt. Financial weakness, coupled with the inter-related problems of multiple kingdoms and religious division, forced Charles to call the Long Parliament and to accede to the demands of its leaders, but he was at the same time waiting for an opportunity to gather a party and restore his position, through armed force if necessary. From the Army Plot of April–May 1641 to the raising of his standard at Nottingham in August 1642, it was the King who made the military running. The leaders in Parliament, however, could count on broad support in 1640 because of Charles' religious policies and his general political incompetence and untrustworthiness. Their aim was to treat Charles 'as if he were a minor, a captive or insane' and to 'impersonalize royal authority' by delegating it to a council and great officers nominated in and answerable to Parliament. This strategy depended on unity for its success as Charles depended on the growth of division: Parliament's strategy was also one with 'precedents going back at least to Simon de Montfort'.[21] This view – that the English Civil War is very like several medieval conflicts – serves, like the comparison with contemporaneous European events, as a challenge to Whig and Marxist claims for the distinctively 'modern' nature of the Civil War.

II

No single positive account of the origins of the Civil War has emerged from revisionist works. The historians we have been discussing would not see this as a failing. They do not regard themselves as a school which ought to present one 'line'. Their initial aim has been to question earlier views and to re-open discussion in areas where 'Whig' and 'Marxist' historians tended to assume that matters had long since been settled. The work of Russell in particular has done much to redirect attention to the structural problems faced by English monarchs: the effects of inflation on crown finances, the consequences of the 'military revolution' for relations between centre and localities, the English monarchy's difficulties in ruling over multiple kingdoms and the legacy of the Reformation in circumstances where contemporaries attached much importance to religious uniformity. Revisionist emphasis on the strength of hierarchy and the desire to maintain unity has led to a much more critical assessment of the application of political ideas. The recognition that Parliament was operating within a political system centred on the court, and that many MPs were responsive to local concerns, has broadened understanding of parliamentary events. Above all revisionists have directed attention back to investigating the actions of individuals in their immediate political and ideological context and have shown that there is a need to go beyond S. R. Gardiner and establish a new narrative of central events. These new perspectives have been immensely stimulating. Rather than simply accepting that conflict and breakdown were inevitable, historians are now being asked to think afresh about their explanations for this. However when it comes to providing these explanations revisionists have been less successful. In particular there are inconsistencies in their account of the origins of the Civil War which have never been adequately resolved.

On the broad characterization of the war, Russell's European comparisons are challenged by John Morrill's view that the Civil War was distinctive because it emerged in a better integrated, 'stronger' political system.[22] In Russell's work, parliaments are usually seen as weak and declining bodies yet they are also capable of causing the monarch serious difficulties. Charles himself is portrayed in a variety of ways. In Russell's account of the 1620s his stance is seen as moderate and reasonable, a picture that Kevin Sharpe at least has extended into the 1630s.[23] By 1642, however, Russell's Charles I has a much greater resemblance to the popular historical image of an untrustworthy king who was both aggressive and ineffectual. There is also a sharp divergence of views over Buckingham. Lockyer and, to some extent, Russell stress that he was the undeserving victim of court conspiracies and jealousy; Sharpe sees his ascendancy as reflecting a 'crisis of counsel'.[24] And while revisionists agree that there was a broad degree of consensus on what the 'constitution' was, they do not agree on the content of this consensus; Sharpe and Morrill, for example, holding that the royal prerogatives were a good deal more extensive than is suggested by Elton.[25] Revisionist inconsistency is seen most clearly in their accounts of religious developments. Puritans have been seen both as a minority of aggressive busy-bodies, and as part of a broad and roughly united spectrum of Protestant opinion. Arminianism in turn is presented as a bolt from the blue which shattered this broad consensus, but its continuity with earlier conformist views has also been stressed. No revisionist work has explicitly addressed these contrasts. In Russell's examination of the problems of religious divisions in the multiple kingdoms of England, Scotland and Ireland, Charles' attempt to impose religious uniformity between England and Scotland, and his reluctance to impose it on Catholics in Ireland are both implicitly accepted as justified.[26] Finally the parliamentarian and the royalist causes are both described in radically different ways. Parliament's supporters are both dogged conservative defenders of traditional rights and irrational extremists driven by millenial exaltation. Royalists are men whose legalism and constitutionalism, affronted by Parliament's excesses, leads them to support an untrustworthy, near-megalomaniac leader.[27] While accepting that both sides in the Civil War were coalitions, the distinctions between religion and politics, or between radicals and moderates, here implied, are surely too sharp to be plausible.

Revisionists have prided themselves on their detailed attention to the sources and on the care with which they have avoided the distortions of hindsight. Nonetheless, they can sometimes be challenged on their use of sources. There are examples in the chapters in this volume by Sommerville and Thompson (Chs 2 and 6) of occasions where a greater sensitivity to context leads to the drawing of different conclusions. Our dissent from revisionist approaches to sources is not merely on technical grounds, however, for we believe their attitudes are sometimes over-literal and unduly narrow. There is often a preoccupation with manuscript sources as if printed material was *ipso facto* tainted, usually in some ill-defined way. Retrospective accounts are frequently rejected as inevitably and irretrievably biased by hindsight and special pleading.[28] This means they sacrifice the valuable insights to be derived from the frameworks in which participants later put their actions; and more straightforwardly they also miss a lot of useful information which can be gleaned once the biases in these retrospective accounts have been allowed for.

Sources are sometimes approached in an over-literal fashion; in particular there is a tendency to argue from silence. If there is no overt and straightforward evidence of ideological conflict or 'opposition' in a particular source, even when it is by no means obvious why such views should be expressed in this context, it is concluded that no ideological stance was present. Insufficient account is taken of what particular sources would be likely to include, or of people's caution in a censored and authoritarian society. The literal approach to sources has been most damaging in the emerging revisionist accounts of the 1630s, where the absence of overt resistance or opposition has led to an overestimation of the stability of Charles' personal rule.[29] Not enough allowance is made for the fear of the consequences of opposition if, for example, imprudent letters were opened by the authorities; or of the fact that the lack of parliaments removed a vital forum for debate. In the absence of parliaments the Privy Council and the court were the principal arenas where grievances could be redressed. As Peter Lake has pointed out in an analysis of ship-money in Cheshire, men who wanted council support in conflicts over ship-money ratings were unlikely to subject Charles and his councillors to a principled constitutional attack on the levy. Private political sources for the 1630s are comparatively rare, and again fear and self-censorship must be important here, but where they do exist they reveal great concern and serious divisions over political and religious developments.[30]

There is also a tendency amongst revisionists to concentrate on the mechanics and the practical functioning of the political system rather than on how people perceived politics. Elton's insistence on studying entities like parliaments through the sources they generated has not been followed in seventeenth-century revisionist work, and indeed has been rejected as a methodology by Russell.[31] But Elton's influence does seem to have produced a narrow focus which tends to stress the more technical aspects of how parliaments, for instance, worked rather than how they were perceived. Thus parliament's journals and the diaries of participants are seen as 'better' sources than those which comment on parliamentary or political affairs such as newsletters or ambassadors' reports. This sort of approach has sometimes obscured the motives and assumptions which prompted individuals to act in the ways they did. For example, revisionists have criticized notions of a 'court-country' split – because as a matter of practical politics many were involved in both the court and the provinces – without making sufficient allowance for the possibility that 'court' and 'country' could operate as an ideological framework within which people viewed politics.[32] Considerable emphasis has also been placed on the effects of inflation and the short-sightedness of MPs in causing financial problems for the Crown. But it is not always recognized that many contemporaries saw the cause of these rather differently. Their perceptions were shaped by a mixture of contemporary moral precepts and classical and medieval precedents. They therefore tended to regard financial difficulties as a consequence of waste, corruption and moral decline; and, as parliaments had done in the past, they came to focus on parasitical courtiers and evil counsellors as the source of the problem.[33] Again Russell refers in his article, 'The nature of a parliament', to Sir John Fortescue who in the fifteenth century, 'began a myth, which has been popular ever since, that there was something especially English about parliaments and estates'. He then points to the inaccuracy of this view – because of the procedural and institutional advantages of several continental estates – but does not stress sufficiently the implications of this patriotic belief in English constitutional superiority for political developments.[34]

However, revisionists do not consistently ignore perceptions of politics, rather they reject some perceptions and take others at face value. There is a particular tendency to take as true some of the more favourable perceptions of Charles and Laud. Thus Russell accepts as accurate Charles' views on parliaments and the financial weakness of the Crown but says little about his fears of popularity, his perception that a popular/Puritan conspiracy aimed at the subversion of the monarchy. Sharpe accepts Laud's and Charles' own account of their programme for the 1630s and can then explain the opposition they aroused only in terms of a 'breakdown in communication' and of arguments over means rather than ends.[35] Many years ago G. R. Elton criticized, 'the coherent explanations of S. R. Gardiner, echoing in reality only the partisan account of the Grand Remonstrance of 1641'.[36] If revisionist historiography has attacked Whig interpretations as parliamentarian, we have come increasingly to regard revisionist accounts as echoes of seventeenth-century royalist views. Their approach has been much influenced by Clarendon's *History of the Great Rebellion* with its emphasis on the short-term causes of the Civil War and contingent events such as the death of the Earl of Bedford. They also reflect less well-known royalist accounts, like that of the historian William Dugdale, writing in the 1680s.[37] For Dugdale the origins of the Civil War lay in the efforts of Anabaptists

> to reduce the king to necessities, and thereby to expose him to the use of such extraordinary ways of supply, as might most conduce to the raising of discontent amongst all his good subjects. Which they did, by engaging first his father in a war for the Palatinate, and their failing to assist him, notwithstanding their most solemn promises,

and then,

> by planting schismatical lectures in most corporate towns and populous places throughout the realm, so to poison the people with anti-monarchical principles.

This view combines Morrill's stress on religious extremism with Conrad Russell's view of the implications of Parliament's activities in the 1620s, although Russell would hardly accept the deliberate intent that Dugdale attributes to MPs. Royalist accounts are also echoed in the emphasis on high politics and the relationships of great men at court as a sufficient explanation of events; and in the rather contradictory stress on the sharp distinctions between central government and local communities.[38] As Hughes shows, this distinction was rarely drawn. When it was, it tended to be royalists who made it in order to limit influence over, or participation in, the processes of government.

III

We can move at last to an indication of the positive aspects of a critique of Revisionism, to how we would interpret the conflicts of early- and mid-seventeenth-century England. We have criticized the sometimes over literal approach revisionist historians have taken to their sources; nonetheless the critique mounted by these scholars has been founded on thorough research, and any response must be equally strongly based. The chapters in this volume try not to engage simply in the counter-assertion which has marked some attacks on revisionism[39]; our intention is to provide an alternative which has a sound empirical basis as well as to challenge revisionist methodologies. All the chapters that follow are thus based on detailed research. Thomas Cogswell and Christopher Thompson (Chs 4 and 6) focus on particular events, but their examinations of the Spanish Match and the 1625 Parliament are developed to illuminate general aspects of the political process. Johann Sommerville, Peter Lake and Ann Hughes (Chs 2, 3 and 8) are concerned to draw out the broader implications of much important recent research, including their own. And Richard Cust and Andrew Foster (Chs 5 and 7) present the results of original research on general topics which have recently been much debated.

Some of the most fruitful and interesting historical research of the past decades has examined the radical groups who emerged in the 1640s and 1650s, rescuing these 'fringe' groups from the condescension of historians. But in the process, historians who do not share revisionist assumptions have often moved away from a close attention to the central, or at least initial conflict between King and Parliament, which was clearly, amongst other things, a split in the ruling élite. We would argue that a challenge to Revisionism must address this central conflict and also take account of the revisionists' insight into some of the structural problems of the English monarchy. Accounts of the English Civil War which do not relate it to the overall 'British' dimension are unsatisfactory, although we would emphasize the ideological, particularly the religious, element in the problems Charles had with his multiple kingdoms rather than seeing the issue merely in a 'functional', practical way. We accept also the revisionist view that it is crucial to examine the court and the peerage as well as the Commons although we do not accept that deference or manipulation provide a convincing explanation of peers' role in politics. We would also agree that an attempt to see the Civil War as a split between progressive and conservative 'forces' is meaningless, although our reasons for rejecting this dichotomy are perhaps different. Both sides in the conflict were grappling with new situations at a time when most commentators understood their problems and sought solutions in terms of precedents, custom and tradition. However this did not imply a real return to a real past. As Sommerville argues in this volume, it was a way of thinking, a habit of mind. Furthermore, as Lake points out here, crucial elements in protestant ideology challenged arguments from mere custom and suggested the need to work for a new and better religious settlement.

Clearly some of the most straightforward 'Whig' assumptions are no longer tenable. There was no simple split between the 'government' and the 'opposition' in early Stuart England; revisionist historians have usefully highlighted the divisions inside the court and the council under James and Charles as well as undermining the notion of the House of Commons as the sole and coherent site of opposition. Neither do we accept the picture of MPs as premature American patriots, defending recognizably modern liberal notions of liberty.[40] We shall argue that there were long-term ideological and social tensions in England but we do not thereby assume that these led inevitably to the type of conflict that emerged in 1642; the moves to war were complex, hesitant and contradictory.

The potential for conflict was there, however. It has become commonplace to emphasize those elements in early Stuart political culture which stressed order, harmony and consensus. Any breach in this stability was consequently attributed to the evil machinations of a conspiratorial minority. Modern historians tend to see these conspiracy theories as irrational as Lake notes in Chapter 3. However an influential current in the social sciences, associated with the structural anthropology of Levi-Strauss, suggests that very many societies have interpreted their world in terms of polarities or pairs of opposites. Far from being irrational this procedure is a crucial and normal means by which the world is described and understood. If we develop this insight it seems that seventeenth-century English people had available several intellectual frameworks within which conflict rather than consensus was normal. Several of these have been described by Stuart Clark and Derek Hirst.[41] The law, which was all-important to how society was seen, as well as to its practical functioning, was founded on an adversarial polarity between the guilty and the innocent. Calvinist theology, in particular, and at a basic level Christianity itself, involved a series of binary opposites between God and Satan, heaven and hell, the saved and the damned. The revival of Platonism helped to establish the popular belief in a world made up of opposites and dissimilarities in fruitful tension. Finally seventeenth-century medical thought provided useful analogies for politics. If the political system was often compared to a body whose parts should function together in perfect, hierarchical harmony, the health of this body was frequently to be secured through a dynamic, even difficult process of purgation or purification. Although consensus was stressed as an ideal, many felt it was an ideal which could only be achieved through vigilance, struggle and sometimes conflict.

Conflict and division were thus perfectly possible within the intellectual framework of early Stuart England. If we turn more directly to politics we can see a series of polarities which operated at the levels of theory and of practice. Although it is convenient to separate these polarities for the purposes of analysis, they were in fact inter-connected and overlapping. As Sommerville's essay demonstrates there were two sharply divergent beliefs about the English 'constitution'. A 'royalist' view held that the king's powers came from God alone and the monarch could therefore issue binding commands even when these orders were contrary to the known laws of the land. On the other hand it was argued that royal power was derived from the people or from the law and that consequently kings should rule according to the law and with consent, consent being especially due when monarchs invaded their subjects' property through taxation. Consent of course would normally be given through a meeting of Parliament which had a crucial role in this latter conception of the constitution. This cleavage of opinion pre-dated Charles' reign but divisions hardened in this reign as the King and some of his councillors promoted 'new counsels'.

Pauline Croft has recently discussed a privately circulated tract, probably written between 1614 and 1621, which called for annual Parliaments. It was argued that the lack of parliaments led to 'many and dangerous enormities' including corruption in the law and the government, and undue enhancement of the prerogative. Copies of this tract have been found in widely scattered gentry collections which suggests a nationwide interest, while the fact that it was anonymous testifies to the contested nature of the views expressed.[42] Charles' increasing fears of 'popularity' focused on views such as those in this tract. By the late 1620s the King and close advisers like Laud had come to believe in a deep-seated conspiracy against monarchical authority, led by popular elements which dominated the House of Commons and supported by seditious Puritans, common lawyers and disloyal members of the lower orders. The attack on Buckingham in the 1626 Parliament and the rejection of the King's request for a benevolence in the summer of 1626 were interpreted as signs that disloyalty was on the increase and the subject could no longer be trusted. This led to the King's decision to adopt 'new counsels', involving resort to prerogative taxes such as the forced loan. The loan was accompanied by statements like the sermons of Sibthorpe and Manwaring declaring that since the King was answerable only to God he could raise taxes without having to consult Parliament. Increasingly the Crown's emphasis was on compelling obedience rather than seeking consent. Charles became reluctant to summon Parliament until forced to do so by financial necessity or foreign policy; and when Parliament met he expected it simply to rubber-stamp royal decisions.[43]

A series of more diffuse polarities is summed up by the contrast between 'court' and 'country'. As we suggested earlier these were ideological polarities, not necessarily concrete separations. In 'real' terms, as Christopher Thompson's essay demonstrates, the court was not monolithic, but contained a range of political factions with differing allegiances and policies; while Hughes suggests the practical links between the court and the provinces. However the term 'court' was also used in political rhetoric, to denote the character of particular politicians and policies. In this sense it was often coupled with the more complex term 'country'.

On one level 'country' indicated a place. Some historians have seen this as synonymous with the county, expressing the loyalty an individual felt for a 'county community'; but it could be used to refer to a whole range of localities from the immediate parish and neighbourhood up to the county and beyond to the 'commonwealth' of England. It is often hard to tell precisely which is being referred to and this in itself was a reflection of how contemporaries envisaged their loyalties. 'Country' expressed in semantic terms the widespread view that each locality was comprehended and integrated within the broad whole of the English nation. Alongside this 'country' also denoted the inhabitants of these different areas. Nearly always it was taken to refer to 'the better sort' – those with a propertied stake in their locality, who served in local offices and paid their rates – as distinct from the 'vulgar' or the 'multitude'. In this sense it sometimes referred exclusively to the gentry, but more often it was seen as also encompassing the 'middling sort', the yeomen, husbandmen and urban artisans. And when employed in this way it was frequently linked with the idea that one owed the 'country' a duty of service. As a collective entity it could place a trust on certain individuals to represent its interests or else acknowledge their role as its 'father' or protector. This trust and these interests were often associated with particular religious and political values. Here the term 'better sort' became as much a moral as a social category. 'Country' could thus refer to particular values and concerns shared by the people and places being described by the same term. It was often politically neutral, indicating something on which nearly all were agreed such as the need to avoid heavy taxes in a time of recession. However increasingly 'country' carried with it a particular ideological slant as it came to refer to the concerns of Puritans and critics of the Crown in Parliament. During the first thirty years of the seventeenth century, by processes which are not entirely clear, these two groups did much to appropriate the term. In the sermons and writings of Puritan ministers like Thomas Scott, the author of *Vox Populi*, 'country' was taken to represent a vision of a godly commonwealth, such as might exist if popery and sinfulness were reduced and England reformed along Protestant lines. For those with a more secular outlook, such as Sir Edward Coke, it tended to mean a commonwealth freed from projectors, evil counsellors and threats to the liberties of the subject; an England in which parliaments met regularly to express and remedy the subjects' grievances. Indeed Parliament stood at the centre of the various notions associated with 'country'. It represented the different social and geographical entities which made up the 'country' and it embodied the ideals and values which it was believed to stand for.[44]

In its more overtly 'political' aspects, the 'country' implied staunch Protestantism, adherence to the rule of law and support for Parliament's participation in the governmental process. The upright and honest 'country' was increasingly, although not necessarily, contrasted with a 'court' that was corrupt and dishonest, inclined to popery and scornful of parliaments. The development of this negative image of the 'court' was another feature of early Stuart politics. It drew on a variety of concerns: resentment at the extravagance of the Scots in James I's Bedchamber; revelations about the corruption of leading councillors and Crown officials; alarm at the popish inclinations of royal advisers such as the Earl of Northampton; and fears about prerogative taxation and its consequences for Parliament.[45] By the end of James' reign this negative image was firmly fixed in the minds of many; but as yet the faults of the 'court' were regarded almost entirely as the responsibility of 'evil counsellors'. The King was usually seen as detached from it and aligned with his people. This view began to alter with revelations about Charles' direct involvement in measures such as the forced loan; and during the early 1640s there was widespread mistrust of the King himself. But even at this stage much of the public rhetoric continued to focus on the disruptive influence of those about the King.[46]

The 'court', then, was a convenient symbol for many of the things that were considered wrong with the body politic of England. To remedy its evil influence 'country' attitudes embraced a dynamic view of politics. Political stability was to be attained through activism and struggle. Here the 'court–country' polarity blends into the rival conspiracy theories current in the 1620s and again in 1642 between Charles and his supporters on the one hand and prominent spokesmen for the 'country' and the parliamentary leadership on the other. Recent work by Cust and Fletcher has elucidated these rival ways of accounting for political conflict and breakdown, and Lake's essay takes this further by exploring the structure and implications of anti-popery.[47] Charles, as we have said, increasingly feared 'popularity', as a threat to monarchy and social order. His solution was to 'close down' the political system; to avoid Parliament if possible, to emphasize hierarchy, order, and honour, and to insist on absolute obedience. Politics was to become a matter of receiving, transmitting and obeying commands from above rather than a process involving consultation and participation. The 'country' diagnosis and proposed treatment of England's political problems differed sharply. Here the central problem was a popish conspiracy with an alarming foothold at court. This conspiracy was aimed against the true Protestant religion and the laws and liberties of English people. It connected with the traditional explanation of political difficulties which blamed evil counsellors for turning the monarch away from his better nature. In the context of Charles' reign, popishly inclined councillors were blamed for the 'new counsels' which undermined Parliament and promoted arbitrary taxation. The solution was active participation by the various social groups comprising the 'country' in free elections to frequent parliaments which would purge the system of corrupt papists and 'evil counsellors', and restore harmony between monarch and people.

The 'country', then, stood for staunch Protestantism while the 'court' was tainted with popery. Religious divisions in early Stuart England were more complex than this, of course, and must be treated in their own right. The notion that there was a clearly defined 'Puritan opposition' in England has been effectively countered by both sixteenth- and seventeenth-century historians.[48] Puritans were not necessarily nonconformists from the English church, still less 'alienated' from the political establishment. On a range of matters from the basics of Calvinist theology to the importance of preaching and of an unceasing struggle against popery, they had much in common with key members of the political and ecclesiastical establishment. However, we do not accept recent work which argues in effect that Puritanism did not exist, that it was part of a broad and indistinguishable Calvinist consensus.[49] At the very least Puritans were the 'vanguard' of English Protestants, the most concerned to eliminate the vestiges of popery from the Church, and to evangelize a population which had not yet satisfactorily absorbed the essentials of Protestantism. As individuals, Puritans emphasized an active, individual understanding or internalization of the fundamentals of faith as revealed in scripture and expounded through preaching. They were those who had tried most determinedly to put into practice a version of Calvinist theology, an approach described by R. T. Kendall as experimental predestinarianism.[50] In practice, if not strictly in theory, they accepted that it was possible to discover in this world who was amongst the elect and embarked on a search for assurance that they were indeed numbered among the saints. On a personal level this produced a tendency towards introspection, assiduous scriptural study, attendance at sermons, and conscientious attempts to live all aspects of life according to God's word. More broadly Puritans sought out like-minded Christians, to form communities of the godly, and distinguished themselves from those who complacently accepted an ungodly world. They also tended to confirm and demonstrate their inner assurance of salvation by an external, activist programme of reform in the world. Thus they attempted to root out popery and establish a godly, moral régime in the Church and in society as a whole.

Puritanism especially, but also evangelical Protestantism in a wider sense, combined with Renaissance humanist ideals which drew on classical exemplars to produce a new model for elements in the ruling élite: the well-informed, conscientious, morally upright governor – the 'godly magistrate'. The obligation of the Puritan to be vigilant against papists and in favour of godly reform produced also a broader notion of active citizenship which had a relevance to many social groups.[51] An influential current in recent scholarship has suggested that Puritanism was particularly important to the 'middling sort' – to yeomen and substantial husbandmen, small merchants and urban craftsmen. Here it is seen as a means by which independent property-holders could distinguish themselves from the rich and the poor and rationalize moves to discipline the poor and reform their unruly and immoral culture.[52] In Chapter 3, however, Lake points out that elements in the Puritan 'world view', particularly the sharp distinction between good and evil, had close affinities with the structures of 'popular culture'. He suggests, therefore, that we should be cautious about too close an equation between Puritanism and a programme of 'social control', too sharp a social divide between a Puritan élite and the ungodly multitude. For at bottom the division between the godly and the ungodly was a moral and not a social categorization. It is true that devout Protestantism, with its emphasis on individual understanding of the word of God embodied in the Scriptures, was achieved most easily by the literate, and literacy was a socially specific accomplishment. However we should not be unduly pessimistic about literacy rates lower down the social scale or forget the techniques for oral transmission and memorization in a society where literate and oral modes of communication were still intertwined.[53] Revisionist emphasis on Puritanism as an ideology of discipline and order is too simple. For the reformed and purified order which Puritans sought did not yet exist in the world; and in their search for a new world and their emphasis on the individual conscience Puritans could speak to the aspirations of people in several different social situations. Seen in this light it is clear that there was a great, and often realized, potential for Puritanism to become a disruptive and divisive influence in local communities and in the realm as a whole. Puritans were not inevitably 'opponents' of the monarchy. A godly prince who headed the struggle against the popish Anti-Christ would receive the support of staunch Protestants. But as Lake demonstrates there was an inescapable tension here. This support was conditional on the monarch actually fulfilling his expected role, something which Charles I manifestly failed to do.[54] In the circumstances of 1641–42, this enabled Puritans to tap a wider constituency committed temporarily to the fight against popery, and mount a remarkably effective challenge to the King.

This view of Puritanism has important implications for an understanding of Arminianism. We mentioned earlier that the rise of Arminianism has been seen as a cataclysmic, unexplained bolt from the blue which fractured the rough and ready unity of the Jacobean Church. Charles' support for Arminianism is a 'contingent fact', explicable purely in personal terms; and Arminians are seen as the aggressive innovators, outraging Puritans and middle-of-the road Protestants alike. These latter two groups are thus both seen as essentially conservative, and part of the establishment. Our account of Puritanism suggests that it included elements which were far from conservative or supportive of the status-quo; and it is as misleading to cast the Puritan–Arminian polarity as a progressive–conservative divide, as it is unhelpful to so categorize conflict in early-Stuart England generally. Both were in many senses innovative attempts to deal, theologically and practically, with new problems deriving from the Reformation. Foster (Ch. 7) deals with the programme of the Arminian party which dominated the church from the later

1620s. Here we wish to highlight and draw together elements in the chapters by Lake and Foster (Chs 3 and 7) which show that Arminianism did not emerge from nowhere, and that Charles' support for Arminians is consistent with his general attitudes. In other words, we wish to emphasize that these developments are explicable in the context of fundamental tensions and problems in the English polity; they are not the random accidents they appear in some revisionist accounts.

The whole thrust of Arminian ecclesiastical policy was incompatible with predestinarianism, although the challenge of English Arminians to Calvinist theology was often muted, partly for tactical reasons. As Peter Lake has shown elsewhere, Arminianism focused on a view of the Church and the Christian community on earth which contrasted sharply with Puritan and evangelical Protestant positions.[55] Puritans stressed the importance of the visibly godly drawing together in the world; and some, who tended to semi-separation, came to equate completely the visibly godly with the true Church. For Arminians, on the other hand, the visible Church was itself a sacred and holy body. Membership of this body and entrance into the Christian community was obtained through a general, communal participation in public worship, in the ordered rituals, sacraments and ceremonial of the Church. Arminians thus elevated the sacraments, and consequently the sacramental role and status of the clergy. They promoted set prayers rather than extempore invocations; and elaborate ceremonial and visual and musical images rather than the lively preaching of the Puritans, which they regarded as both dangerously subversive and irrelevant to the creation of a true Church. Crucial also was the stress on hierarchy, order and seemliness. Arminianism can thus be seen as a response to the 'popular', activist and participatory elements in Puritanism, and here of course was a major part of its appeal to Charles. It paralleled his adoption of 'new counsels' in the political sphere for it was another 'closing down' of the system, a means of enjoining obedience on subordinates. In turn the Arminian stress on obedience within a strictly ordained hierarchy harmonized with an authoritarian or absolutist view of monarchy as revealed in the support of clerics like Sibthorpe for the forced loan.

The roots of Arminianism can be traced back to conformist attacks on Puritanism in the early years of Elizabeth's reign. At a broad level most of the earlier conformists, like Archbishop Whitgift, shared the Calvinist theology of their Puritan or Presbyterian opponents; however they represented a different tendency within the Calvinist tradition. Whitgift's Calvinism was a matter of belief; it had few implications for religious practice. As far as he was concerned, the impossibility of distinguishing between the saved and the damned in this life meant that it was not possible to derive a view of the Christian community from the distinction. The visible or national Church included both the elect and the reprobate and should thus be accepted as an imperfect institution. Equally, Whitgift regarded Puritan preaching on election and assurance as subversive, and ultimately irrelevant to salvation since the elect were, and remained, the elect, no matter what sermons they heard. This view effectively emptied the visible Church of much of its substantive religious content, and conformity to it was justified on pragmatic and political grounds rather than for positive religious reasons. It was conformist practical domination of the Church, not their success in theological debate which secured their position. It was left to the isolated figure of Richard Hooker to promote a more attractive vision of an inclusive national Church when he argued that membership of the Christian community was attained through participation in the sacraments and rituals of public worship. This Christian community was equated with the visible Church which was seen as part of Christ's mystical body.

Hooker never attacked Calvinist theology overtly but his ideas clearly contributed to Arminian positions. Arminians were an organized group that could be more effective than one individual; their break with the implications of predestinarianism enabled them to mount a much broader and more coherent attack on Calvinists and Puritans than conformists like Whitgift could mount. Furthermore, Arminians from the late 1620s achieved a dominating position in the ecclesiastical hierarchy which was vastly different from the more muddled divisions between evangelical Protestants and conformists in the Elizabethan and Jacobean Church. For a large part of his reign James held Arminians responsible for divisions in the Church and promoted moderate evangelical Calvinists like Thomas Morton or Samuel Ward. It was not until the agitation against the Spanish match, described here by Cogswell (Ch. 4) that James became really alarmed at the implications of Puritanism and susceptible to the anti-Puritans like Richard Montague.[56] Charles, however, from the start of his reign unhesitatingly blamed Puritans for subversion and division and with his support writers like Montagu effectively recharged the anti-Puritan rhetoric which derived from the 1580s and now applied it to all Calvinists. Moderate Puritans like Ward and Thomas Gataker, and even Calvinist bishops

like Morton felt themselves to be victims of Arminianism as much as
more thoroughgoing Puritans. Arminian dominance under Laud
and Charles was accompanied by a vengeful stance towards their
enemies. For as Foster demonstrates the Arminians ironically
continued to see themselves as the embattled minority they had
been in their struggle to power against Archbishop Abbot and
his allies. Finally Arminian attempts to increase the powers of the
clergy, particularly in local government, were an unprecedented
attack on the very lay élites who had been vital in the development
of a Protestant England. Arminianism may not have shattered a
cosy ecclesiastical consensus – because such a consensus had never
existed – but it seriously deepened religious divisions in England and
alarmed a broad range of Protestant opinion as nothing before.

We agree with some revisionists, notably Morrill, that religion
was crucial to the divisions which brought about Civil War, but
we do not share the tendency to see religion as a phenomenon
hermetically sealed from other aspects of life. In the preceding
discussion we have tried to show the interconnections between
religion and political attitudes or divisions. The Puritan emphasis
on active citizenship, for example, had clear political implications.
The need to combat popery in all its guises led to an emphasis on
freely elected parliaments which were seen as the means to uphold
true religion and protect the King from popish counsellors at the
same time as defending property and the law. Those who were
more fearful of the popular implications of Puritan activism tended
to support an authoritarian monarchy. Hence the close parallels
between Arminianism and the 'new counsels', both emphasizing the
necessity of obedience within a divinely ordained hierarchy.

IV

We have sketched a view of early Stuart England as seriously divided
over intertwined, fundamental questions of religion and politics. It
is not our intention to provide a narrative of the 1620s and 1630s,
but it is worth drawing out the important features, many of which
are covered further in the chapters which follow.

One of the most significant of these is the character and role
of the court and Privy Council, particularly insofar as this affected
the making of policy. Revisionists have rightly urged the need to
understand the more permanent features of seventeenth-century
government rather than concentrating on occasional meetings of

Parliament; but, as yet, little detailed work has been done on either court or Privy Council. What there is, however, suggests that many of the conflicts of the period had their origins here, in the adoption of misguided or politically provocative policies. The basic problem was that during the late 1620s and 1630s both court and Privy Council were becoming less accessible to the political nation, less open to the earlier pro-Protestant/pro-Parliament approaches. Under James the court had for the most part remained broad and tolerant in its outlook, able to accommodate royal favourites and also some of those who were hostile to them. James did not always listen to advice, but at least a broad range of opinions was available to him, as became evident when the council openly divided over the advisability of the Spanish Match. Under Charles, however, this was to change.[57]

As Thompson indicates (Ch. 5), from the time of his first Parliament Charles was reluctant to listen to moderate advice and ready to turn to the prerogative whenever he was resisted. These tendencies were reinforced by the vindictiveness of the Duke of Buckingham who, particularly after the 1626 Parliament, carried through a purge of those who had opposed him. This swept out of office not only leading court politicians such as Lord Keeper Williams and Archbishop Abbot, but also a large number of local governors, several of whom were mainstays of the commission of the peace or the lieutenancy. However Buckingham's vindictiveness was tempered with a basic sensitivity to political realities; and in 1628 access to the court became more open again as the Duke reconciled himself to former enemies, such as Wentworth and Arundel, in recognition of the need to work with future parliaments. The greater problem was caused by Charles himself. He found it hard to forgive those whom he felt had been disloyal; and his definition of loyalty tended to be much narrower than Buckingham's, depending on ideological as well as personal considerations. With the Duke's assassination in 1628 – if not before – it became clear that it was the King who was setting the tone of the court and closing down the range of policy options.[58] It was still possible to put the case for a forward Protestant foreign policy – often, as Malcolm Smuts and Martin Butler have shown, through influence with the Queen – but the basic agenda was tightly controlled.[59] For those who disagreed with Charles the choice was generally either to shut up or get out. Whereas early in the reign it had been possible for Calvinist councillors, such as Pembroke or Sir John Coke, to challenge the rise of Arminianism, by the 1630s one hears no more of this; and the most outspoken opponent of Arminians, Sir Robert Heath, was removed from his post in 1634. Discussion of a summons of Parliament also became more difficult. In 1628 financial necessity and Buckingham's concern to keep his options open allowed a relatively open council debate on the subject. After 1629, however, such discussion became extremely restricted. Charles was able to stifle proposals for a summons, from councillors such as Dorchester and Pembroke, by insisting that Parliament could not be trusted to display the requisite loyalty.[60] The King's influence was particularly apparent in the policy towards Scotland in the 1630s for which the Privy Council had no formal responsibility. As Russell has shown Charles tended to make his own policy in consultation with individuals such as Laud or Hamilton.[61] Had the King's political judgment been sounder, this need not have been disastrous; but the escalation of the conflict with the Scots revealed again and again his inability to make sensible compromises or to comprehend the concerns of his subjects.

Setbacks and miscalculations over high policy were the more serious because, by the 1620s, these had become matters of great public interest. As Cogswell's essay on the Spanish Match demonstrates (Ch. 4), foreign affairs were being widely discussed outside Parliament, in sermons, newsletters and ballads. This was in part a consequence of recent developments in the dissemination of political news. The Privy Council maintained strict controls over what was printed, but it was unable to prevent material circulating in manuscript, either as newsletters or what were known as 'separates' (containing transcripts of proceedings in Parliament, state trials, diplomatic negotiations, etc.). These formed the basis for networks of information which faithfully reproduced what was being reported at St Paul's Walk and the Exchange in London. News of national events was thus transmitted not only to the literate gentry and 'middling sort', but also – by means of local gossip – to the 'lower orders'. The Crown had opportunities to manipulate these networks and adapt them for its own purposes, but for the most part it failed to take them. Its main concern, as in other areas, was to close down discussion, to ensure that matters such as the Spanish Match remained *arcana imperii*. In this it was largely unsuccessful. Informed discussion continued and the existence of a relatively developed public opinion was to place important constraints on James and Charles' freedom for manoeuvre.[62]

The circulation of political news also helped to broaden the extent of political participation and to introduce a more overtly ideological dimension into local politics which tended to work in ways detrimental to the Crown. News naturally focused on dramatic events and often presented politics in terms of conflict between two sides, sometimes described as 'court and country'. This helped to undermine the emphasis on consensus which pervaded contemporary rhetoric. It also attuned public opinion to the idea of political polarity. The effects of this are explored in Cust's essay on the electorate (Ch. 5). This shows that freeholders were not simply voting fodder for the leading gentry, but were often sufficiently prosperous and independently minded to make their own political judgments. In doing this they were influenced by the information and assumptions in the news. Increasingly it was the case that MPs, particularly those serving in county seats, were expected to represent the concerns and ideals associated with 'the country'. This created important additional pressures when they reached Westminster. Their actions were subject to regular scrutiny back in their localities which limited their freedom of action and sometimes encouraged opposition to the Crown.

The implications of this have not been fully understood by revisionists. Russell has acknowledged the importance of constituency pressures, but has stressed that what mainly concerned MPs were local issues, in particular defending their localities against taxation and the other burdens arising from war. Thompson shows in Chapter 6 that these concerns were usually linked to broader matters of high policy.[63] MPs were much more worried at the prospect of giving away taxpayers' money if they thought this would be misspent. Fears that the Crown might allow a toleration for Catholics, much in evidence at the time of the Spanish Match, seriously disrupted Charles' efforts to secure an adequate grant of supply in 1625. The nature of the war itself was also a central issue in the parliaments of the mid-1620s. In 1624 there were high hopes of a successful war against Spain based on a 'blue-water' policy of attacking colonies and treasure fleets. But, as the war developed, the main effort was directed to expeditionary forces and a continental land war; and the failures of Mansfeldt's expedition and the attempt on Cadiz raised questions about the direction of strategy. These were coupled with concern at the influence of Buckingham, and came to the surface with criticisms late in the 1625 Parliament and the attempt to impeach him in 1626. By 1628, with the recent setback at the Isle de Rhé, MPs were thoroughly disillusioned with the war and, as a result, reluctant to discuss it or make adequate provision for it. But this did not reflect a reaction against war itself so much as the experience of a war which almost from the outset had gone very badly.

A rather different set of parliamentary concerns is discussed by Sommerville in Chapter 2. This was the unease at the growth of unparliamentary taxation and the consequent fears for the future existence of Parliament. It was these which gave a hard edge to the debates on impositions in 1610 and 1614 and the attacks on prerogative government in 1628. They also tended to make the Commons extremely sensitive when it felt that its privileges were being challenged. Infringements on freedom of speech or the right to hold free elections were all too often viewed in the context of a broader threat to dispense with Parliament altogether.

Russell has argued that fears for the future of Parliament stemmed from the fact that it was of less and less value to a Crown which no longer wished to legislate and found its grants inadequate. This view of Parliament is not entirely shared by the contributors to this volume. Thompson, and Cogswell writing elsewhere, have stressed the importance of parliamentary subsidies, particularly in wartime.[64] These were not sufficient to meet all the needs of the Crown, but during the 1620s they were more numerous and more frequent than ever before; and to judge by the lengths to which the Crown was prepared to go to obtain them, particularly in 1628, they were much sought after. The Commons' leaders recognized this fact and for much of the 1620s displayed considerable flexibility and tactical skill in using it to secure redress of the subject's grievances. It was only in 1621 and 1625 that grants were made with no strings attached. Otherwise the Commons drove a hard bargain; and in 1624 – with substantial concessions over domestic and foreign policy – and in 1628 – with the Petition of Right – they appeared to achieve what they had set out to. Negotiations over supply and grievances were very much the central focus of parliamentary debate. The Commons' leaders and those acting as the Crown's spokesmen or 'undertakers' recognized this and, for the most part, accepted the principle of *quid pro quo*. However it is not clear that this was ever accepted by Charles; and herein lay another source of conflict.

MPs had become accustomed to dealing with James who, if rather touchy, was still prepared to go along with the fudges and accommodations needed to achieve a settlement. Charles for the most part was not; and, as Thompson's essay on the 1625 Parliament shows, this initially caused MPs considerable bemusement. They were uncertain how to proceed with a king who did not appear to play the game. In 1625 and 1626 they miscalculated and overreached themselves in trying to strike directly at Buckingham; by 1628 they recognized that this was unlikely to succeed and changed their tactics to limiting the King's freedom of action through the Petition of Right. Charles, however, effectively reneged on even this concession by ordering a second printing of the Petition as soon as the session was over. By 1629 trust in the King was rapidly diminishing, as was reflected in the divided tactics of the Commons' leadership. Some were still pressing for a realistic accommodation while others had abandoned hope of this and were determined to strike at the King's 'evil counsellors' before it was too late.[65]

Growing distrust of Charles is one of the themes which link together the 1620s and the 1630s. Another, particularly prominent in revisionist accounts, is the impact of war on a government system close to 'functional breakdown'. This, it is suggested, was the basic cause of the conflicts of the late 1620s and the collapse of the 'personal rule'. However we would argue that, while war undoubtedly placed a strain on political relationships, it alone is not a sufficient explanation for the level of conflict. This is indicated by the experience of the 1590s, when some coastal shires faced heavier burdens than during the 1620s with much less evidence of overt protest.[66] Conflict was crucially linked to broader political considerations, as is shown by a study of the billeting of soldiers in the localities. This service proceeded relatively smoothly – apart from complaints about Scots and Irish soldiers and central government's slowness in reimbursing charges – until the meeting of the 1628 Parliament. What transformed it, and led local inhabitants to turn soldiers out of doors, was Parliament's questioning of the legal basis of billeting. News of this quickly spread to the localities and effectively undermined the legitimacy of the whole service.[67]

Parallel conclusions can be drawn from a study of ship-money in Cheshire by Peter Lake. He has demonstrated that the levy was collected with considerable success in the short term and that this was actually facilitated by the administrative disputes and rating struggles which it tended to generate. These encouraged different groups within local society to compete in collecting the money efficiently in order to demonstrate their loyalty and win conciliar favour. In the long run the service was undermined by more overtly political considerations. After 1637, at the same time as it was becoming apparent that the levy was legally contentious, local officials were increasingly being subjected to the direct and hectoring authority of the King. Sheriffs and constables were continually reminded that their loyalty and obedience to the Crown could only be demonstrated by prompt and efficient collection of the levy. This necessarily raised the possibility of dissent and encouraged the questioning and, ultimately, the undermining of royal authority.[68] Demands for money, then, did not translate automatically into political conflict. In spite of its inadequacies the administrative system retained considerable scope for constructive interaction. What destroyed this were the ideological concerns discussed earlier.

With regular meetings of Parliament in the 1620s there was plenty of scope for these to be voiced openly; but in the absence of Parliament the only effective source of central power became the court and Privy Council. This made the expression of dissent much more difficult. The council was obviously unlikely to look kindly on complaints couched in legal or ideological terms; therefore public protests took a more restricted form, focussed on practical issues. This has led some revisionists to argue that most people were unconcerned at the broader implications of royal policy and that the 'personal rule' would have continued to be acceptable had it not been for the Scots' war.[69] Such a verdict, however, is not borne out if we look at recent studies of this decade which draw on private sources.

Ken Fincham has elucidated the debates amongst the Kentish gentry following the testing of ship-money in the courts which indicate a clear understanding of the constitutional issues underlying the levy, and sharp differences in the positions taken on these issues. The reluctance of the government to allow Saye and Hampden to force a legal case against the levy was clearly well-placed.[70] The deep anxiety generated by the government's religious policies is clearly indicated in some contemporary diaries. Robert Woodford, the steward of Northampton recorded his association with wide-ranging groups of godly Calvinists, his alarm at attacks on Calvinist theological orthodoxy and the rise of Arminian ritual, and much sympathy for the Scots' resistance to Charles.[71] A significant minority of the godly were driven to despair of the English church and emigrated to build a true Church in New England. Even an apparent conformist like Thomas Dugard, the schoolmaster of Warwick, was part of a circle of the godly which comprised men and women who risked emigration and clergy deprived of livings for opposition to Laudian developments, as well as more amenable figures. During the difficult years of Laud's ascendancy such networks had a defensive role, which made possible the survival of godly preaching, the discussion of sermons and the training of 'orthodox' ministers. However through contacts made at the university and the connections of his patron Lord Brooke, Dugard had become part of a national network including important opposition figures like Pym and Saye. When the Long Parliament met, his circle, like several others, became transformed into a positive movement working for reform.[72]

V

Thus far our attention has been largely directed towards political and ideological developments. But it is important to integrate a social dimension into our understanding of the outbreak of the Civil War.[73] Early in the introduction we noted that revisionists had simply dismissed most Marxist-influenced attempts to link the Civil War to various interpretations of social change. This dismissal was facilitated partly by the unsophisticated and sometimes confused theoretical assumptions of some of the social and economic history of early modern England, especially when compared to many studies of the nineteenth century. There is, for instance, no agreement on how to categorize the English economy as a whole. More importantly, there is little overt discussion of the sharp differences of view. Alan Macfarlane sees England from an early date as a market-orientated, individualistic, 'capitalist' society. Brian Manning's work on the Civil War as a social conflict draws on Porchnev's studies of seventeenth-century France to suggest that early Stuart England was still a feudal society where fundamental conflicts arose through the efforts of feudal landlords to extract a surplus from the rents and dues of their tenants, and through the exploitation of commons.[74] There are similar problems with analyses of social status or 'class' in the seventeenth century; work tends to oscillate between using very broad categories, often no more than the élite, the middling sort and the poor, and multiplying categories defined in a very technical way. In part this reflects both varieties of social analysis used by seventeenth-century commentators themselves, and the fluidity of early modern English society,[75] but too often it again reveals a failure on the part of modern historians to address directly the theoretical basis of their work. The middling sort are especially elusive: for Brian Manning they are initially part of the 'people' engaged in a struggle against their social superiors although their position and allegiance become increasingly uncertain as the Civil War goes on. In Keith Wrightson's very influential account of social change in early modern England, many of the middling sort gradually became assimilated to the élite as social differentiation intensified. Far from allying with poorer groups against the rich, the middling sort were attempting to distance themselves from the poor and trying also to reform and discipline the unruly, ungodly poor through energetic use of the organs of local government.[76]

The conceptual confusions in some of the social and economic analysis of early modern England compounded the disarray following the failure of any attempts to link patterns of élite allegiance in the 1640s to processes of social change. Many of these attempts were shaped by Marxist notions of a 'bourgeois revolution', although the influential pioneer of such analysis, R. H. Tawney, cannot be described as a Marxist. Tawney, drawing on his interpretation of the work of the seventeenth-century political philosopher James Harrington, argued that the Civil War was the product of the rise of the gentry and the corresponding decline of the aristocracy.[77] In the century following the dissolution of the monasteries the wealth of the gentry had risen at the expense of the peerage and the Crown, and this economic advance was accompanied by a rise in self-confidence and a desire for political power. The Civil War was thus the gentry's attempt to win through Parliament a political position commensurate with their new-found wealth. There were many problems with this interpretation: in the first place it is not clear that the gentry and the peerage should be treated as two separate economic groups as opposed to two different legally defined status groups; the evidential basis for Tawney's argument has not been widely accepted; while at the most obvious level both Charles and the Parliament attracted support from peers and from gentlemen during the Civil War. Part of Tawney's argument was that the gentry were less wedded to traditional attitudes to estate management than were the peerage and so were better able to take advantage of the inflation and expansion of the sixteenth century. This argument was developed by Christopher Hill who suggested that the cleavage of 1642 was not between peers and gentry but between landowners (titled and untitled) with 'progressive' attitudes to their estates, and those with a more traditional, or feudal approach. Thus landowners who sought to extract a maximum return from their estates through raising rents, engaging in industrial enterprises and in commerce, tended to support Parliament which was seen as the best protection of property rights and economic advance. Paternalist landlords who regarded their estates more as a source of social influence were more likely to be royalist.[78] A very different explanation for gentry allegiance was proposed by Trevor-Roper. He argued that those gentry who depended solely on land for their wealth were in economic difficulties before 1642. The parliamentarians were such declining 'mere' gentry: men who both resented and hankered after the spoils of office and the court perks that would, they hoped, improve their economic situation.[79]

Research into the economic backgrounds of Long Parliament MPs, and particularly county studies of gentry allegiance such as those by Cliffe and Blackwood, gave little support to any of the hypotheses (or conclusions) suggested during the 'gentry controversy'.[80] Few significant economic differences between royalists and parliamentarians were discovered. The *per capita* income of each side was similar; both the royalists and the parliamentarians included prospering gentry and those in difficulties; they both included 'traditionally' minded, paternalist gentry, and those who exploited their estates to the limit; families with professional, official, commercial and industrial links were found on both sides. In fact it was discovered that a greater proportion of parliamentarian families were prospering, but the difference is not sufficient to justify characterizing the parliamentarians as rising gentry, still less as a bourgeoisie bent on overthrowing a political system which blocked their further advance. In both Yorkshire and Suffolk parliamentarian gentry were of more recent origins than the royalist families, but, in Suffolk especially, the royalists were considerably younger than the parliamentarians. The same pattern was found among MPs in the Long Parliament. As being young and being a parvenu are both associated (in the unelaborated assumptions of many analyses) with being 'progressive', the whole enterprise of finding social patterns to match élite allegiance floundered in a confusion where it has largely remained for over a decade.

Nonetheless it must be emphasized that the Civil War arose after more than a century of significant economic and social change.[81] Between the 1520s and the 1620s, the population of England probably doubled from about 2.3 million to 4.6 million; in the same period prices rose dramatically, if by 'fits and starts'. By the end of the sixteenth century grain prices had risen sixfold and the prices of industrial products had more than doubled, compared to their cost in the late fifteeenth century. The value of real wages had been halved. The price of agricultural products peaked in the 1630s and 1640s because of a succession of bad harvests and the disruption of the Civil War. Between 1500 and 1650 also there was a general expansion of overseas trade and important advances in agriculture. More land was taken into cultivation, new crops and farming practices began to be adopted; in general there was a trend towards commercial farming and more efficient exploitation of the land although there were complex regional variations. These developments provided risks but also opportunities for some sections of the population while other groups faced serious difficulties. Those from the upper and middle ranks of the population who could produce a surplus for the market, and whose profits rose in value faster than outgoings such as rents, could reap great rewards. Thus most research has shown that the gentry did 'rise' both in numbers and in overall prosperity and this economic advance is an important element in the emergence of the conscientious, Protestant public men of local government and the House of Commons. Nonetheless these were anxious times and many families could not adjust to the rising prices and faced mounting debts. For the 'middling sort' the implications of economic trends were more ambiguous: many did not produce a surplus sufficient to take advantage of rising prices and declined into the expanding ranks of landless labourers. Others, probably a majority, could profit from the inflationary trends and formed the prosperous, literate, well-informed public already mentioned; these were the men who participated in elections, sat on juries and increasingly monopolized village offices. For as much as a third of the population, however, these were dreadful decades. People who had to buy their basic foodstuffs, who were the victims of richer groups' attempts to exploit their lands more efficiently, often lost what little land they had. Population rose faster than the resources to support it; and those resources were in any case concentrated on the most prosperous sections of society. Consequently there was in many areas a decline in the numbers of small landholders and an expansion in the ranks of landless labourers, a rise in the numbers receiving poor relief, and in wayfaring vagrants.

In the century or so before the Civil War, then, there was an intensification in social differentiation. The pace of change was slowing down by 1640 and convincing recent research has suggested that the poor were much less threatening to social order than social élites feared. The expansion of poor relief, opportunities for casual labour, the increasing identification of sections of the 'middling sort' with local government and with the upper classes, meant that the poor were both less able, and less prone to mount violent challenges to authority from the latter part of the sixteenth century.[82] The anxieties of middling and wealthy groups clearly lagged behind these developments, however, and were particularly intense at times of trade depression and bad harvests such as the 1620s and the early 1640s. The crisis of the early 1640s, in particular, seems to have produced something of a moral panic amongst élites. All these developments suggest that the approaches used in the gentry controversy, of focusing on broad categories moving like real entities up and down an economic system, were not very helpful. In the sixteenth and seventeenth centuries, social categories were shifting and being restructured in complex and often alarming ways and the crucial social context of the Civil War should be sought in the consequent problems of relationships between different social groups. It is surely not overly deterministic to suggest that the political and religious divisions we have already discussed can be connected to the variety of ways in which élites and other social groups reacted to the problems which arose from social change. There were great local variations in the pace and character of economic change; social issues and political and religious attitudes interrelated in very complex ways; and much more research needs to be done in these areas. In Chapter 8 Hughes explores these matters a little further, and here we suggest some general linkages.

The increasing numbers of the poor and uncertainty about the attitudes of independent middling groups were a crucial factor in the fears of Charles and his supporters at the growth of 'popularity'. The unrest of the early 1640s, particularly in London and in the fens, played a large part in attracting gentry support to the king and to his emphasis on order, obedience and hierarchy. Worries about the divisive and challenging implications of Puritanism were exacerbated by the tense social context and led some groups to defend or even to recreate a more communal, festive, and ceremonial religious practice at parish level. On the other hand the improving material conditions of existence of many of the solid middling sort attracted them to a 'country' position, characterized by a staunch and conscientious Protestantism, a concern for legal processes and property rights, and a commitment to participation at all levels of the legal, administrative and political structures of England, from village affairs to parliamentary elections. For some of the middling sort a sharp Calvinist belief in the dichotomy between the saved and the damned paralleled the risky enterprises of their lives, while a Puritan sense of assurance and adherence to duty helped mitigate these risks. At a higher social level, the social alliance of the respectable in defence of true religion and English laws and liberties can be seen as an alternative response to the social tensions of the century. By 1642, these attitudes had, in some cases, become transformed into a rousing, popular, godly crusade against popery and for the thorough reformation of a corrupt and ungodly society.[83]

The existence of these divergent groups within a comparatively broad, participatory political structure marked England off from most continental states. It also led to the emergence of an increasingly separate 'political' sphere of life which is one of the most crucial transformations of the seventeenth century. Hence for Parliament's leaders an ideological alliance became a means of achieving local influence and a national political role at a time when social change meant that a landlord's economic power by itself was no guarantee of political power. This is not to argue, however, that élites could manipulate the lower orders as they wished. Rather the adherence to particular sets of attitudes by people from below the gentry's ranks, and the social changes affecting the 'middling sort' and the poor, helped to structure élite behaviour.[84] Nor is it intended to suggest that people's religious and political beliefs are reducible to the social and economic context. Our argument is simply that this context is vital to an understanding of how and why certain beliefs were developed and adopted.

VI

In the long period of social change from the early sixteenth century, sharp divisions emerged over religion and politics and different choices on the future development of England slowly and ambiguously emerged. This is not to argue that a conflict in the form which erupted in 1642 was in any sense inevitable. However we would argue that in these circumstances settlement was much harder to achieve because of earlier developments, in religion, politics and ideology, as well as in society and the economy.

Some historians have tried to explain the outbreak of civil war almost wholly in terms of Charles' personality. We do not accept this, although we would argue that his style of rule was vital to the type of struggle that took place. Thompson well outlines the fatal combination in Charles' approach, with his stress on the need for absolute obedience being joined by an almost complete lack of mundane political skills and a deviousness which destroyed trust. Charles' religious affiliations were also clearly crucial to the seriousness of the divide. We have argued that there were structural reasons for his adoption of Arminianism; it was not merely a matter of personal choice, but neither was his enthusiasm inevitable. We do not agree with a recent suggestion that an absolute monarchy was acceptable in England, providing it was based on a thoroughly

Protestant dynasty; we have tried to show that Protestantism in England was closely identified with notions of law, property rights and support for parliaments. It is hard to conceive, however, of a broad military struggle against a monarch who was regarded as a defender of the true Protestant religion; and Charles' religious policies had the very drastic consequences of unleashing the anti-monarchical implications of anti-popery.

The immediate occasions of civil war in England were that conflict had already broken out in Charles' other kingdoms of Scotland and Ireland; but this was only possible because of the severe, longstanding divisions in England. These multiple conflicts reveal more differences than similarities with contemporary events in continental Europe. In the first place ideology, particularly religious commitment, was vital to the Scottish rebellion. The Scots were not merely concerned with the perennial problems of subordinate kingdoms, such as lack of access to a remote monarchy and inadequate mechanisms for the dispensing of patronage. Charles' attack on their Church meant that their struggle was a religious and national crusade as well as an aristocratic revolt. It was religion also which led sections among the English political nation to see the Scottish struggle as their own. There was thus very widespread reluctance to help Charles fight the Scots, much sympathy for their plight, and a remarkable degree of co-operation between the English and Scots leaders of opposition to the King. No such level of co-operation was found in the struggles of French provinces or Spanish kingdoms against their central authorities. These revolts remained fragmented and isolated.[85] The complex origins of the Irish Rising of 1641 were lost on the English who saw it simply as a monstrous papist assault on religion and all goodness. English terror was intensified by the coming together of the old Irish suffering from generations of colonial oppression with the Anglo-Irish affronted by Strafford's rule.[86] In the 'British' context and in a 'European' perspective it is remarkable that the English opponents of the Crown were very anxious that the Irish be suppressed; indeed the most implacable opponents of Charles in England were the most committed to the defeat of the Irish revolt. There were no moves to take direct advantage of this diversionary challenge to Charles as there would have been in superficially similar federal kingdoms. The political and religious frameworks, particularly that of anti-popery, within which the Irish conflict was perceived were again vital.

From the perspective of divisions in England, the successive revolts in Scotland and Ireland were a terrible practical embodiment of the rival conspiracy theories frequently discussed in this volume. For Charles, the Scots rebellion was proof of the subversive and popular implications of Calvinist, reformed religion and of the treacherous inclinations of many of his English subjects; for his opponents the Irish Rising was an almost unimaginable fulfilment of their anti-popish and xenophobic nightmares. In more direct ways the Scots and Irish conflicts provided the raw materials for the hesitant, slow but inexorable resort to violence in England.[87] The idle and disaffected remnants of the forces he had gathered against the Scots rebels, plus dissident elements in Scotland itself, were fatally tempting to Charles, and he sought from 1641 ways he could use them to recover his position in England by force. The parliamentary leaders were determined that the Irish be crushed, but more than half convinced that Charles himself was implicated in this popish rising – a conviction that was only plausible because of the triumph of Arminianism in the 1630s. They were determined that Charles should not be entrusted with the forces needed to suppress the Irish. 1642 saw the increasingly ominous working out of these two perspectives in England with political violence in Ireland and Scotland providing the fatal context. Charles' failed military coup against the Parliament sabotaged the moderate constitutionalism of some of his advisers; he fled London and began to raise forces to subdue the Parliament. The Parliament reluctantly adopted the militia ordinance and moved to take control of the existing financial, administrative and military resources of the royal government. By the summer two major field armies had been raised; by October 1642 they had clashed in bloody but indecisive battle at Edgehill and a long civil war was underway.

Notes and References

1. D. Cannadine, 'British history: past, present and future', *P&P*, 116 (1987), 169–91.

2. R. Mitchison, *London Review of Books* 20.11.86; J. C. D. Clark, *Revolution and Rebellion* (London, 1986) and *English Society 1688–1832* (London, 1985).

3. A thorough survey is R. C. Richardson, *The Debate on the English Revolution* (London, 1977). H. Tomlinson, 'The causes of war: a historiographical survey', in H. Tomlinson (ed.), *Before the English Civil War* (London, 1983), pp. 7–26 provides a briefer version. J. G. A. Pocock, 'Introduction' in J. G. A. Pocock (ed.), *Three British Revolutions: 1641, 1688, 1776* (New Jersey, 1980), pp. 3–20 is an especially sparkling account.

4. Most Whig accounts derive from the monumental work of S. R. Gardiner in his *History of England 1603–1642*, 10 vols (1883–84). The summaries of this are generally much cruder and less well-informed than the original. An interesting account of changes in Marxist-influenced interpretations of seventeenth-century England is included in Raphael Samuel, 'British Marxist Historians 1880–1980', *New Left Review*, 120 (1980), 21–96. For a range of such interpretations see Christopher Hill, *The English Revolution* (London, 1940); C. Hill, 'Recent interpretations of the Civil War', in C. Hill, *Puritanism and Revolution* (London, 1968), pp. 13–40; C. Hill, *The World Turned Upside Down* (London, 1972); B. Manning, *The English People and the English Revolution* (London, 1976). P. Corrigan and D. Sayer, *The Great Arch* (Oxford, 1985) represents a different Marxist approach.

5. J. P. Cooper, 'The counting of manors', *Ec.HR*, 2nd ser. vii (1956), 377–89; J. H. Hexter, 'Storm over the gentry' in *Reappraisals in History* (London, 1961); H. R. Trevor-Roper, 'The Gentry 1540–1640', *Ec.HR* Supplement 1 (1953); L. Stone, *Social Change and Revolution in England 1540–1640* (London, 1965); A. M. Everitt, *The Community of Kent and the Great Rebellion 1640–1660* (Leicester, 1966); J. N. Ball, 'Sir John Eliot at the Oxford Parliament, 1625', *BIHR* 28 (1955), 113–27; T. G. Barnes, 'County politics and a puritan cause célèbre; Somerset churchales, 1633', *TRHS*, 5th ser., 9 (1959), 103–22; G. R. Elton, 'A high road to Civil War', in his *Studies in Tudor and Stuart Politics and Government*, 2 vols (London, 1974), ii, pp. 164–82; C. S. R. Russell, 'Introduction', in C. S. R. Russell (ed.), *The Origins of the English Civil War* (1973), pp. 1–31. See also Russell's later work which has been crucially influential, in particular: C. S. R. Russell, 'Parliamentary history in perspective, 1604–29', *Hist.*, 61 (1976), 1–27; C. S. R. Russell, *Parliaments and English Politics 1621–1629* (Oxford, 1979).

6. J. S. Morrill, *The Revolt of the Provinces* (London, 1976); K. Sharpe, 'Introduction: parliamentary history 1603–29; in or out of perspective?' in K. Sharpe (ed.), *Faction and Parliament* (Oxford, 1973), pp. 1–42; M. Kishlansky, 'The emergence of adversary politics in the Long Parliament', *JMH* 49 (1977), 617–40; M. Kishlansky, *Parliamentary Selection* (London, 1986). See also J. P. Kenyon, *The Stuart Constitution 1603–88* (2nd edn, London, 1986).

7. Russell, *Parliaments and English Politics*, pp. 1–84; Kishlansky, 'The emergence of adversary politics', 617–28; D. Hirst, 'Court, country and politics before 1629' in Sharpe (ed.), *Faction and Parliament*, pp. 105–37.

8. W. Notestein, *The Winning of the Initiative by the House of Commons* (London, 1924); Russell, 'Parliamentary history in perspective', 1–27; C. S. R. Russell, 'The nature of a parliament in early-Stuart England', in Tomlinson (ed.), *Before the English Civil War*, pp. 123–50.

9. Everitt, *The Community of Kent*; Kishlansky, *Parliamentary Selection*; Morrill, *Revolt of the Provinces*, pp. 13–31; A. Fletcher, *A County Community in Peace and War; Sussex 1600–1660* (London, 1975).

10. N. R. N. Tyacke, 'Puritanism, Arminianism and counter-revolution', in Russell (ed.), *Origins of the English Civil War*, pp. 119–43; P. Collinson, *The Religion of Protestants* (Oxford, 1983); P. Collinson,

English Puritanism (Historical Association gen. ser. 106, London, 1983).

11. This is the phrase used by Derek Hirst in *Authority and Conflict: England 1603–1658* (London, 1986), p. 77.

12. K. Sharpe, 'Archbishop Laud', *History Today*, 33 (Aug. 1983), 26–30; K. Sharpe, 'Archbishop Laud and the University of Oxford', in H. Lloyd-Jones *et al.* (eds), *History and Imagination* (London, 1981), pp. 146–64; P. White, 'The rise of Arminianism reconsidered', *P&P*, 101 (1983), 35–54

13. C. Haigh, 'The Church of England, the Catholics and the People', in C. Haigh (ed.), *The Reign of Elizabeth I* (London, 1984), pp. 195–219.

14. J. S. Morrill, 'The religious context of the English Civil War', *TRHS*, 5th ser., 34 (1984), 155–78; J. S. Morrill, 'The attack on the Church of England in the Long Parliament, 1640–42' in D. Beales and G. Best eds., *History, Society and the Churches* (London, 1985), pp. 105–24.

15. Russell, *Parliaments and English Politics*, pp. 64–84, 417–33.

16. Sharpe, 'Introduction' in *Faction and Parliament*, pp. 37–42; Russell, *Parliaments and English Politics*, pp. 26–32, 404–12; see the works cited in footnote 10.

17. C. S. R. Russell, 'Monarchies, wars and estates in England, France and Spain *c.* 1580–1640' in *Legislative Studies Quarterly*, vii (1982), 205–19; C. S. R. Russell, 'Why did Charles I fight the civil war?', *History Today* 34 (June, 1984), 31–4.

18. Morrill, 'The religious context of the English Civil War', 178.

19. A. Fletcher, *The Outbreak of the English Civil War* (London, 1981).

20. This account summarises very baldly the argument in the introduction to Russell ed., *The Origins of the English Civil War*.

21. Russell, 'Why did Charles I fight the civil war?', 31–4.

22. J. S. Morrill, 'Sir William Brereton and England's Wars of Religion', *JBS*, 24 (1985), 311–32.

23. K. Sharpe, 'The personal rule of Charles I', in Tomlinson (ed.), *Before the English Civil War*, pp. 53–78.

24. R. Lockyer, *Buckingham* (London, 1981).

25. For this point see Sommerville (Ch. 2), p. 62.

26. Russell, 'Why did Charles I fight the Civil War?', 34; see also C. S. R. Russell, 'The British problem and the English Civil War', *Hist*, 72 (1987), 404.

27. Morrill, 'The religious context of the English Civil War', 155–78; Morrill, 'The attack on the Church of England in the Long Parliament', 105–24.

28. The most overt justification for not using retrospective accounts is in the preface to M. Kishlansky, *The Rise of the New Model Army* (London, 1979).

29. Morrill, *Revolt of the Provinces*, 24–8; Sharpe, 'The personal rule of Charles I', 67–78.

30. P. G. Lake, 'The collection of ship money in Cheshire during the 1630s: a case study of relations between central and local government', *NH*, xvii (1981), 44–71; K. Fincham, 'The judges' decision on ship money in February 1637: the reaction of Kent', *BIHR*, 57 (1984), 230–7; A. J. Fielding, 'Opposition to the personal

rule of Charles I: the diary of Robert Woodford, 1637–41', *HJ* (forthcoming)

31. It is worth pointing out that Elton and Russell, the two most eminent revisionists, disagree over this question of sources. In a review of Russell's *Parliaments* in the *TLS*, 23.11.79, Elton implies that too wide a range of sources was used with too much credence given to parliamentary diaries while more recently Russell has criticized Elton's *The Parliament of England 1559–1581* (Cambridge, 1987) for his reliance on a very *narrow* range of sources: *THES*, 9.1.1987.

32. Russell, *Parliaments and English Politics*, pp. 5–26; R. P. Cust, 'News and politics in early-seventeenth-century England', *P&P*, 112 (1986), 75–8.

33. Russell, *Parliaments and English Politics*, pp. 49–53 and *passim*; Hirst, *Authority and Conflict*, pp. 84–6. For the existence of similar sets of attitudes in Spain see J. H. Elliott, 'Self-perception and decline in seventeenth-century Spain', *P&P*, 74 (1977), 41–61.

34. Russell, 'The nature of a parliament', pp. 123–50.

35. Russell, 'Why did Charles I fight the Civil War?', 33; Sharpe, 'The personal rule', pp. 53–78; Sharpe, 'Archbishop Laud and the University of Oxford', p. 161.

36. Elton, 'A high road to civil war', p. 164.

37. Earl of Clarendon, *History of the Rebellion and Civil Wars in England*, ed. W. D. Macray (Oxford, 1888), iii, 191–2; William Dugdale, *A Short View of the Late Troubles in England* (Oxford, 1681), Preface.

38. Clark, *Revolution and Rebellion*, p. 57 usefully points out the distinctions between 'high political' and 'localist' Revisionism.

39. This criticism can be applied to the response of T. K. Rabb, 'The role of the Commons', *P&P*, 92 (1981), 55–78.

40. This view has pervaded much of the recent work by J. H. Hexter: 'Power struggle, parliament and liberty in early Stuart England', *JMH*, 50 (1978), 1–50; 'The birth of modern freedom', *TLS*, 21.1.83.

41. S. Clark, 'Inversion, misrule and the meaning of witchcraft', *P&P*, 87 (1980), 98–110; D. Hirst, 'The place of principle', *P&P*, 92 (1981), 79–99; Hirst, *Authority and Conflict*, pp. 84–7.

42. P. Croft, 'Annual parliaments and the Long Parliament', *BIHR*, 59 (1986), 155–71.

43. R. P. Cust, *The Forced Loan and English Politics 1626–1628* (Oxford, 1987), pp. 13–90, 324–31; R. M. Smuts, *Court Culture and the Origins of a Royalist Tradition in Early Stuart England* (Philadelphia, 1987), esp. pp. 258–62; R. P. Cust, 'Charles I and a draft Declaration for the 1628 Parliament' (forthcoming).

44. R. P. Cust and P. G. Lake, 'Sir Richard Grosvenor and the rhetoric of magistracy', *BIHR*, 54 (1981), 40–53; P. Zagorin, *The Court and the Country* (1969), pp. 33–9; L. Stone, *The Causes of the English Revolution 1529–1642* (London, 1972), pp. 105–8; P. G. Lake, 'Constitutional consensus and puritan opposition in the 1620s; Thomas Scott and the Spanish Match', *HJ*, xxv (1982), 805–25; S. D. White, *Sir Edward Coke and the Grievances of the Commonwealth* (Manchester, 1979), pp. 18–23, 187–276.

45. N. Cuddy, 'The revival of the entourage; the Bedchamber of James I, 1603–25', in D. Starkey *et al.* (eds), *The English Court* (London, 1987), pp. 173–225; L. L. Peck, 'Corruption at the court of James I; the undermining of legitimacy', in B. Malament (ed.), *After the Reformation* (Manchester, 1980), pp. 75–93; Cust, *The Forced Loan and English Politics*, pp. 151–8.

46. Cust and Lake, 'Sir Richard Grosvenor', 40–53; Lake, 'Constitutional consensus and puritan opposition', 805–25; Cust, *The Forced Loan and English Politics*, pp. 170–85, 329–30; Fletcher, *Outbreak of the English Civil War*, pp. 42–90, 228–63; Morrill, 'Sir William Brereton and England's Wars of Religion', 317.

47. Cust, *The Forced Loan and English Politics*; Fletcher, *Outbreak of the English Civil War*.

48. Collinson, *The Religion of Protestants*; P. G. Lake, *Moderate Puritans and the Elizabethan Church* (Cambridge, 1982); Tyacke, 'Puritanism, Arminianism and counter-revolution', pp. 119–43.

49. M. Finlayson, *Historians, Puritanism and the English Revolution* (Toronto, 1983); P. Christianson, 'Reformers and the Church of England under Elizabeth I and the early Stuarts', *JEH*, 31 (1980), 463–82.

50. R. T. Kendall, *Calvin and English Calvinism to 1649* (Oxford, 1979), pp. 1–13; P. G. Lake, 'Calvinism and the English Church 1570–1635, *P&P*, 114 (1987), 32–76.

51. V. M. Larminie, *The Godly Magistrate: the private philosophy and public life of Sir John Newdigate 1571–1610* (Dugdale Soc., occasional papers, 28, 1982); Lake, 'Constitutional consensus and puritan opposition', 805–25.

52. W. Hunt, *The Puritan Moment* (Cambridge, Mass., 1983); K. Wrightson and D. Levine, *Poverty and Piety in an English Village: Terling 1525–1700* (London, 1979), B. Manning, *The English People and the English Revolution* (London, 1976).

53. M. Spufford, *Small Books and Pleasant Histories* (London, 1981), pp. 111–26; K. Wrightson, *English Society 1580–1680* (London, 1982), pp. 193–9; P. G. Lake, 'William Bradshaw and the community of the godly', *JEH*, 36 (1985), 570–89.

54. For this point see also: C. S. R. Russell, 'The parliamentary career of John Pym 1621–9', in P. Clark *et al.* (eds), *The English Commonwealth, 1547–1640* (Leicester, 1979), pp. 147–65.

55. This discussion is developed further in Lake, 'Calvinism and the English Church', 32–76.

56. K. Fincham and P. G. Lake, 'The ecclesiastical policy of King James I', *JBS*, 24 (1985), 169–207.

57. D. H. Willson, *The Privy Councillors in the House of Commons 1604–1629* (Minneapolis, 1940); ch. 2 provides an excellent discussion of the political outlook of the court.

58. Cust, *The Forced Loan and English Politics*, chs 1 and 4.

59. R. M. Smuts, 'The puritan followers of Henrietta Maria in the 1630s', *EHR*, 93 (1978), 26–45; M. Butler, 'Entertaining the palatine prince: plays on foreign affairs 1635–7', *English Literacy Renaissance*, 13 (1983), 319–44.

60. Cust, *The Forced Loan and English Politics*, pp. 72–85; L. J. Reeve, 'The Secretaryship of State of Viscount Dorchester 1628–1632' (University of Cambridge, Ph.D, 1983).
61. Russell, 'The British Problem and the English Civil War', 395–415.
62. Cust, 'News and politics', 60–90.
63. For this see also an important forthcoming article by T. E. Cogswell, 'Parliament, liberty and the continent: the actuality'.
64. Ibid.
65. E. R. Foster, 'Printing the Petition of Right', *HLQ*, xxviii (1974), 81–3; J. A. Guy, 'The origins of the Petition of Right reconsidered', *HJ*, 25 (1982), 289–312; C. Thompson 'The divided leadership of the House of Commons in 1629', in Sharpe (ed.), *Faction and Parliament*, pp. 245–84.
66. P. Clark, *English Provincial Society from the Reformation to the Revolution* (Hassocks, 1977), pp. 226–8.
67. T. G. Barnes, *Somerset 1625–40* (Oxford, 1961), pp. 256–8; A. Fletcher, *A County Community in Peace and War: Sussex 1600–60* (London, 1975), pp. 197–8; R. P. Cust, 'Billeting in Hampshire, 1626–8' (unpublished paper).
68. Lake, 'The collection of ship money in Cheshire', 44–71.
69. Morrill, *The Revolt of the Provinces*, pp. 19–31; Sharpe, 'The personal rule of Charles I', pp. 53–78.
70. Fincham, 'The judges' decision on ship money', 230–7; N. Bard, 'The ship money case of William Fiennes, Viscount Saye and Sele', *BIHR*, 50 (1977), 177–84. For evidence of widespread concern with the constitutional implications of ship-money in Northamptonshire see N. Jackson, 'The collection of ship money in Northamptonshire 1635–40' (University of Birmingham, M.Phil., 1987), ch. 3.
71. Fielding, 'The diary of Robert Woodford'.
72. A. L. Hughes, 'Thomas Dugard and his circle in the 1630s: a parliamentary–puritan connection?', *HJ*, 29 (1986), 771–93.
73. K. Wrightson, 'Estates, degrees and sorts in Tudor and Stuart England', *History Today* (Jan. 1987), 17–22.
74. A. McFarlane, *The Origins of English Individualism* (Oxford, 1978); Manning, *The English People and the English Revolution*.
75. Wrightson, 'Estates, degrees and sorts', 17–22.
76. Manning, *The English People and the English Revolution*; K. Wrightson, *English Society 1580–1680* (London, 1982), chs 5–7; K. Wrightson, 'Aspects of social differentiation in rural England, c. 1580–1660', *Journal of Peasant Studies*, 5 (1977–78), 33–47.
77. 'Harrington's interpretation of his age', in J. M. Winter (ed.), *History and Society: Essays by R. H. Tawney*, (London, 1978), pp. 66–84. For a survey of the 'gentry debate' see Stone, *Social Change and Revolution in England 1540–1640*.
78. Hill, 'Recent interpretations of the civil war', in *Puritanism and Revolution*, 13–40.
79. Trevor-Roper, 'The Gentry 1540–1640'.
80. D. Brunton and D. H. Pennington, *Members of the Long Parliament* (London, 1954); B. G. Blackwood, *The Lancashire Gentry and the Great Rebellion* (Chetham Soc., 3rd ser., xxv, 1978); B. G. Blackwood, 'The

cavalier and roundhead gentry of Suffolk', *The Suffolk Review*, nos 5 and 7 (1985–6).

81. C. G. A. Clay, *Economic Expansion and Social Change: England 1500–1700*, 2 vols (Cambridge, 1984), i, pp. 2–3, 42–4. Clay's two volumes and J. A. Sharpe, *Early Modern England: a Social History 1550–1760* (London, 1987) provide an up-to-date introduction to social and economic developments.

82. J. S. Morrill and J. D. Walter, 'Order and Disorder in the English Revolution', in A. Fletcher and J. Stevenson (eds), *Order and Disorder in Early Modern England* (Cambridge, 1985), pp. 137–65.

83. Manning, *The English People and the English Revolution*, chs 3 and 4; C. Holmes, *Seventeenth Century Lincolnshire* (History of Lincolnshire Committee, 1980), ch 9; Hunt, *The Puritan Moment*; D. Underdown, *Revel, Riot and Rebellion* (Oxford, 1985).

84. See the chapters by Cust and Hughes (Chs 5 and 8) in this volume.

85. R. Bonney, 'The English and French civil wars', *Hist.*, 65 (1980), 365–82; J. H. Elliott, 'Revolts in the Spanish monarchy', in R. Foster and J. P. Greene (eds), *Preconditions of Revolution in Early Modern Europe* (London, 1970), pp. 109–30.

86. T. W. Moody, F. X. Martin and F. T. Byrne (eds), *A New History of Ireland*, 9 vols (Oxford, 1976–86), iii, chs. vii–xi.

87. Fletcher, *The Outbreak of the English Civil War*; Russell, 'Why did Charles I fight the civil war?', 31–4; Russell, 'The British problem and the English Civil War', 395–415.

2   Ideology, Property and the Constitution

Johann Sommerville

I

Early in August 1642 the Lords and Commons, assembled in
Parliament, issued a *Declaration* 'setting forth the grounds and
reasons that necessitate them at this time to take up defensive arms
for the preservation of his majesty's person, the maintenance of true
religion, the laws and liberties of this kingdom, and the power and
privilege of Parliament'. In this document the Houses spelled out
why they were willing to go to war. They spoke of 'the design which
hath so long been carried on to alter the frame and constitution of
this government, both in church and state'. They referred to 'that
violence so long intended, and often attempted for the alteration of
religion, and subversion of the laws and liberties of the kingdom'.
They alleged that the King's wicked advisers planned 'to make us
slaves, and alter the government of this kingdom, and reduce it to
the condition of some other countries, which are not governed by
Parliaments, and so by laws, but by the will of the Prince, or rather
of those who are about him'. According to their own account, then,
one major reason why the two Houses took up arms in 1642 was
to preserve the 'frame and constitution of this government'. They
believed that there had long existed a plan to subvert English laws
and liberties, and to subject the realm to the will of the King or
those who had his ear. In August 1642, so the case ran, only force
would ensure that this plan failed.[1]

This interpretation of the origins of the Civil War was common
throughout the 1640s. At the beginning of the decade Henry
Parker claimed that 'the common court doctrine is that kings
are boundless in authority'. 'From this doctrine', he asserted, 'hath

grown all the jealousies of late between the King and his best subjects; and this is that venomous matter which hath lain burning, and ulcerating inwardly in the bowels of the commonwealth so long'. On 7 November 1640 Pym told the House of Commons that there was 'a design to alter the kingdom both in religion and government'. A month later Falkland declared that the ship-money judges had not merely intended 'to subvert our fundamental laws, and to introduce arbitrary government', but had actually done so, 'there being no law more fundamental than that they have already subverted, and no government more absolute than they have really introduced'.[2]

In 1641 Pym charged the Earl of Strafford with attempting to 'subvert the fundamental laws of England and Ireland, and to introduce an arbitrary and tyrannical government'. 'It hath been the general belief of this nation', said a pamphleteer in 1642, 'that the design of his majesty's late father King James was to wind up this government to the height of France', and the scheme had been revived under Charles – as the Forced Loan, monopolies and the illegal collection of tonnage and poundage proved. 'The world hath long been abus'd by court preachers', declared Charles Herle in the same year, 'first crying up the sole divinity of monarchy in general, and then (what must follow) the absoluteness of this in the King's sole person.'[3]

In 1643 William Prynne spoke of 'a more than probable long-since resolved design in his majesty's evil counsellors, to make him an absolute sovereign monarch, and his subjects as mere vassals as those of France'. 'From whence are our state-divisions, our wars', asked the congregationalist minister Jeremiah Burroughes in 1646, 'but because Princes have been persuaded their power was boundless?' Henry Marten took much the same line, affirming that 'for sixteen years without intermission' King Charles 'broke the law, turned the government upside down, null'd Parliaments, and when craft and cruelty would not suffice, rais'd a most unnaturall war against this Parliament.' A pamphlet of 1649 claimed that the King had fought 'to introduce an arbitrary and tyrannical power into the civil state', and the Levellers likewise blamed the wars upon 'the exercise of an unlimited and arbitrary power'.[4]

So there is good contemporary evidence for supposing that many Parliamentarians in the 1640s believed they were fighting against the attempts of the King or his evil counsellors to subvert the English system of government and to introduce 'arbitrary' power. There is evidence, too, that they believed these attempts dated back at least to 1625. Yet, in much recent writing on the origins of the Civil War, this type of explanation has been given short shrift, and the suggestion has been advanced that the war had few if any long-term origins. Perhaps the most important assumption which underlies this approach is that there were no major differences of political principle amongst Englishmen in the decades before the Civil War. Far from attempting to subvert English liberties, so the argument goes, the King and his advisers in fact shared the same broad political outlook as the rest of the nation. There were, of course, disputes over particular royal policies in the years before 1642. For example, under James I impositions attracted some controversy, and in the reign of Charles I the collection of ship money proved contentious. But questions of property and taxation are likely to provoke dispute in any age, and under the early Stuarts (it is argued) such disputes usually had more to do with the local effects of the levies, or with administrative problems, than with any high constitutional principles – for a remarkable degree of unity prevailed in constitutional thinking. Indeed, the coming of the Civil War itself did not wholly shatter this unity, and a good many royalists subscribed to constitutional principles which were scarcely if at all different from those held by many of their Parliamentarian opponents.[5]

The main purpose of this paper is to challenge the claim that broad unity on constitutional questions prevailed in early Stuart England. We shall see that at least two markedly different constitutional theories were voiced throughout the period. Of course, some men were confused, or apathetic, or ill-informed on constitutional questions. Others attempted to tone down their claims for the sake of preserving harmony. Nevertheless, differences of constitutional principle contributed to political conflict, especially when they were applied to issues involving property and taxation. It was in connection with such issues that the king or his ministers were usually accused of attempting to introduce arbitrary government. The king's extra-parliamentary levies became contentious not merely because of their local effects but also because of their constitutional implications. I shall argue that from the late sixteenth century onwards a number of men claimed that the king could tax without consent in what he regarded as emergencies. We shall see that this claim was frequently associated with the contentions that kings derive their powers not from the people, nor from the law of the land, but from God alone, and that kings could issue binding commands which contradicted the law. Next, I shall show that many Englishmen rejected these views and argued that the King's powers *were* derived from the people or from the laws of the realm, and that the king did not have to be obeyed if his orders conflicted with law. Finally, we shall examine some of the evidence which has been put forward in favour of the idea that unity prevailed amongst Englishmen on constitutional questions.

II

What were the acts and assertions which led men to fear the growth of 'arbitrary power'? By far the most important were royal levies of money without the consent of the subject in Parliament. A number of men put forward principled justifications of such levies. In Parliament it was often said that his majesty might tax only with consent, and this was portrayed as a fundamental law of the land. But such opinions did not achieve anything like universal approval, and among highly placed clerics – who looked to the king to further their careers – the view was widely rejected. In 1585 Thomas Bilson (later Bishop of Winchester) asserted that kings 'may justly command the goods and bodies of all their subjects in time both of war and peace, for any public necessity or utility'. Similarly, Edwin Sandys (Archbishop of York) preached that taxation was a 'tribute due to the King and not a gift freely given'. In 1593 the cleric Hadrian Saravia affirmed that necessity justified kings in taxing without consent. In 1606 John Buckeridge (Laud's old tutor, and later Bishop of Ely) informed subjects that 'you pay tribute and custom and subsidies of duty and justice: you give them not of courtesy'. In 1608 Archbishop Bancroft's chaplain Westerman claimed that loyal subjects would willingly pay subsidies and customs, and would 'hold nothing too dear for a gracious King if his necessity require it'. He denied that the subject could 'resist the exactions, no not of a tyrant'.[6]

In 1610 Archbishop Bancroft told a conference of the two Houses of Parliament that 'this I know in speculative divinity: the King must be relieved in his necessity'. In the same year Samuel Harsnett (Bishop of Chichester, and later Archbishop of York) allegedly preached that 'goods and money were ... not to be denied unto' the king since he was empowered to take them anyway. In 1622 George Montaigne (Bishop of London) justified an extra-parliamentary levy by attempting to 'prove that what we have is not our own, and what we gave was but rendering and restoring'.

Bishop Lancelot Andrewes similarly held that the king had a divine right to be relieved in a case of necessity.[7]

Tribute, said Robert Sibthorpe in 1627, was 'due to princes . . . by the law of God, as a sign of our subjection; by the law of nature, as the reward of their pains and protection', and 'by the law of nations, as the sinews of the state's preservation'. Subjects, he remarked, were bound in conscience to pay even an immoderate or unjust tax. In passing, it is worth noting that the committee which licensed Sibthorpe's work for the press included Buckeridge and Montaigne, as well as Bishop Laud himself. The clergy's *Constitutions and Canons* of 1640 similarly asserted that 'Tribute, and custom, and aid, and subsidy, and all manner of necessary support and supply, be respectively due to kings from their subjects by the law of God, nature, and nations'. In the same year William Beale (Master of St John's College Cambridge) was accused of preaching that 'all we had was the king's. He might command all wives, children, estates and all'.[8]

So the idea that the king could tax without consent was asserted by many clerics, and not just by Mainwaring in his notorious sermons of 1627 in favour of the Forced Loan. The same idea was also expressed by laymen. Subsidies, said the writer Patrick Scot in 1622, were 'as due to' kings 'from their people, as justice, clemency and protection is from Princes to subjects'. The anonymous author of *A true presentation of forepast Parliaments* was no cleric but a courtier and former member of the House of Commons. Writing in 1629 he asserted that the king could 'justly and honestly' raise levies 'without a Parliament'. Many men, he noted, believed that in ancient times 'there were no subsidies granted or had, but by grant or consent of the House of Commons'. He rejected this notion, claiming that the Commons had not been summoned to Parliament before the time of Henry I, and that later Parliaments had often met without them. He denied 'that our present sovereign' or his ancestors 'did ever necessitate themselves by any act, to summon the Commons'. The king, then, could tax without Parliament and could summon parliaments without the Commons. So the idea that taxation required the consent of the subject represented in the Lower House was utterly mistaken.[9]

James and Charles themselves expressed similar views. All free monarchs, said James, had the same 'right over all the land, and subjects thereof', and he went on to relate how William the Conqueror had 'changed the laws' and 'inverted the order of government' in England. He made it clear that the right of levying subsidies rested with the king alone, and insisted that the privileges of the House of Commons were derived from the grace of the monarch. Parliament possessed no authority independently of his majesty. Indeed, its functions were merely advisory, for it was the king alone who made law in England. Where he could, a good king should indeed respect traditional constitutional arrangements. But if he failed to do so his subjects had no remedy against him except prayers and tears. Kings, said James, had to be obeyed unless their commands directly contradicted the decrees of God. So the king could bindingly order his subjects to break the law of the land. Moreover, if he thought that the public good required it, he could justly as well as validly suspend laws.[10]

Although he believed that parliaments had wilfully obstructed his attempts to rule in the public interest, Charles I nevertheless agreed to consult one in 1628. Yet he made it clear that if Parliament did not vote him money he would be justified in taking it without their consent.

> If you (which God forbid) should not give that supply, which this kingdom and state requires at your hands in this time of common danger, [he told both Houses] I must, according to my conscience, take those other courses, which God hath put into mine hands.

God had entrusted the king with the government of the realm. If Parliaments proved unco-operative, or if some other reason made it necessary for the monarch to raise funds without their approval, then he was empowered by God to do so.[11]

Charles and James believed that their powers were derived from God alone and that they were not accountable for the exercise of these powers to any human institution. The same belief was expressed by a great many clerics, and was enshrined in the abortive ecclesiastical canons of 1606. Andrewes and Buckeridge – who, as we have seen, maintained that kings could tax without consent – both insisted that the monarch drew his power only from God. 'Neither pope nor people stand between God and the king', said Buckeridge in 1618, 'for he is God's minister, not man's: he is . . . greater than all men, and *solo Deo minor*, lesser than God only, from whom he immediately receives his power over all men.' 'The king is not bound to give account either to pope or people', said the cleric Lionel Sharpe, 'but to God, from whom he received all his power immediately.' Andrewes insisted that all royal power was directly derived from God alone. Mainwaring's sermons cited such passages from works by Buckeridge, Andrewes and similar writers to justify the Forced Loan in 1627. 'Kings do hold their crowns by no other tenure than *Dei gratia*', said Peter Heylin (a royal chaplain) in 1637, 'and . . . what ever power they have, they have from God.' The 'law of monarchy', he claimed, was founded on God's eternal law of nature and not on the positive (i.e. changeable) laws of the realm: 'and positive laws I trow are of no such efficacy, as to annihilate anything, which hath its being and original in the law of nature'. 'The most high and sacred order of kings is of divine right', said the canons of 1640, 'being the ordinance of God himself, founded in the prime laws of nature, and clearly established by express texts both of the old and new Testaments'.[12]

The implications of such statements did not go unnoticed by critics of royal policy. Speaking against the canons in 1640 the leading MP Nathaniel Fiennes spelled out their meaning:

> If kings were of divine right, as the office of a pastor in the church, or founded in the prime laws of nature, as the power of a father in a family; then it would certainly follow, that they should receive the fashion and manner of their government only from the prescript of God's word, or of the law of nature.

In other words if the monarch did indeed derive his powers from God alone, he would be limited only by God's law and not by the customs or wishes of the people. So, 'consequently, if there be no text, neither of the Old nor New Testament, nor yet any law of nature, that kings may not make law without Parliaments, they may make laws without Parliaments'. Again, if Scripture and the law of nature did not forbid kings 'to lay taxes or any kind of impositions upon their people without consent in Parliament, they may do it out of Parliament'. God's law did not rule out extra-parliamentary taxation. To assert that his majesty was limited only by God's law was therefore to permit him to tax without consent. Fiennes confirmed his point by observing that the canons in fact granted Charles the right to levy taxes without the approval of Parliament.[13]

According to Fiennes, kings derived their power not *immediately* from God but from the people: 'give me leave to say they were the ordinances of men, before they were the ordinances of God'. Jeremiah Burroughes said much the same thing: the king is 'an ordinance of man, and therefore to be limited by man. He may be the chief man in authority, and yet limited in authority; he is supreme but not absolute'. In Burroughes' opinion, kings derived their authority from the consent of the people, and popular consent could impose limitations upon it. If the king were limited only by the laws of God and nature, then he would be free to tax without consent. But if he received his power from the people, and if they imposed upon him an obligation to tax only in Parliament, then he could not validly tax without consent. The point was spelled out by Henry Parker in 1642. 'If nations by common consent', he said, 'can neither set limits, nor judge the limits set to sovereignty but must look upon it as a thing merely divine and above all human consent... then all nations are equally slaves'. To derive royal power from God alone was to deprive Englishmen of the protection of their laws and to condemn them to the fate of the 'asinine peasants of France ... whose wooden shoes and canvas breeches sufficiently proclaim what a blessedness it is to be born under a mere divine prerogative'.[14]

Parker rejected the idea that all kings possess equal power. James I, by contrast, asserted precisely that all free monarchs held the same rights. Fiennes rejected the notion that kings, like fathers, derive their powers from God alone. So too did Selden (a lawyer hostile to Puritanism) and the Puritan ministers Mather and Herle. On the other hand Buckeridge, Andrewes, Filmer, Saravia and the royalist pamphleteer Ferne (to name only a few) asserted that both royal and fatherly power stemmed directly from God. Clearly there were differences of opinion on the origins and nature of royal power. Moreover, some men thought that the derivation of the king's authority from God alone had the crude practical consequence of jeopardizing the subject's property rights. In fact, many of those who granted his majesty a right to tax without consent nevertheless admitted that Englishmen held property (or 'propriety' as it was often spelt) in their lands and goods. They argued not that the king could justly take his subjects' goods *at will*, but that he could take them whenever he found that his God-given task of promoting the public welfare required such action.[15]

The notorious John Cowell (whose *Interpreter* was condemned by the House of Commons in 1610) came as close as anyone to asserting that English land was the monarch's property, and that subjects had no more than a right to use it. 'Property', he said, 'signifieth the highest right that a man hath or can have to any thing. . . . And this none in our kingdom can be said to have in any lands, or tenements, but only the king.' Elsewhere Cowell distinguished between '*dominium directum*' (which he took to include both property and rights of use) and '*dominium utile*' (which he equated with rights of use only). James drew a similar distinction, giving the king '*dominium directum*' over English land, and Saravia and Camden both claimed that after the Conquest, William had reserved '*dominium directum*' for himself. Yet it is unclear that much of substance can be deduced from these distinctions and definitions. In particular, it is doubtful that any of these authors thought that the king could justly deprive his subjects of the use of their land *at will*. Saravia, indeed, insisted that in a monarchy that was not 'herile' (or despotic) the king had no authority to deprive his subjects of their land *arbitrarily*. England was not a 'herile' monarchy. Even Cowell never argued that the monarch might take land at will.[16]

Charles I acknowledged that subjects held property. The canons of 1640 similarly declared that 'subjects have not only possession of, but a true and just right, title and property, to, and in all their goods and estates, and ought so to have'. It was commonly recognized, however, that private rights gave way to the public good. Charles I justified ship-money and the Forced Loan by claiming that public necessity required the levies. In 1633 the Oxford graduate William Evans contended that 'we should be willing to be at charge and to take pains for the maintenance of the king and state' because money was used by the king in ways which redounded to the public benefit. 'I would have you learn not to mutter, or to think it much what ye do for the king and state', he told his readers, 'for what they receive at your hands they employ it to the general good of the whole kingdom.' Even those who opposed the king argued that the public good took precedence over individual rights. In 1642 the parliamentarian John March affirmed that 'a man (contrary to the opinion of the vulgar) may not do with his property as he pleaseth; for that the commonwealth hath an interest paramount in the property of any private man'. But March denied that the king alone should be judge of what constituted the common good. By insisting that the king derived his power immediately from God, others asserted just this.[17]

The author of the *True presentation of forepast Parliaments* claimed that 'the king is the head of the country, and to whom God Almighty by his grace hath given the whole country', making him 'the immediate instrument of the people's harm or welfare'. Kings, he said, were 'only directed, formed, and inclin'd by God himself, and by no earthly mortal power or policy'. The king, therefore, was the supreme custodian of the public good, and the *True presentation* recommended that no one should 'be so arrogant as to think that he hath a greater care of the commonwealth, or a greater interest in the commonwealth than the king hath'.

> Let no man [the author concluded] think himself a good patriot, that under a pretence of the liberty of subjects, or the commonwealth's welfare, stands in opposition to the king's pleasure, or is too rigid and strict for legality in a business that the king directs to be done.[18]

According to the *True presentation* the king's interpretation of the common good had to be accepted by his servants unless his majesty commanded anything that was 'contrary to God's honour or word, or derogatory to God's true religion and worship'. 'If the king command a thing to be done which is only . . . grievous to the subject, or contrary to the laws of the kingdom', however, he ought to be obeyed. In this case the king alone would take responsibility for the subject's obedience, and he would have to answer to 'God, the king of kings, to whom all kings are only accountable'. The servant was guiltless, he said, and ought not to be called in question by Parliament. Only the law of nature limited royal power, wrote Peter Heylin in 1637. 'All sovereign Princes in themselves are above the laws', he concluded, and stated that they could rule in the tyrannical manner described by the prophet Samuel if they wished, though it would not be just to do so. As John Rawlinson (principal of St Edmund Hall in Oxford) put it in 1619, 'a king in his absolute and unlimited power is able to do more than a good king will do'.[19]

So far we have seen that a number of early-seventeenth-century writers asserted that the king could tax outside Parliament, and that he could do so justly if necessity demanded such a course. Both James and Charles did in fact raise extra-parliamentary levies, and gained far more in this way than they ever did from Parliament – a fact which put the continued existence of that institution in jeopardy. Their majesties did allow the judges to pronounce on the legality of impositions and ship-money in the cases of Bate and Hampden, but there is little reason to think that either monarch regarded royal power itself as subject to judicial determination. The commission for the collection of impositions of 1608 did not ground the king's right upon the law of the land, but upon the law of nations. Charles collected ship-money for years before it was tested in court. Bate's Case and Hampden's Case did indeed convince many gentlemen that the law was being perverted, but in other respects their significance should not be overestimated. The judges in these trials were, of course, required to comment only on the particular cases before them, and not on the far wider issue of the extent of royal authority. It is not, therefore, surprising that much that was said in these trials was circumspectly confined to narrow legal questions.

What *is* surprising is that some of the judges did broach the wider problems. Fleming in Bate's Case, for example, argued that in matters of public as opposed to private concern decisions were to be made 'according to the wisdom of the king, for the public good', and such decisions were always to be treated as legal. Though Fleming judiciously refrained from spelling this out, his words could easily be construed as meaning that if the king in his wisdom decided that the public good required any extra-parliamentary levy whatever, that levy would automatically be legal.[20]

III

In the Commons the judgement in Bate's Case was not welcomed. On 23 May 1610 the House told James that 'a general conceit is had, that the reasons of that judgement may be extended much further, even to the utter ruin of the ancient liberty of this kingdom, and of your subjects' right of propriety of their lands and goods'. The dominant view in the Lower House throughout the early seventeenth century was that by the law of the land subjects held property in their goods and estates, and that this property could not be taken from them without their consent. To say that something was a man's property was indeed to admit that it could not be taken from him without consent. So if the king taxed without consent, upon whatever pretext, he infringed the laws and liberties of England. True, subjects should contribute subsidies to the king in cases of necessity. But in the words of Sir John Strangeways, 'if the king be judge of the necessity, we have nothing and are but tenants at will'. As long as the will of the king determined necessity the government of England was literally arbitrary. Since subjects did have property it was up to them to decide what constituted necessity. The institution in which they did this was Parliament, which represented the whole realm. Unless subjects had property Parliament would be pointless, for Englishmen would have nothing to give the king. To deprive the subject of property was to reduce him to the status of a villein or slave. To deprive him of parliament would be to permit the king to invade all his liberties.[21]

In 1610 the House of Commons declared that English subjects had 'such a propriety' in their goods 'as may not without their consent be altered and charged'. 'If the liberty of the subject be in this point impeached', said Hedley 'that their lands and goods be any way in the king's absolute power to be taken from them, then they are . . . little better than the king's bondmen.' When Sir Robert Hitcham suggested that the king *could* raise extra-parliamentary levies in emergencies, William Hakewill upbraided him for his error: 'this position in my opinion is very dangerous', he said, 'for to admit this were by consequence to bring us into bondage'. Since the king alone would judge what constituted an emergency, 'will it not follow that the king may levy a tax at his own pleasure, seeing his pleasure cannot be bounded by law?'. To concede that the king could tax in what he deemed to be emergencies was, therefore, to grant him arbitrary power.[22]

In 1628 the Lower House declared that 'the ancient and undoubted right of every free man is that he hath a full and absolute property in his goods and estate', and they condemned all extra-parliamentary taxation. If the king could take his subjects' goods 'when it pleaseth him', said Sir Francis Seymour, 'I would gladly know what we have to give'. In 1610 Whitelocke pointed out that unless impositions were removed there would be little likelihood of frequent parliaments. In 1628 Eliot asserted that extra-parliamentary taxation 'gives leave to annihilate acts of Parliament, and Parliaments themselves'. He added that 'what the consequence may be is plain, and what the danger is'. By 1640 no Parliament had been called for eleven years – the longest period since the beginnings of that institution. In Pym's view this was responsible for the ills which plagued the state: 'the intermission of Parliaments', he said, 'has been a true cause of all these evils to the commonwealth'.[23]

In 1610, 1628–29 and 1640 the House of Commons attacked extra-parliamentary taxation because it undermined the subject's property and jeopardized the future of parliaments. The King might indeed claim that he respected property and the canons of 1640 argued likewise. In the Commons this was treated as humbug. Fiennes noted that the canons asserted both that the King could tax without consent and that subjects had property. This, he said, 'is nothing but the bare assertion of a contradiction', for 'to take my goods without my consent must needs destroy my propriety'. The judgement in Bate's Case arguably applied to Bate alone and affected not his property but that of foreigners – for when the imposition was levied the imports in question were still Venetian and did not belong to an English subject. But in the Commons impositions were seen as an assault on the property of all Englishmen. Whatever the pleasantries which kings occasionally chose to mouth, however narrow and technical the grounds of judicial decisions, the Commons feared that property was in danger and that arbitrary government was being introduced. They feared these things because the king's actions and the public statements of his servants – particularly clerics – strongly suggested that there was every reason for them to do so.[24]

In 1610 the House proceeded against John Cowell because he denied that the King was bound to rule in accordance with the laws of the land. Cowell was Vicar-General to the Archbishop of Canterbury. In the same year Whitelocke inveighed against churchmen who attempted 'by application of the text of Scripture to overthrow the ancient laws and liberties of the kingdom'. A Bill was read which would have deprived clerics of all their offices in the Church for 'preaching and publishing books against the laws of the land'. When the clergy at the universities spoke ill of parliamentary proceedings, a complaint was lodged against them in the Commons by John Hoskins – who had brought Cowell's case to the attention of the House, and whose activities helped to addle the session of 1614. It was in 1614 that Bishop Neile cast aspersions upon the loyalty of the House of Commons on the grounds that they opposed impositions. Of course, many in the Lower House believed that impositions were contrary to the laws and liberties of the kingdom. 'If in public they will speak thus', said Sir Dudley Digges, referring to Neile's remarks, 'what will he speak, when he is alone, to the king?' It may be worth noting that Neile was another of those who licensed Sibthorpe's book in 1627.[25]

The idea that many clerics advocated arbitrary government and that they were polluting the King's mind with such notions was commonplace by 1628. One member of the Commons wished that 'there were none near his Majesty that do infuse this doctrine of absolute sovereignty'. Pym claimed that Mainwaring 'went about to infuse into his majesty that which was most unfit for his royal breast – an absolute power not bounded by law'. Digges thought that Mainwaring was not the only guilty ecclesiastic, arguing that 'a great many churchmen are gone too far in this kind'. In the Short Parliament Seymour denounced clerics who 'betrayed the king to himself' by telling him that 'his prerogative is above all laws and that his subjects are but slaves, to the destruction of property'. At the beginning of the Long Parliament Pym decried 'preaching for absolute monarchy that the king may do what he list'. In 1641 Laud was accused of attempting 'to bring in an arbitrary government', of encouraging the King 'to levy money without the consent of the subject', and of causing 'divers . . . sermons . . . to be printed which might . . . establish that arbitrary way'. Writing in the following year Charles Herle declared that it had recently been 'good pulpit stuff with court doctors, that safety being the end of government, and the king only by God solely entrusted with it, he was not bound by or to any human laws in the managing it to that its end'. These clerics, he said, had preached that the king could take whatever subjects possessed, 'to the very parings of their nails'. Fears of arbitrary government, then, were closely connected with the belief that an influential section of the clergy advocated such government.[26]

The notion that kings might tax without consent was underpinned by the contention that the monarch is entrusted by God alone to govern the country. One way of arguing against extra-parliamentary taxation, therefore, was to claim that royal power was derived directly from the people, and not from God. This was the opinion of Fiennes, Burroughes and Parker. Much the same thing was said by Hoskins in 1610, by Sandys in 1614, and by Phelips in 1628. A second approach was to admit that kings had *at first* drawn their power immediately from God and that they had once validly ruled by laws of their own making, but to argue that in the course of time customs grew up which set unbreakable limits to their power. This opinion was frequently expressed by common lawyers, including Coke and Hedley. According to both views, the king did not derive his power from God alone, but from the law of the land. This law prevented the king from taking his subjects' goods without consent. The laws limited royal power and protected the property of the subject. The sacrosanctity of property was inscribed in Magna Carta, along with other English liberties. To overthrow Magna Carta would be to make Englishmen slaves.[27]

In the early seventeenth century almost everyone agreed that the king's power was in *some* sense limited by the law. But there were two different attitudes to the nature of the limitations. Peter Heylin (like James I) believed that it was kings who had made the laws of the land and that good kings would abide by their promise to rule in accordance with them. But if a king failed to do so, his subjects were nevertheless obliged to obey him. The laws of the land could not, then, give the subject any grounds for disobedience. Nor did laws necessarily impose limitations upon the king even in the weak sense of giving him a moral obligation to rule in certain ways. A clause saving the right of the Crown was necessarily 'express'd or imply'd' in any agreement made by the king, said the author of the *True presentation*, and others agreed. So if the right of the Crown included a divine prerogative to do whatever the king thought the public good required, no law or promise could deprive him of it.[28]

In the House of Commons a very different attitude towards limitations prevailed. Here, men said that the king possessed only those powers which the law granted to him, and that he need never be obeyed if he commanded against law. "'Tis the highest prerogative of a king that he cannot do against law', said Heneage Finch in 1610, and in 1621 Sir Edward Coke told the House that 'every grant against the liberty of the subject' was 'void'. People obeying such commands were liable to punishment for breaking the law, as Glanville observed in 1628. In the following year the House proceeded against customs officers who had been collecting tonnage and poundage without parliamentary approval, though the King made it perfectly clear that they had been acting on his command. In effect, the doctrine that the king's servants are punishable for executing his commands permitted active resistance to the king's will.[29]

IV

I have argued that there were differences of opinion in early-seventeenth-century England on whether the king could tax without consent, and on the related question of the relationship between royal authority and the law. Yet a number of recent commentators have asserted that consensus prevailed in political thinking. Two main arguments have been put forward to substantiate this claim. The first emphasizes the conservative nature of English thinking, pointing out that 'innovation' was commonly agreed to be evil, and stressing the extent to which political or constitutional claims were based on appeals to history. Given that almost everyone subscribed to political principles which were hostile to change, we might conclude that political changes which did occur (for example the Civil War) cannot be explained in terms of divisions of principle. The second argument admits that differences existed on points of detail, but claims that on most matters of substance harmony prevailed. In what follows we shall examine both of these positions in more detail.

Innovation was wrong, said Englishmen, and they looked to past practice to justify their present actions. But they interpreted the past in the light of preconceived political attitudes, selecting and rejecting precedents in accordance with what they believed to be right or wrong. No one adopted the absurd attitude that all that had happened in history constituted binding precedent for the present. In 1626 William Vaughan (a civil lawyer and poet) noted that Catholics justified their 'enormities' by appeals to history. 'You may as well allege', he said, 'that the wearing of codpieces, which men used in ancient times, ought still to be continued.' Because primitive peoples 'did eat acorns like savages', he asked rhetorically, 'will you have men to return to their old vomits? Speak no more of antiquity', Vaughan concluded, 'for without truth and Scripture it is but an old doting sin.' Questions of right could not be answered by mere reference to matters of fact, said Henry Parker in 1644, and Buckeridge said the same thing in 1614. So if men disagreed on what was right, it mattered little that they agreed in appealing to the past to confirm their various views.[30]

Moreover, hostility to innovation need not imply hostility to change, for change may restore the past rather than usher in some unprecedented future. In the sixteenth century, Protestants claimed that they wished for reformation according to the word of God and the practice of those ancient Christians who had lived before the Anti-Christian papacy first began to pollute the Church with corrupt innovations. Catholics likewise looked to the past to confirm their doctrines, but interpreted Scripture and history differently and regarded Protestants as the innovators. Men on both sides displayed deeply conservative habits of mind, but this manifestly did not prevent fundamental disagreement and on occasion such disagreements resulted in bloodshed.

It has been suggested, however, that there were few fundamental disagreements amongst Englishmen in the early seventeenth century. What, then, were the principles which all or virtually all Englishmen supposedly endorsed? Surprisingly, there is little consensus on this question, even amongst those who assert most vigorously that harmony prevailed. Some commentators claim that the conventional opinion was that kings were not ultimately limited by law and that they could take property without consent when they thought this necessary. What caused dispute, then, was merely whether it was appropriate for his majesty to collect extra-parliamentary levies in certain particular circumstances. Other commentators, by contrast, argue that the king's powers were rigidly limited by law, and that virtually everyone believed that the royal prerogative was no more than 'a set of rights defined in law and subject to its rule'. Which of these two views is correct? Or is there something to be said for both?[31]

Dr Kevin Sharpe has rightly argued that historians should examine the manuscript treatises of gentlemen who wrote on the subject of Parliament. He suggests that these treatises have too often been dismissed because their authors 'clung to the ideal of harmony and order' – an ideal which Whig historians have mistakenly supposed was becoming increasingly unrealistic in the early seventeenth century. To illustrate his contention that consensus prevailed on fundamentals Dr Sharpe draws particularly on Ralph Starkey's *Priviledges and practice of Parliaments in England*, and on the anonymous *True presentation of forepast Parliaments*, which replied to Starkey. He asserts that the writers of these two treatises disagreed 'about the honourable achievements which were to be attributed to parliament' after the reign of Henry I. But on questions of royal authority, he tells us, consensus prevailed between them, and both agreed that 'though it was desirable to make laws by the consent of the whole realm, "simply to binde the King to or by those Lawes were repugnant to the nature of an absolute Monarchy" '. It is useful to be reminded that early Stuart gentlemen could endorse such sentiments. But it is unlikely that all did so. For these words about the king and the laws are a direct quotation from Cowell's *Interpreter*, and these very words were included in the Commons' charge against Cowell of 1610. In the early Stuart Commons many believed that the king *was* simply bound by the laws. But Dr Sharpe's evidence serves to show that not all did so. Nor was this the only point on which the author of the *True presentation* differed from other gentlemen. As we have seen, he held that the king could justly tax without consent, and that illegal royal commands had to be obeyed. He also believed that Magna Carta derived its force not from ancient law but 'from the goodness of kings of this realm', arguing that it had in any case 'been extorted by strong hand from kings', and had only been 'confirm'd . . . *de facto*, not *de jure*'. Such views, it need hardly be said, would not have gone down well in the Commons.[32]

Dr John Morrill has recently advanced an interpretation which in many respects resembles that of Dr Sharpe. When the Long Parliament met in 1640, he claims, many men had 'a limited but clear and firm belief in a partial royal tyranny'. Yet even then, he continues, 'the king was not accused of . . . claiming new prerogatives or emergency powers'. Men asserted 'that the king was using approved powers in inappropriate circumstances', Dr Morrill tells us, and the king was 'criticised for raising emergency taxation in non-emergency situations'. Even when religious issues had wrecked the relative harmony of 1640, the argument continues, men still clung to their old beliefs about royal power. Even in 1642 Henry Parker still recognized the 'absolute and unlimitable power of the king's sword and sceptre', though he lamented the fact that this power had fallen under the sway of the Queen. Once more, it is useful to be reminded that some laymen expressed such views.[33]

Though Dr Morrill's thesis is persuasively argued, it is not easy to sustain the view that most men acknowledged the king's emergency powers of taxation. The Petition of Right of 1628 condemned all taxation without consent, and there is little reason to suppose that this position had been abandoned in 1640. On 7 January 1641 Oliver St John told the House of Lords what the Commons thought about ship-money. The levy, he asserted, was contrary to the Petition of Right. The principles underlying ship-money – namely that the king could take goods in what he saw as emergencies – delivered up the subject 'to bare will and pleasure', reducing him 'to the state of villeinage, nay to a lower'. In August a statute was passed declaring that ship-money was illegal because it was 'contrary to . . . the right of property, the liberty of the subjects . . . and the Petition of Right'. Later, replying to the commissions of array, the two Houses declared that the Petition of Right had been 'made to free subjects from all taxes and charges, although for the defence of the kingdom'. 'To defend the kingdom in time of imminent danger', they said, 'is no sufficient cause to lay any tax or charge upon the subjects without their consent in Parliament.' So the king was not abusing an approved power. Rather, he was claiming a power which he did not have, and his claim threatened to enslave his subjects and introduce arbitrary government.[34]

Within the House of Commons men frequently argued that the king possessed only those powers which the law of the land conferred upon him, and that the law gave him no right to take his subjects' goods without their consent. They regarded the royal prerogative as a 'department of law', and not as some supra-legal power conferred on the king by God. It has been suggested that this attitude was virtually universal in Tudor and Stuart England. Undeniably it was common. However, it is plain that a good many men dissented from this view, including James and Charles themselves. Peter Heylin castigated the view that the king's prerogative was limited by law, and many clerics shared his opinions. If the arguments of Drs Sharpe and Morrill are to be believed, a good many laymen likewise recognized that the king possessed the powers he claimed, though on occasion they expressed misgivings about the way these powers were used.[35]

Disagreements on the nature of royal power were voiced in England throughout the early seventeenth century. These disagreements often contributed to friction between the king and the House of Commons – for instance over impositions in 1610 and 1614, over the privileges of the Lower House in 1621, and over the Forced Loan and the illegal collection of tonnage and poundage in 1628–29. Of course, there were disagreements on other issues too, and in particular on religion. Yet it is arguable that the religious issue would have caused fewer problems if it had not fused with constitutional grievances. 'Unless the body of the commonwealth had been sick of convulsion fits, that men had smarted in their purses, and bodily privileges', said the Puritan minister Nathaniel Holmes in 1641, 'God knows how long the soul of the church had lain speechless with unutterable sorrow.' In 1640 the higher clergy were widely seen as proponents and instruments of royal tyranny. So those who complained of their conduct on religious grounds were given a hearing which they would otherwise not have had.[36]

Of course, royal religious policies *were* widely attacked, both before and after 1640. To assert that Englishmen cared about their secular liberties is *not* to deny that they also cared about religion. Some, perhaps, mouthed religious sentiments hypocritically, for there was little to be lost by appearing to be pious. Others, by contrast, were so obsessively concerned with religion that they scarcely mentioned civil affairs. Lady Brilliana Harley, for example, paid little attention to royal taxation and a great deal to the interests of the godly in Herefordshire. But most critics of the king's policies perceived misgovernment in *both* the religious and secular spheres. As Peter Lake shows in Chapter 3, the anti-popish ideology of so many Englishmen in the early seventeenth century reached far beyond narrow doctrinal questions. Tyranny and liberty had religious overtones, since the Pope was seen as the quintessential tyrant, and popery as the logical opposite of liberty. So actions which infringed English liberties could be straightforwardly characterized – and denounced – as popish.[37]

Divisions on constitutional principle, when added to royal incompetence and to religious differences, explain much about politics between 1625 and 1640. But what of 1640–42? Did Englishmen divide over constitutional issues in those years? The answer is that many did not. Such men as Sir Francis Seymour and Viscount Falkland had spoken as tellingly as anyone against arbitrary government in 1640. Yet when war came both sided with the King. The idea that the Civil War was fought between advocates and opponents of arbitrary royal rule has little to recommend it. Men joined the King for a variety of reasons which had little to do with support for tyranny. Some no doubt hoped for office, power or titles. It may be no accident that Seymour was elevated to the peerage in 1641. Others came to fear that the two Houses posed a greater threat to English laws and liberties than the King, and the question of Church government proved particularly divisive. Falkland feared that the abolition of episcopacy would place religious liberty in still greater peril than it had been under Laud, while others, such as the Cheshire gentleman Sir Thomas Aston, believed that social upheaval would follow if the government of the Church were changed, and the activities of the London mob lent evidence to this thesis.

So the King gained support by 1642 for a number of reasons which had little to do with constitutional issues. It would be wrong, however, to conclude from this that constitutional questions somehow ceased to matter after 1640. One vital reason why the King acquired a party was that he conceded constitutional ground – assenting to the reforming legislation of 1641–42. An equally vital reason why so many continued to oppose his will was the belief that if he were able he would destroy the legislation and revert to his old methods of arbitrary government.

> The ill satisfaction the people receive, notwithstanding the king's mighty protestations to govern by the laws [said one pamphleteer in 1642] springs out of this jealousy, that if it come into his majesty's power to do otherwise, he will do so. For who can think (say they) having the same maxims in his mind, and the same counsel in his ear that he hath had, that he will do otherwise than he hath done.[38]

The lesson of 1625–40 was that the King's high constitutional views rendered his promises untrustworthy. By such actions as the attempt on the five members, his majesty later demonstrated that his views were unchanged, and persuaded many that royal tyranny could be averted only by force. Constitutional divisions between the King and some of his most powerful subjects were crucial in destroying trust, and the destruction of trust was a fundamental prerequisite – and reason – for war in 1642.

Notes and References

Earlier versions of this paper were read at the Institute of Historical Research and at the Universities of Kent and Sheffield. I am grateful to all those who commented on them. In the text, quotations have been modernized and all dates are old style, though the year is taken to begin on 1 January. In the notes and references, the titles of primary sources, and the dates of these works, are as given on the title-page.

1. *A declaration of the Lords and Commons assembled in Parliament, setting forth the grounds and reasons, that necessitate them at this time to take up defensive arms . . . August ·3 . . . 1642* (1642) title-page, pp. 4, 5, 14; also in *Journal of the House of Lords* v. 257–60 at 257, 259. For a somewhat different interpretation of this document see John Morrill, 'The religious context of the English Civil War', *TRHS*, 5th ser., 34 (1984), 155–78, at 174.

2. Henry Parker, *The case of shipmony briefly discoursed* (1640) 34. Pym quoted in Wallace Notestein (ed.), *The Journal of Sir Simonds D'Ewes from the Beginning of the Long Parliament to the Opening of the Trial of the Earl of Strafford* (New Haven, 1923), p. 8. Falkland in *Speeches and passages of this great and happy Parliament* (1641), p. 339; cf. Notestein, *The Journal of D'Ewes*, p. 117. Falkland spoke of the judges as introducing an 'absolute' government, and the views which he opposed are sometimes characterized as 'absolutist'. Though this term is sanctioned by tradition, and is useful if employed with care, it has been drawn to my attention that some recent commentators have found it confusing. To prevent confusion as much as possible I have therefore refrained from using it in this essay.

3. John Pym, *The speech or declaration of John Pym Esquire: after the recapitulation or summing up of the charge of high-treason, against Thomas, Earle of Strafford* (1641), p. 2; *A discourse upon the questions in debate between the King and Parliament* (1642), p. 2; Charles Herle, *A fuller answer to a treatise written by Doctor Ferne* (1642), p. 6.

4. William Prynne, *The soveraigne power of Parliaments & Kingdomes* (1643), p. 27; Jeremiah Burroughes, *Irenicum to the lovers of truth and peace* (1646), p. 153; Henry Marten, *A corrector of the answerer to the speech out of doores* (1646), p. 5; Κολλούριον, *or eye salve* (1649), p. 4; *An agreement of the free people of England . . . May and 1. 1649* (1649), p. 2.

5. See especially C. Russell, *Parliaments and English Politics 1621–1629* (Oxford, 1979); K. Sharpe, 'Parliamentary history: in or out of perspective?', in Sharpe (ed.), *Faction and Parliament: Essays on Early Stuart history* (Oxford, 1978); G. R. Elton, *Studies in Tudor and Stuart Politics and Government*, 2 vols (Cambridge, 1974) ii, pp. 164–89.

6. Thomas Bilson, *The true difference between Christian subiection and unchristian rebellion* (Oxford, 1585), p. 356. Nicholas Tyacke, 'Puritanism, Arminianism and Counter-Revolution', in Conrad Russell (ed.), *The Origins of the English Civil War* (London, 1973), pp. 119–43, at p. 140 (I am grateful to Dr Tyacke for drawing my attention to this passage); Hadrian Saravia, *De imperandi authoritate* (1593), reprinted in *Diversi tractatus theologici* (1611) 4th count, pp. 107–314, at p. 178; John Buckeridge, *A sermon preached at Hampton Court before the Kings Maiestie* (1606) sig. A3a. W. Westerman, *The faithfull subiect: or Mephiboseth* (1608), p. 36.

7. Bancroft in E. R. Foster (ed.), *Proceedings in Parliament 1610*, 2 vols (New Haven, 1966), i, p. 79. Harsnett paraphrased by George Abbot in W. Cobbett and T. B. Howell (eds), *State Trials*, 33 vols (1809–26) ii, col. 1463; Montaigne summarized in a letter of John Chamberlain to Sir Dudley Carleton, 1 July 1622, in N. E. McClure (ed.), *The Letters*

   of John Chamberlain, 2 vols (Philadelphia, 1939) ii, p. 443. Andrewes
   is discussed by G. L. Harriss, 'Medieval doctrines in the debates
   on supply, 1610–1629', in Sharpe (ed.), *Faction and Parliament*, pp.
   73–103 at p. 87.

8. Robert Sibthorpe, *Apostolike obedience* (1627), quoted in G. W. Prothero,
   *Select Statutes and Other Constitutional Documents Illustrative of the Reigns
   of Elizabeth and James I*, 3rd edn (Oxford, 1906), p. 437. On the
   licensing of Sibthorpe's book see J. P. Sommerville, *Politics and Ideology
   in England, 1603–1640* (London, 1986), pp. 128–9. *Constitutions and
   canons ecclesiasticall* (1640) sig. Clb; E. S. Cope and W. H. Coates
   (eds), *Proceedings of the Short Parliament of 1640* (London, 1977), p.
   204 (on Beale).

9. Patrick Scot, *A table-booke for Princes* (1622), pp. 87–8. 'A true
   presentation of forepast Parliaments, to the view of present times
   and posteritie', B. L. Lansdowne MSS 213, ff. 146a–76b, at ff. 147a
   (courtier and MP), 146a cf. 169a (date); 172a, 153a, 152a, 154a,
   158a, 158b. 'A true presentation' may be by Sir Francis Kynaston (or
   Kenaston): see SP 16/233, ff. 75a–77b, at 77b (notes by Windebank
   on a treatise on Parliament, ascribing it to 'Sr Fr: Ken:'; the treatise in
   question is manifestly 'A true presentation'. I am grateful to Professor
   Conrad Russell for drawing Windebank's notes to my attention).
   Internal evidence tends to confirm the attribution to Kynaston. If
   this is correct it provides first-hand evidence of what was thought
   about parliaments in Charles I's immediate circle, for Kynaston was
   esquire of the body to the King. After this essay was written it came to
   my attention that the *True presentation* is also attributed to Kynaston by
   Esther Cope in *Politics without Parliaments 1629–1640* (London, 1987),
   pp. 27–8, 40n, 122.

10. James I, *The workes* (1616), pp. 202 (free monarchs and William);
   178 (subsidies); 200 (duty of obedience); 203 (suspending laws); W.
   Notestein, F. H. Relf and H. Simpson (eds), *Commons Debates in 1621*,
   7 vols (New Haven, 1935) i, p. 4 (king as lawmaker); Foster (ed.),
   Proceedings in Parliament 1610 ii, p. 103 (prayers and tears); Prothero,
   Select statutes, p. 313 (Commons' privileges).

11. R. C. Johnson, M. F. Keeler *et al.* (eds), *Proceedings in Parliament 1628*,
   6 vols (London, 1977–83) ii, p. 3.

12. Buckeridge, *A sermon preached before his maiestie at Whitehall, March 22.
   1617* (1618), p. 4. Lionel Sharpe, *A Looking-Glasse for the Pope* (1616),
   p. 181. Lancelot Andrewes, *Tortura Torti*, ed. J. Bliss (Oxford, 1851),
   pp. 472–3; this is cited in Roger Mainwaring, *Religion and alegiance*
   (1627), i, p. 26; Mainwaring quotes Buckeridge at i, pp. 17, 18, 26.
   Peter Heylin, *A briefe and moderate answer, to the seditious scandalous
   challenges of Henry Burton* (1637), pp. 32–3; *Constitutions and canons*
   (1640), sig. B4b.

13. Fiennes in *Speeches and passages of this great and happy Parliament*
   (1641), pp. 51–2.

14. Fiennes in ibid., p. 51. Burroughes, *The glorious name of God, the
   Lord of Hosts* (1643), pp. 122, 126, 129. Parker, *Some few observations
   upon his Majesties late answer* (1642), p. 15; cf. Parker, *An answer to the
   poysonous sedicious paper of Mr. David Jenkins* (1647), pp. 5–6.

15. John Selden, *Titles of honor* (1614), pp. 2–5; Richard Mather, *Church government and church-covenant discussed* (1643), pp. 21–2; Herle, *An answer to Doctor Fernes reply* (1643), p. 16; cf. *Maximes unfolded viz. 1. The election and succession of the Kings of England are with the consent of the people* . . . (1643), pp. 8, 19. Buckeridge, *De potestate papae in rebus temporalibus* (1614), p. 282; cf. Buckeridge, *A sermon preached before his maiestie at Whitehall* (1618), p. 7: 'the power of the King is no other but *Patria potestas*, that fatherly power that was placed by God immediately in Adam over all the families that issued from him'; Andrewes, *A sermon preached before his maiestie, on Sunday the fifth of August last, at Holdenbie* (1610), p. 13; Sir Robert Filmer, *Patriarcha and other political works*, ed. Peter Laslett (Oxford, 1949), *passim*; Saravia, *De imperandi authoritate*, pp. 167–8; Henry Ferne, *Conscience satisfied. That there is no warrant for the armes now taken up by subjects* (Oxford, 1643), pp. 8–9.

16. John Cowell, *The interpreter* (Cambridge, 1607), sig. 3F4a–b; Cowell, *Institutiones iuris Anglicani* (Cambridge, 1605), p. 65. James I, *The workes*, p. 202; Saravia, *De imperandi authoritate*, pp. 288, 176. William Camden, *Britannia* (1586), p. 50.

17. Charles I, *His majesties declaration: to all his loving subjects, of the causes which moved him to dissolve the last Parliament* (1640), p. 19; *Constitutions and canons* (1640), sig. C1b; William Evans, *A translation of the booke of nature, into the use of grace* (Oxford, 1633), sig. E4b–F1a; John March, *An argument or, debate in law: of the great question concerning the militia* (1642), p. 9.

18. B. L. Landsdowne MSS 213, ff. 167a–b, 171a.

19. Ibid., ff. 171a–b. Heylin, *A briefe and moderate answer*, p. 33. John Rawlinson, *Vivat rex. A sermon preached at Pauls Crosse* (1619), p. 6. The sermon was preached in 1614 according to the title-page.

20. Fleming in Cobbett and Howell (eds), *State Trials*, ii. col. 389. A good commentary on Fleming's judgement is in G. R. Elton, *Studies*, i, p. 269.

21. *Journal of the House of Commons*, i, 431; Cope and Coates (eds), *Proceedings of the Short Parliament*, p. 159 (Strangeways).

22. Foster (ed.), *Proceedings in Parliament 1610*, ii, 266 (House of Commons petition of 7 July 1610); 194 (Hedley). William Hakewill, *The libertie of the subject: against the pretended power of impositions. Maintained by argument in Parliament An° 7°; Jacobi Regis* (1641), p. 22.

23. Johnson *et al.* (eds), *Proceedings in Parliament 1628*, ii, 276, 291 (Commons' resolution); 56 (Seymour), 57 (Eliot). Cobbett and Howell (eds), *State Trials*, ii, col. 487 (Whitelocke) Cope and Coates (eds), *Proceedings of the Short Parliament*, 155 (Pym).

24. Fiennes in *Speeches and passages of this great and happy Parliament* (1641), p. 52. Fleming on Bate's Case in Cobbett and Howell (eds), *State Trials*, ii, col. 390.

25. Cobbett and Howell (eds), *State Trials*, ii, col. 485 (Whitelocke); S. R. Gardiner (ed.), *Parliamentary debates in 1610* (1862), 131; cf. Foster (ed.), *Proceedings in Parliament 1610*, ii, 328–9 (Bill of 1610). Ibid., 384; 278 (Hoskins and the universities). *Journals of the House of Commons*, i, 496 (Digges).

26. Johnson *et al.* (eds), *Proceedings in Parliament 1628*, iv, 170; iii, 408 (Pym); iii, 405 (Digges); Cope and Coates (eds), *Proceedings of the Short Parliament*, 142 (Seymour); Notestein (ed.), *The Journal of D'Ewes*, 9–49, M. Jansson (ed.), *Two Diaries of the Long Parliament* (Gloucester, 1984), p. 99 (Laud). Herle, *A fuller answer*, p. 6.

27. J. P. Sommerville, *Politics and Ideology*, pp. 66, 79, 64 (Hoskins, Sandys, Phelips), 86–108 (Coke, Hedley); Johnson *et al.* (eds), *Proceedings in Parliament 1628*, ii, 64 (Coke on Magna Carta and slavery).

28. Heylin, *A briefe and moderate answer*, pp. 32–3, 36–7, 179; Lansdowne MSS 213, f. 159b; cf. Sir Walter Raleigh, *The prerogative of Parliaments in England* (1628), p. 15; William Laud in State Papers 16/102/14.

29. Foster (ed.), *Proceedings in Parliament 1610*, ii, 234 (Finch). Notestein, Relf and Simpson (eds), *Commons Debates in 1621* v, 59 (Coke). Johnson *et al.* (eds), *Proceedings in Parliament 1628*, iv, 393 (Glanville). Notestein and Relf (eds), *Commons Debates for 1629* (Minneapolis, 1921), p. 11 (Charles I on the customs).

30. William Vaughan, *The golden fleece* (1626), p. 58. Parker, *Jus populi* (1644), p. 53. Buckeridge, *De potestate papae* (1614), p. 909. Cf. Christopher Lever, *Heaven and earth* (1608), p. 71; Thomas Morton, *The encounter against M. Parsons* (1610), p. 188.

31. Elton, *Studies*, ii, p. 269 (set of rights).

32. Sharpe, 'Parliamentary history: in our out of perspective?', pp. 14–15. Dr Sharpe does not note that the passage on the king and the laws is a quotation from Cowell. The original (Cowell, *Interpreter*, sig. 3A4b) prints 'prince', but Ralph Starkey, *The priviledges and practice of Parliaments in England* (1628), p. 41, has 'King'. Starkey does not endorse the quotation, though Dr Sharpe suggests that he does ('Parliamentary history', p. 15). Foster (ed.), *Proceedings in Parliament 1610*, i, 25 (condemnation of Cowell). Lansdowne MSS 213, f. 160b. Contrasting views on Magna Carta are in Foster (ed.), *Proceedings*, ii, 190 (Hedley); Johnson *et al.* (eds), *Proceedings in Parliament 1628*, iii, 95 (Coke).

33. Morrill, 'The religious context of the English Civil War', 160, 174 n83. Though Dr Morrill's general point – that some gentlemen held such views – is doubtless sound, Parker did not in fact maintain this position. In the passage cited he asserted of Henrietta Maria that 'some think she has an absolute and unlimitable power over the king's sword and sceptre'. He did not assert that the king possessed absolute and unlimited power: Parker, *The contra-replicant, his complaint to his maiestie* (1642), p. 15.

34. Oliver St John, *Mr S.-John's speech to the Lords in the upper house of Parliament* (1640), sig. B4b, A2b. 'Act Declaring the Illegality of Ship-Money', in S. R. Gardiner (ed.), *The Constitutional Documents of the Puritan Revolution 1625–1660*, 3rd edn (London, 1906), pp. 189–192 at p. 191; I am grateful to Professor Conrad Russell for reminding me of this passage. *A second remonstrance or declaration of the Lords and Commons . . . concerning the commission of array . . . Jan 18. 1642* (1642), pp. 39–41, in *A collection of severall speeches, messages, and answers* (1642).

35. Elton, *Studies*, i, pp. 268–9. Heylin, *A briefe and moderate answer*, p. 179.

36. Nathaniel Holmes, *The new world, or the new reformed church discovered* (1641), p. 29.
37. *Letters of the Lady Brilliana Harley*, ed. T. T. Lewis (1854), *passim*, esp. pp. 111, 115. On the Harleys see J. Levy's important University of London Ph.D thesis, 'Perceptions and Beliefs: The Harleys of Brampton Bryan and the Origins and Outbreak of the Civil War' (1983).
38. *A discourse upon the questions in debate between the King and Parliament* (1642), pp. 3–4.

3 Anti-popery: the Structure of a Prejudice

Peter Lake

I

Religion is back in fashion as an explanation for the English Civil War. This might seem unsurprising given the currency, until relatively recently, of the notion of the 'Puritan Revolution'. We are surely dealing here only with another revolution of the wheel of historiographical fortune of the sort produced by the institutionalized need for novelty of interpretation amongst professional historians. However, the interpretation now in vogue does not focus on the purposive, radical, even revolutionary ideology which earlier commentators liked to ascribe to the 'Puritans', but rather on the irrational passions and prejudices stirred up by the threat of 'popery'.

To take a few examples; Anthony Fletcher has written of two myths clouding contemporaries' perceptions and effectively concealing the enormous areas of common ideological ground still shared by the King and his opponents. The most pervasive and persuasive of these myths, according to Fletcher, was that of a popish plot to subvert the civil and religious liberties of England and it was the prevalence of this view that enabled Parliament to mobilize support so effectively against the King. William Lamont has emphasized the sheer oddness and irrationality of anti-popery. Kevin Sharpe can only explain the extreme reaction of many Englishmen to the activities of William Laud (who, for Sharpe, was a simple Whitgiftian disciple of order and uniformity) by seeing it as a function of the irrational anti-popery of the period. John Morrill, too, locates the roots of conflict in the fanaticism of two relatively small groups of religious engagés. His account can, at least, accommodate a positive role for the Puritan drive for further reformation; Michael Finlayson has, however, effectively collapsed Puritanism into anti-popery. For Finlayson Puritanism is a mere chimera, produced by modern historians fixated on the so-called 'English revolution' and consequently in desperate search for an appropriately revolutionary ideology. As for anti-popery, it was a cloud of unknowing through which contemporaries blundered into civil war. As such it can be considered as a wholly irrational and unitary 'thing' which merely has to be identified rather than analysed or explained.[1]

This emphasis on religious passion and anti-popish fear fits very neatly within recent trends in 'revisionist' writing on the causes of the Civil War. For, if everyone wanted accommodation, if there were no major differences of secular ideology dividing contemporaries, if radical Puritanism was an illusion and religious innovation was a preserve of the Arminian right rather than the Puritan left, and if the majority of even the ruling class were more concerned with local than national issues, then the revisionists' greatest need was for a positive explanation of conflict.[2]

I want here to provide a framework for re-evaluating the religious component in the political crisis of the early seventeenth century, not by resurrecting a view of Puritanism as a revolutionary ideology (although, as Conrad Russell observed in 1973,[3] it was fulfilling that role by the early 1640s), but rather by examining the phenomenon of anti-popery. I want to see it as, as least in England, the most obvious and important example of that process of binary opposition, inversion or the argument from contraries which, we are increasingly being told, played so central a part in both the learned and popular culture of early modern Europe.[4] Certainly to many, if not most, educated Protestant English people of the period popery was an anti-religion, a perfectly symmetrical negative image of true Christianity. Anti-Christ was an agent of Satan, sent in to the Church to corrupt and take it over from within. He was not an overt enemy like the Turk, but rather rose by stealth and deception, pretending piety and reverence while in fact inverting and perverting the values of true religion. For the Cambridge Puritan divine William Fulke popery was tantamount to devil worship, while for the conformist John Bridges it represented a more serious threat to the true Church than the pagans, the Jews or the Turk.[5]

Since the Protestant analysis of popish anti-Christianity proceeded through a series of binary oppositions, every negative characteristic imputed to Rome implied a positive cultural, political or religious value which Protestants claimed as their own exclusive property. Thus the Protestants' negative image of popery can tell us a great deal about their positive image of themselves. What follows is an attempt to read off from their negative image of Rome the Protestants' own self image and then to present anti-popery as a 'rational response' to situations in which values central to that self image came under threat.[6] Whether the Protestant image of popery was accurate is therefore a question of no significance for the present enquiry. Clearly anti-popery was not an early exercise in the study of comparative religion. It was, however, a way of dividing up the world between positive and negative characteristics, a symbolic means of labelling and expelling trends and tendencies which seemed to those doing the labelling, at least, to threaten the integrity of a Protestant England.

II

The Protestant rejection of Rome was based fundamentally on a brutal dichotomy between the authority of man and the authority of God, the claims of the Church and the dictates of scripture, the creature and the creator. For Protestants popery had allowed merely human authorities, traditions and practices to take over the Church. The most obvious of these was the pope's usurpation of Christ's role as head of the Church.

Once established, the authority of the pope was used to set up and confirm in the Church a whole series of ceremonies, forms of worship and beliefs which were of entirely human origin. Crucial to the Protestant analysis of the falseness of these practices and beliefs was the concept of idolatry. That the worship of the one true God had been supplanted and subverted by the worship of his creatures was evident in the papists' reverence for the worship of idols and images, their use of the saints as intercessors and their virtual deification of the Virgin Mary. Perhaps the central example of this tendency toward idolatry was the doctrine of transubstantiation which sanctioned what Protestants contemptuously referred to as the 'bread worship' associated with the Catholic mass.[7]

Christ's sacrifice on the cross was no longer at the centre of popish belief and practice; the papists had substituted the doctrine of justification by works for one of justification by faith. Their insistence on the importance of religious works of human devising as a means to achieve salvation established hypocrisy as a central characteristic of popery. The guilt of virtually any sin could be assuaged and salvation attained through some form of external religious observance or act of clerical absolution.[8] Here Protestant treatments of popish attitudes to sex provide a useful encapsulation of the inverted, hall-of-mirrors quality that pervaded much anti-popish writing. For William Perkins the Catholic attempt to confer on celibacy a peculiarly exalted religious significance was a prime example of the pope's usurped and tyrannical claim to be able to set aside and alter at will the laws of God and nature, which had, after all, established marriage as an honourable estate. By so doing, of course, the papists forced many men and women into chaste lives for which they had no calling, with predictable results. Indeed, for many Protestants buggery became an archetypically popish sin, not only because of its proverbially monastic provenance but also because, since it involved the abuse of natural faculties and impulses for unnatural ends, it perfectly symbolized the wider idolatry at the heart of popish religion. Again the Protestants made great play with the papists' notorious laxity towards heterosexual promiscuity, citing here the stews of Rome and the papal revenues produced by licensing them.[9]

The capacity of the clergy to extract a profit from the vicious cycle of hypocrisy and guilt which such beliefs produced provided the Protestants with a convincing sociological explanation for the rise of Popery. But if the prevalence of popery was based on the greed and vainglory of the clergy it was also founded on the ignorance and credulity of the laity. The surface glitter of popish ceremonies and images were all intended to appeal to 'the heart of carnal man, bewitching it with great glistering of the painted harlot'. Popery was a religion based on illusion and trickery. The mass itself was compared to conjuring or magic, as were the false miracles and powers of exorcism claimed for saints and the priesthood respectively. Crucial popish doctrines were also designed expressly to appeal to the corrupt common sense and self love of the natural man. Justification by works was 'an opinion settled in nature'; human self-love and presumption were fostered by the doctrine of free will and merit.[10]

Popery was, therefore, an anti-religion, whose rise in the Church and popular appeal the Protestants explained by the accuracy with which it reflected and played upon the weaknesses and corruptions of man's fallen nature. The differences between this anti-religion and true religion were described by Protestants in terms of a whole series of opposites or contraries; one was carnal, the other spiritual, one inward, the other outward and so on. Here I want to concentrate on the contrasts they drew between tyranny and liberty and light and darkness. The tyranny of popery consisted most obviously in the pope's usurped claim to be the head of the Church. Through the exercise of that claim he trampled on the rights and liberties not only of other bishops and patriarchs but also those of Christian princes.[11] However, the tyranny of the pope was not limited to the 'high politics' of Church government. It consisted also in the spiritual oppression inherent in popish religion, whereby the spiritual rights and liberties of ordinary believers were subverted and destroyed. Their sense of a full and free redemption in Christ was undercut by the popish stress on works; in consequence their consciences were oppressed by the vain human traditions and laws laid upon them by the pope and his clergy.[12]

Of course, this tyranny could not exist without the ignorance of the laity. The papists realized that their hold over the laity would not survive exposure to the clear light of the gospel and had in consequence always opposed the spread of 'good letters' amongst the learned and scriptural knowledge amongst the people. According to Perkins and others the papists really did believe that ignorance was the mother of devotion. Thus the division between popish tyranny and Christian liberty led straight into that between popish darkness and the light of the gospel.[13] For Protestants the Reformation was a gradual process of enlightenment which, started by the likes of Wycliffe and Huss, culminated in the activities of the reformers of the sixteenth century and, in England, in the establishment of the gospel under Elizabeth. Protestants assumed that once the clear light of the gospel had been revealed to the people via the press and the pulpit it would inevitably cut a swathe through the clouds of ignorance and superstition left behind by popery.[14]

Thus Protestants claimed that while popery, through magic, symbols, false miracles and seeming common sense, appealed to the lower, carnal and corrupt side of human nature, their own religion sought to free all Christians from this world of illusion and inversion through the propagation of the unvarnished word. Obviously Protestant confidence in the power of the word was based primarily on the status of scripture as the divinely inspired word of God (and on God's promise that the action of the spirit would attend upon the exposition of his word from the pulpit). But there was also a sense in which Protestants regarded their faith as more rational, more internally coherent than popery. William Perkins, for one, was quite happy to prove that popery was self-contradictory.

Transubstantiation was a nonsense, he wrote, involving as it did the simultaneous presence of Christ's body in heaven and in the bread and wine. Also contradictory were claims that man was saved by grace and then works and that sin was remitted by Christ only to be punished subsequently in purgatory.[15] The mindless acceptance of beliefs and practices merely because they had been held for centuries was also seen by Thomas Scott (the author of *Vox Populi*) and others as a defining mark of popish darkness. Faced with popish appeals to custom and tradition, Matthew Hutton, the future Archbishop of York, replied that 'custom without truth is but old error'. In a culture which, we are often told, was dominated by the claims of custom and tradition the reformation of the Church gave contemporaries at least one prominent example of the reordering of established institutions and value systems according to the dictates of abstract criteria, rationally applied.[16]

Thus the whole Protestant view of popery not only associated it with a ritual-based vision of ignorance, superstition and unthinking traditionalism but it also appropriated for Protestantism an essentially word-based vision of rationality, enlightenment and knowledge. This opinion combined with the repudiation of popish tyranny both secular and spiritual revealed a strain of populism running through the centre of the Protestant image of Rome. Since true reformation could only be brought about as each individual came to a proper understanding and possession of his spiritual liberties and duties as a Christian, Protestant enlightenment was, almost by definition, popular enlightenment. In John Foxe's account of the struggle between the true and false Churches, underground groups of humble believers had kept the true Church alive while the ecclesiastical hierarchy of priests and bishops, aided by the princes of this world, had proved the leading agents of persecution.[17]

The logical culmination of this populist strand was reached in Presbyterianism. Presbyterians saw the rule of one minister over another as a direct emanation of the pope's tyrannical rule over the Church; popery had removed not only the spiritual liberties of ordinary believers but also their civil liberties as Church members. For Thomas Cartwright the right to a say in the election of Church governors and in the conduct of Church government was one of the liberties bought on the cross by Christ for all Christians and subsequently removed by the rise of Antichrist.[18]

Despite such trends and tendencies it would be absurd to see the political legacy of anti-popery as unequivocally populist. After all Foxe himself had made it clear that a central element in the supposed tyranny of Antichrist was his usurpation of the just rights of Christian princes. Moreover, the resumption of those rights had a crucial role to play in the expulsion of Antichrist from the Church. While John Bridges denounced the power of the pope as absolute and therefore tyrannical he did not understand that tyranny to flow from denial of the rights of ordinary believers or ministers to a consent-giving say in ecclesiastical government. Rather it resided, firstly, in the pope's denial of Christian princes' just and God-given powers over the church and secondly in his claim to be able to dissolve and alter the dictates of both natural and divine law.

According to Bridges the powers lawfully exercised by sovereign Christian princes were limited, but only by the dictates of natural and divine law not by the consent of their lay or clerical subjects. In this way conformist writers like Bridges were able to denounce the pope's power as absolute and therefore tyrannical without at the same time committing themselves to a view of political power inherently limited by the ruler's obligation to seek the consent of the ruled. Rather for them tyranny was to be avoided by the subjection of the ruler's will to the laws of God and nature; a subjection to which the pope would not submit.

In part in reaction to the papists' claim about the power of the pope to depose princes and in part in reaction against Presbyterian opinions that had similar implications for religious and secular authority, conformist divines came more and more to emphasize the sovereign powers of Christian princes. Popish tyranny was thus to be avoided not by the retrieval of any popular liberties but by the vindication of the rights of sovereign Christian princes as ecclesiastical governors. In so far as such writers retained any vision of the Reformation as an open-ended process of change, a genuinely popular movement, they limited that vision to the spiritual sphere of individual conversion and collective growth in grace. For them the institutional consequences of the reformation consisted solely of the princes resumption of his or her powers over the Church and the use of those powers to re-establish right doctrine. Of course, consent by both the laity and the clergy was presented even by the most drily conformist writers as a good thing. In practice, they claimed, English monarchs did govern the Church with the consent and co-operation of their (orthodox) subjects. However, the real difference between monarchic and papal power lay not in the consent of either the clergy or the laity but rather in the monarch's submission to natural and divine law.[19]

For these writers the extra-human origins of popery conferred an aura of eschatalogical significance on any régime that successfully contrived to resist it. The success of Elizabeth and James in expelling the pope, restoring the gospel, resisting the assaults of foreign princes and preserving England from the confessional strife which engulfed so many other countries all seemed to prove God's providential care for the English. They certainly provided many conformist defenders of the status quo with powerful arguments against Puritan attacks on the popish remnants within the English Church.[20]

To this can be added another central characteristic of popery in the eyes of English Protestants – it was foreign, involving allegiance to a foreign ruler (the pope) and acceptance of his right to excommunicate and depose Christian princes. The experiences of Elizabeth's reign served to associate popery indelibly with the aggression of foreign popish powers, particularly Spain. Precisely the same process of inversion and name-calling was applied by Protestants to the Spanish as had been used against the papists, a process which culminated, by the second half of Elizabeth's reign, in the so-called 'black legend' of Spanish cruelty and tyranny. Associated as it was with foreign powers, popery appeared to Protestants to be a solvent of the ties of political loyalty. In making that point Protestants tended to emphasize the populist theories of power which Catholic authors advanced to vindicate the rights of subjects to resist and remove heretical rulers. Politically, therefore, the legacy of anti-popery was decidedly ambiguous. Concern with the popish threat could prompt the development of authoritarian as well as of populist readings of the powers of the English Crown and of the nature of authority in the English church.[21]

The legacy of anti-popery was also polemically ambiguous. In the debates between different strands of English Protestant opinion, Presbyterians used popery to emphasize the need to extend the process of reformation from the sphere of doctrine to that of discipline. Conformists invoked it to underwrite the essential soundness of the régime which had stood so long in the breach against Rome. Moderate Puritans and conformists both used it to play down the significance of the internal divisions among English Protestants in the face of the 'common adversary' and to stress the value, as a bulwark of order and obedience, of evangelical Calvinist preaching, even by nonconformists and erstwhile presbyterians.[22]

However, the ambiguity of anti-popery operated at deeper levels than the conscious polemical and political manipulations of contemporaries. Arguably the power of anti-popery as a source of ideological leverage and explanatory power was based on the capacity of the image of popery to express, contain and, to an extent, control the anxieties and tensions at the very centre of the experience and outlook of English Protestants. In part, the roots of those anxieties were obvious enough. There really was a popish threat to the autonomy of Protestant England for much of Elizabeth's reign. Under James the war with Spain ended, but as Tom Cogswell has pointed out, if the alarm over the Spanish Match is added to the traditional list which stretches from the Armada, through the gunpowder plot, the various invasion scares of the 1620s and the Irish revolt, then every generation of English people between the 1580s and the 1640s had personal experience of a popish assault on English independence.[23]

However, the anxieties which lay behind anti-popery had other, less obvious cultural roots. Kai Ericson in his seminal study of the witch craze in New England has argued that the production of such threatening ideal types of deviance and 'otherness' should be located within moments when the moral and cultural boundaries of groups or societies shift or are placed under threat. Clearly the reformation itself was just such a major shift. John Bossy has recently written of the sixteenth century as a period dominated by the emergence of an austerely word-and-doctrine-based view of true religion. In the English context the Protestant image of popery was perhaps the most important ideological means produced for explaining and controlling the strains associated with the transition to that word-based vision of true religion.[24] The image of popery as the natural religion for the fallen man drew on at least three elements within the situation of English Protestants. Firstly it explained and labelled as popish and undesirable the continuing appeal of ritual and symbol and visual imagery in a society still drenched in all three. Secondly it spoke to and helped to account for the pronounced religious conservatism of the English provinces;[25] and thirdly it keyed in with the Protestants' own very pessimistic view of human nature after the fall.

It has become increasingly obvious of late that the cultural struggles upon which English Protestants embarked at the Reformation lasted well into the seventeenth century.[26] This ensured that many of the anxieties about the potential popularity of 'popery', characterized in terms of what had become the inherently popish attributes of sin, sexual licence, superstition and the mindless acceptance of custom, retained their relevance for committed Protestants well into the seventeenth century. That relevance could only be heightened by the continued political threat from foreign popish powers and, increasingly under James and Charles, from popish influence at court. Insofar as this situation might rationally be taken to induce anxiety in Protestants, anti-popery allowed them to label, externalize and hence to act upon that anxiety and, to an extent, therefore, to quell it.

Another parallel explanation for the prevalence and appeal of anti-popery in this period may be found in the political system and its ideology of consensus decision-making. The early seventeenth century was a period of increasing political conflict in Parliament. While revisionist scholars like Conrad Russell have demonstrated that the parties to that conflict are not best seen as a monolithic government and opposition it remains the case that the parliamentary history of the early seventeenth century was hardly a story of untroubled agreement and co-operation between Crown and Parliament. And yet revisionists like Russell and Mark Kishlansky have convincingly argued that despite these difficulties the practical and ideological assumptions of contemporaries remained dominated by the need for agreement between the king and his subjects. Parliament, it seems, drew its prominence in the world view of contemporaries from its supposed capacity to bring about such unanimity and harmony. In view of all this the political history of the period must have come as something of a shock and a disappointment to contemporary observers.[27] Such a basic failure on the part of the political system to produce the goods for which it was supposedly designed called not only for disappointment, it called also for explanation.

Whether the failure of the ruling class assembled in Parliament to meet the financial needs of the Crown was due to ideological principle or penny-pinching localism or some mixture of the two, the fact remains that as the crown resorted to new and unparliamentary sources of revenue what Dr Sommerville has revealed as two mutually exclusive views of political authority were brought increasingly into conflict. It is perhaps worth reminding ourselves that there was an ideological as well as a financial logic which led from impositions to the forced loan and then to ship-money. Given the relationship in contemporary thought between liberty and property it was inevitable that, however great the impulse towards ideological agreement, the functional breakdown delineated by Professor Russell would bring with it ideological conflict. At the level of theoretical argument, as Johann Sommerville has shown, there was precious little room for compromise and yet the workings of the political system and the assumptions of contemporaries were still predicated on the need for agreement and the existence of ideological consensus.[28]

At this point the spectre of popery and popish conspiracy came to the rescue. For the popish threat provided an unimpeachably 'other', foreign and corrupt origin and explanation for conflict, to which those elements in the political system deemed noisome or divisive could be assimilated, while yet leaving the basic structure of the English political system and Church pure and unsullied. As the political crisis of the period deepened during the 1620s the extent of the ideological differences dividing contemporaries came to be reflected in the development of an alternative conspiracy theory, this time centring on the threat of Puritanism.

We will return to that development below. For the present it is sufficient to note the way in which the Protestant image of popery allowed a number of disparate phenomena to be associated to form a unitary thing or force. That force could then be located within a certain eschatological framework, which, by explaining where popery came from, accounted for its awful more-than-human power, but did so in a way that made it quite clear that in the end Antichrist would fall and the gospel triumph. Viewed in this way, the world took on the shape of a progressive and therefore ultimately predictable struggle between Christ and Antichrist, and thus became the ground for the collective action of Protestants, who had been called together positively by their common apprehension of the truths of right doctrine and negatively by their common opposition to the threat of Rome. Popery thus became a unifying 'other' in the presence of which all those not directly implicated in the problem (popery) became part of the solution (non-popery).[29] In this way Protestants, who had started Elizabeth's reign as a minority (probably a small minority) had been able to produce an image of England as inherently Protestant because Protestantism's opposite, popery, was inherently foreign.

Until recently that image of England was associated with the notion of 'the elect nation', but as a number of scholars have recently pointed out, the whole idea of an elect nation was a theological nonsense for Protestants. While it was certain that ultimately Antichrist would lose and Christ would win, it was still an open question whether England would triumph with Christ or be destroyed with Antichrist. The answer depended on whether the English responded to God's commands expounded to them from the pulpit. If they did, God would protect them from the papists; if they did not he would surely use the papists as a stick with which to chastise his erring flock. Both here and in their vision of popery as appealing to those elements in human nature and contemporary society of which they most disapproved, committed Protestants were in grave danger of producing a perfectly circular argument. Elements in their objective situation were taken up and interpreted by Protestants as confirming central strands in their own view of the world, and in the process they produced an ideal type of deviance and evil against which all true Protestants should unite. This image was then employed as an ideological tool with which to label and repress the very impulses from which it was supposed to draw its strength and appeal. Thus what was an inherently purposive and dynamic vision of popery could be employed to underwrite an equally purposive and dynamic vision of further reformation, since only an active campaign against those things upon which popery fed could keep popery at bay.[30]

Whether the notion of further reformation thus canvassed was limited to the active propagation of the gospel and the repression of sin, or whether it was taken to include broader political and ecclesiastical initiatives, either way it is tempting to observe, paraphrasing Sartre's remark about anti-semitism, that if popery had not existed Protestants and, in particular Puritans, would have had to invent it.[31] Indeed, in one sense in the various images of popery that was precisely what they were doing. And yet popery did exist and intermittently throughout the period seemed to call into question the very existence of a Protestant England.

Among the committed minority the continuous cultural threats to Protestant values (compounded by the activities of recusants and missionary priests) were enough to keep the anti-popish pot boiling. However, at the popular level, as the researches of Dr Clifton have shown, anti-popery was crisis-related,[32] representing a symbolic means of dealing with an inherently foreign popish threat and latterly of expressing and controlling worries about internal divisions in terms of such a threat. While the anti-popish spasm lasted, the most committed Protestants were offered an opportunity to lead bodies of opinion far broader than those normally deemed Puritan. That, of course, was one of the things that happened between 1640 and 1642. In order to understand a little more of how and why that happened we need to turn to a more detailed analysis of the relationship between religious ideology and politics in early-seventeenth-century England.

III

From fairly early on in James' reign there were those about the king, including relative moderates like Ellesmere, who saw the Crown's parliamentary difficulties as stemming from 'popular spirits' in the Commons who sought to reduce the power of the crown by playing up to the people. After the collapse of the 1610 Parliament James blamed the Commons in the most acrimonious terms. By 1621 he was complaining of various 'firey and popular spirits' who had debated 'publicly of matters far above their reach and capacity tending to the high dishonour and breach of prerogative royal'.[33]

Conformist writers under Elizabeth had habitually associated a populist threat to monarchy with Puritanism. It was, however, possible to be worried about popularity and not to equate it with Puritanism. Ellesmere, for one, was a Calvinist with many moderate Puritan clients. However, it seems clear that for James the two concepts were integrally linked. Certainly in 1621 his complaints were centred on Parliament's treatment of the Spanish match and the issue of the marriage of his son, the motivations for which were largely religious.[34] By 1626 an anonymous author was explaining the assault on Buckingham in Parliament as the work of popular spirits in the Commons who sought 'the debasing of this free monarchy'. Amongst the malcontents likely to support such a conspiracy the author numbered Puritans and sectaries. Moreover, he located the origins of this movement in the Presbyterian programme first canvassed in 1584. Here he was consciously keying into a rhetoric of anti-Puritanism which had been established in the 1590s during the campaign against Presbyterianism when it had been argued that, since the Presbyterian platform gave the people a considerable role in the election of ministers and the government of the Church, Puritanism was an inherently populist and thus subversive movement.

William Laud in his sermon before the 1626 Parliament made this connection newly explicit, in the course of an assault on what he took to be a Presbyterian plot against authority in Church and state. Such sentiments bulked large in the printed works of Richard Montague in which he repeatedly attempted to persuade King James of the evils of English Calvinism and of the need formally to realign the theological position of the Church of England *vis à vis* the church of Rome.[35]

The agitation over the Spanish match reactivated James' fears of a Puritan plot against monarchy. A similar concern about a populist threat influenced Charles' decision to dissolve the 1626 Parliament as Richard Cust has shown. Such fears, felt by both James and Charles, clearly presented the Arminians, with their vision of a populist Puritan conspiracy against all constituted authority, with a window of polemical opportunity. This they exploited to good effect at the end of one reign and the beginning of the next. However, men like Montague and Laud were moved by more than a desire to curry favour with the King; their vision of Puritan popularity was integrally related to their own positive image of what constituted true religion. According to Howson, Laud and Buckeridge the errors of Calvinism (labelled by the Arminians as distinctively and definitively Puritan) were contrary to all civil government in the commonwealth as well as 'preaching and external ministry in the church'.[36]

Why was Calvinism taken to be incompatible with good government? As a religion of the word it was thought to stir up the lower orders by giving them a spurious interest in matters above and beyond them. In particular the Arminians took the doctrine of predestination, so central to Puritan practical divinity and the spiritual experience of the godly, to lead either to desperation or still worse to presumption. The habitual division between the godly and the ungodly, and the equation of those two groups with the elect and the reprobate, which was taken to typify Puritan piety was regarded by Arminians as inherently divisive and likely to lead to all sorts of anti-nomian excess and political disorder on the part of the godly, whose spurious claims to a status based on 'grace' undercut existing hierarchies of political office, birth or property. To shut up all the worship of God in the hearing of sermons was fatally to underestimate the value of outward ceremony, public prayer and the sacraments in the life of the Church. To this almost idolatrous addiction to sermons could be attributed the appallingly disordered state of many English parishes. Here, as elsewhere, the misguided enthusiasms of the Puritans fitted all too closely with the natural parsimony and anti-clericalism of the laity. The resulting chaos produced an irreverence not only towards God but also towards all constituted authority and where there was irreverence overt disobedience could not be far behind. Over against the Calvinist or Puritan emphasis on preaching the Arminians sought to elevate the role of worship – the solemn administration of the sacraments and public prayer – in the life of the Church. It was this predilection which prompted the liturgical experiments and innovations, the changes in the internal arrangements and decorations of many churches, to which their opponents objected so strongly in the late 1620s and 1630s. Not only did the Arminians take all this to be conducive to the beauty of holiness in the Church, they also believed that it would lead to greater respect for authority and obedience in secular affairs. Beliefs such as these underlay Laud's sermon to Parliament in 1626 and his speeches at the show trials of the 1630s.[37]

Many commentators have got this far in their analysis of Laudian rhetoric, but of late they have tended to cut their argument short, to observe how misguided, even irrational, were Laudian fears of Puritan Calvinism.[38] Certainly Presbyterianism, either as a movement or even an expressed preference, was conspicuous by its absence from the Jacobean Church. This presented few difficulties for the Laudians, who, more convinced than recent historians of the existence of a distinctively Puritan strain of divinity, were quite happy to see in it the cunning of a subversive movement driven underground, waiting its chance under a thin veneer of formal and totally insincere conformity. In response to this view modern scholars have been quick to point out that Calvinism was little short of the received orthodoxy of the high Elizabethan and Jacobean Churches and that its carriers among both laity and clergy were essentially conservative pillars of the establishment in Church, state and locality. Certainly, it would be absurd, with the Laudian avant garde, to see men like George Abbot as crypto-Presbyterian or Puritan incendiaries or semi-republican enemies of monarchy. And yet there was a kernel of truth in the Laudian case. The whole cult of the godly prince and magistrate, to which nearly all Calvinists subscribed, was deeply ambiguous. Certainly it involved the exaltation of royal power but only within an eschatological schema predicated on the pope's identity as Antichrist and the Prince's opposition to popery. Thus when Sir Richard Grosvenor sang the praises of the English King as 'the immediate vice-gerent of God', subject to no rival or superior jurisdiction in this world, he did so in the context of the struggle with Rome.[39]

What happened, however, if the Prince failed to live up to his divinely appointed role as the champion of the gospel and the hammer of the papists? As doubts about the religious reliability of Charles I grew during the 1620s even relatively radical spirits like Henry Burton responded by simply increasing the stakes and assuring Charles that, of course, he must and would fulfil his role as a godly prince in the final struggle between Christ and Antichrist, which Burton felt sure would arrive during Charles I's reign. Yet by 1628 Burton was warning Charles not to slide from godly rule into its opposite, tyranny, and by 1636 he was expressing the sarcastic hope that the people would not conclude from Charles' actions that 'this king hath no regard to his sacred vows'. The logical culmination of this train of thought was reached in 1641 when Richard Baxter, convinced that Charles was implicated in the Irish rebellion, concluded that in effect the king had abdicated and thus become subject to legitimate resistance.[40] Of course in the second and third decades of the century such ultimate decisions were a long way off. Yet, given the tightly defined view of what constituted popery to which men like Archbishop Abbot subscribed,[41] and the context of confessional strife within which European diplomacy was increasingly being conducted, the role of the godly prince, at least as defined by many of his subjects, placed very considerable constraints on James' freedom of manoeuvre.

As Conrad Russell and a number of foreign ambassadors of the 1630s have all pointed out, during the sixteenth century various English monarchs had changed the religion of the nation more or less at will. James I was, however, unable even to arrange the marriage of his son to the Infanta without rousing a storm of protest from his subjects. Orchestrated by Calvinist bishops like Abbot and moderate and not so moderate Puritans like John Preston and Thomas Scott, the rise of a stolidly Protestant and rabidly anti-papal public opinion thus represented a real limitation on the Crown's autonomy.[42] No monarch, who was not a Calvinist zealot, could be expected to welcome this intrusion on his or her traditional prerogatives. From that perspective the Laudian rhetoric which equated Calvinism with Puritanism and Puritanism with popularity and subversion must have taken on a new credibility.

IV

Of course from the outside looking in things appeared rather different. From the outset James's ecclesiastical policy had involved the representation at court of a wider range of religious opinions than had ever made it into the inner circles of the Elizabethan régime. In particular James admitted crypto-Catholics like the Earl of Northampton to positions of real influence. Even amongst members of the establishment the activities of those men caused dismay; Archbishops Bancroft and Abbot both complained about the presence of papists and crypto-papists on the Privy Council. Nor was this alarm limited to the court; in 1614 Sir Peter Bucke was hauled before Star Chamber for claiming that Northampton and other court Catholics had petitioned the king for a formal toleration for their co-religionists. Dark hints about Northampton's religious opinions appeared in some satirical poems by Thomas Scott, published in 1616. Commenting on news of the Overbury murder the Cheshire gentleman William Davenport noted that 'it is plain that my Lord of Northampton had he now been living would have had his head in shrewd hazard for he was a most dangerous traitor'. If Dr Peck is right that Northampton was innocent of any plot to addle the addled Parliament then the fact that he was immediately blamed by the populace for its failure takes on renewed significance. Clearly by 1614 popular perceptions of politics cast Northampton in the role of evil counsellor; a role rendered conceptually necessary by the need to account for Parliament's failure – of which the addled Parliament provides so spectacular an example – to bring the king and his subjects together. It was a role for which Northampton's known crypto-popery fitted him all too well.[43]

Of course it was the Spanish match that really sparked widespread worry about undue popish influence at court and that associated the notion of evil counsel with popery. Davenport passed smoothly from an interest in the spectacular scandal of the Overbury murder to concern over Spanish schemes to undermine English religion through a match with the prince.[44]

Some observers, perhaps more politically sophisticated than Davenport, developed a dichotomy between court and country of the classic sort. The court, argued Thomas Scott, as the ultimate source of power and wealth could not but attract ambitious, self-seeking men as well as foreign papists and ambassadors like Gondomar. The country, however, being relatively free from such influences remained uncorrupt, Protestant, patriotic. In order, therefore, to keep things within bounds, the virtue of the country had to be brought into contact with the actual or potential corruption of the court. The obvious way to do that was through Parliament.

Parliament's importance thus rested on its status as a genuinely representative institution. For pamphleteers such as Scott and country gentlemen such as Sir Richard Grosvenor that status could best be guaranteed if each freeholder stood up and cast his vote according to the dictates of conscience, true religion and the common good. Since such strictures applied even to uncontested elections their significance would appear to have been as much symbolic as practical. Nevertheless, they represented the direct application to politics of the evangelical Protestant or Puritan view that if England were to stand before God as a genuinely godly commonwealth each individual believer had to internalize fully and act on the ground of his or her salvation. This applied with particular force to the need to oppose the mystifications and spiritual tyranny of Antichrist. Such notions must, therefore, have seemed particularly apposite to both Scott and Grosvenor, whose crucial concern was indeed the need to counteract the influence of foreigners and papists at the centre of power.[45]

In all this we can see central elements in contemporary moderate Puritan or evangelical Calvinist thought becoming enmeshed with native traditions of representative government, centred on Parliament, and concepts of active citizenship based on essentially classical models which members of the ruling class had encountered during their years at university. Again, it is not going too far to see the basic paradigm for all the lesser oppositions between good and evil counsel, the public and the private good, through which many contemporaries looked at politics, in the master opposition between Christ and Antichrist, popery and true religion. For, as we have seen, the Protestant image of popery contained within itself all those other oppositions and inversions, and popery as the ultimate model of false order was an awful warning of what would happen if the process of decay and corruption were not halted and the pursuit of the public good and true religion not placed above merely private concerns and gratifications. There was, of course, a basic structural similarity between the Protestant view of the effects of popery on the Church and, say, Sir Edward Coke's view of the effects of corruption on the commonwealth. In both cases a sinister force, based on the corruption of human nature, spread gradually through what had started out as a perfectly stable and sound institutional structure, until it was utterly subverted and undermined.[46]

Of course, it might be possible to write off the likes of Scott, if not of Grosvenor, as unrepresentative firebrands but for the fact that nearly all the central elements in Scott's religio-political outlook were shared by as central a member of the establishment as George Abbot. With Scott, Abbot saw popery as a genuinely international threat. He was consistently worried by the influence of papists and crypto-papists at court and passionately opposed to the Spanish match. Again like Scott, Abbot saw Parliament as a crucial means to bridle the influence of popery at court, enforce the recusancy laws at home and provide money for war abroad. In moments of crisis, again like Scott, although not so openly, Abbot was quite capable of appealing to wider bodies of Protestant opinion in order to put pressure on the King.

There were, of course, differences between the two men, differences summed up by their diametrically opposed estimations of the United Provinces. Where for Scott the Low Countries were the epitome of the godly commonwealth and England's natural allies against popish Spain, Abbot was more suspicious. He particularly disliked the popular structure of their government in Church and state and blamed it, along with the Low Countries' venal tolerance of other religions, for the prevalance of Arminianism there. This seemingly small difference of opinion shows two very different attitudes towards popularity and hierarchy in Church and state in general, and episcopacy in particular.[47] Twenty years later such nuances often made the difference between siding with the king or Parliament. In the 1620s however, such definitive choices were a long way off and Scott and Abbot remained on essentially the same side, particularly as the rise of Arminianism raised the spectre of a crypto-popish fifth column taking over the Church from within.[48]

To committed Calvinists that was precisely what Arminianism looked like and not without reason. Arminian rejection of the central Calvinist doctrines of assurance and perseverance opened the way to what the godly regarded as a popish doubtfulness on the issue of personal salvation and an equally popish reliance on human works to merit salvation. Arminian deprecation of the sermon and revaluation of the role of ritual and outward reverence in the life of the Church also raised the spectre of popery, as did their agnosticism on the hitherto axiomatic identification of the pope as Antichrist. Add to that the undoubted prominence of Laud and Neile in the counsels of the King when the decision to resort to the forced loan was taken and their continuance in royal favour after the Parliament of 1628 and the grounds for implicating the Arminians in a popish plot against the secular and religious liberties of England become clear.

Whether one dates the emergence of Arminianism as a major issue in Parliament relatively early in the 1620s or, with Professor Russell, somewhat later, it remains the case that by the end of the decade innovation in religion had become associated with an assault on the subjects' liberties.[49] That was no mere accident, a product of the contingent adoption by Charles I of an Arminian ecclesiastical policy, but rather the culmination of a longstanding ideological tension between the populist aspects of the English Protestant tradition and the desire in some circles to control and, indeed, even to suppress such tendencies. Thus Arminian religious opinions came to be associated with a jaundiced view of Parliament and strongly absolutist accounts of royal power. This association was based on more than the politique consideration that Parliament, left to its own devices, would have impeached the likes of Richard Montague or Roger Mainwaring. The link between the two positions, while scarcely rooted in the logical structure of Arminian theology itself, was founded on the polemical situation within which English Arminianism was formed and thus on the populist Puritan threat against which the Arminians felt themselves to be in reaction and the political values of hierarchy and obedience inscribed within Arminian piety itself.

On the other side, central elements in the Protestant image of popery rendered it an ideal polemical tool against a régime widely held to be adopting 'new counsels', antipathetic to the rights and liberties of the English. Men like Archbishop Abbot had long assumed that Parliament could be relied upon to oppose popery and that in the struggle against crypto-popish influence at court an appeal both through and outside Parliament to wider bodies of opinion was a useful card to play.[50] Thus it was natural to assume that papists would oppose Parliament and equally natural, if there seemed to be a move afoot to suppress Parliaments, to look for popish involvement. Here practical politics intersected with Protestant theory, since, as we have seen, the arbitrary, unlimited and thus tyrannical power of the pope was seen as the result of a gradual erosion of the liberties of all Christians – an erosion parallel to that supposedly taking place in Church and state in England during the 1620s and 1630s.

Thus by the end of the 1620s there were two structurally similar but mutually exclusive conspiracy theories, both of which purported to explain the political difficulties of the period. The one was centred on a populist Puritan plot to undermine monarchy, the other on a popish plot to overthrow English religion and law. Both theories offered a way out of the political impasse of 1629 by providing an explanation of conflict in terms of the activities of relatively small groups of ideologically motivated men. Thus the integrity of the political system as a whole was left untouched and each side, by labelling the other as intrusive and un-English subverters of a settled system of government, was able automatically to legitimate its own position as the guardian of English good government. As Professor

Russell has suggested, the failure to achieve or maintain political and religious unity could push contemporaries into a sort of collective anxiety fit, for which the conspiracy theory might provide a very effective placebo. And yet, as Dr Sommerville has shown, there were two mutually exclusive visions of the English political system current among contemporaries. By adopting either the popish or the Puritan conspiracy as an explanation for conflict contemporaries were hence doing more than deciding between more or less interchangeable models of deviance; they were choosing between two very different sets of political, cultural and religious values.[51]

V

These two parallel but mutually exclusive conspiracy theories provided the conceptual framework through which many contemporaries viewed the events of the 1630s and early 1640s. It was precisely in terms of an international Calvinist conspiracy against monarchy that the papal agent George Con and Archbishop Laud described the Scots revolt to Charles I. Both Dr Hibbard and more recently Richard Cust have concluded that Charles himself viewed events through these same ideological spectacles. Conversely, the researches of John Fielding have revealed fears of a popish plot centred on the court current in the provinces as early as 1637. It was precisely on such fears that Pym and the other leaders of the Long Parliament intended their propaganda to play.[52]

Of course, the whole notion of a popish conspiracy offered considerable advantages to the parliamentary leadership. It provided a compelling explanation of the course of events from the 1620s until the outbreak of the war; an explanation which allowed them to put the blame for the political crisis squarely on the court and to excoriate the King's policies and advisers without directly attacking his person. A variant of the evil-counsellor argument, it had the advantage of not being limited to any one adviser or faction. Since popery was a principle of evil, with roots in foreign conspiracy and papal influence, it was infinitely extendable, retaining its explanatory force long after the fall of individual favourites like Laud or Strafford.[53]

Popery was not only able to perform this function within the political élite, it also struck a sympathetic chord among the populace. Riots, anti-popish panics and petitioning campaigns testified to popular concern over the issue, as the researches of Manning,

Clifton and Hunt have all shown.[54] But how were these popular feelings related to the coherent ideological positions outlined in the first half of this essay? Of late we may have been seduced into taking too adversarial a view of the relationship between Puritanism and popular culture. It is certainly true that, when it suited them, Puritan ministers could use a brutally clear-cut division between the godly and the ungodly. Yet, as Eamonn Duffy has recently pointed out, they did so within a set of practical assumptions that left room for far more subtle distinctions between the different types or degrees of Christian profession. The ministers' use of the simple godly/ungodly dichotomy might best be understood, therefore, as a rhetorical device, designed to convince all those in some sense within the Church of how stark the choice that lay before them was and how seriously their duties as Christians had to be taken if they were to make good their membership of Christ's body and be saved. Many of the structures of thought and feeling employed by the ministers in this process may not have been so very different from those of their parishioners. Michael McDonald has suggested that popular views of illness and affliction as products of a cosmic struggle between light and darkness had much in common with the Puritan view of a world caught in struggle between God and Satan, Christ and Antichrist. Clive Holmes has made a related point, seeing Puritan and educated Protestant views of witchcraft as feeding off and attempting to control and organize more popular manichaean, even animist ways of looking at the world.[55]

As we have seen, anti-popery operated through precisely the same sort of binary oppositions and inversions as those underlying the attitudes to healing and witchcraft analysed by McDonald and Holmes. In particular, popish religious practices – the mass, miracles, exorcisms – were assimilated, via the pope's identity with Antichrist, to Satan. Like witches' maleficium, popish miracles and exorcisms were either simple tricks and illusions, or else, if they had any substance in reality, they were a product of Satan's complete mastery over second causes and natural forces, employed to deceive the human eye and lead the simple or the unwary to spiritual destruction. Perhaps, therefore, popular anti-popery was the product of Puritan or educated Protestant attempts to organize and enlist for their own purposes deep-rooted popular traditions and ways of looking at the world.[56]

Certainly Dr Clifton's analysis of the structure of the normal anti-popish scare indicates similarities and parallels between these popular 'performances' and the élite 'scripts' analysed above. Panics

93

were normally started by the suspicious antics, often reported by children, of strangers and outsiders, whose actions were seen as part of a popish, often an Irish popish, plot. Clifton attributes to the intense localism of the period this suspicion of people from outside the immediate community or neighbourhood boundary, but then goes on to note that such panics were clustered around the political crises between 1640 and 1642. That the panics and national political crises coincided so closely might be used for purposes other than the demonstration of the strength of localism. Rather it surely provides further evidence of provincial and popular sensitivity to national political events and the intense worry such crises could generate. Richard Cust's recent findings on the circulation of political news and rumour among the classes beneath the gentry would seem to substantiate this view and further to illustrate the way in which the passage of news and rumour at a number of social levels was gradually creating a genuinely national political consciousness in this period.[57]

In fact the role of strangers in many anti-popish panics fits rather well with what we know of anti-popery at higher social levels and in the propaganda of the Long Parliament. There popery worked as a unifying 'other', an inherently un-English or alien force whose intrusive influence within the English Church and political system brought disagreement and conflict in its wake. The role of strangers, often taken to be Irish, in popular panics, dramatized that otherness and the resulting panic expressed, directed and thus helped to control anxiety generated by political events at the centre. The result was cathartically unifying local action, the structures of thought and feeling underlying which were essentially the same as those that underlay the polemics of the most educated and sophisticated of contemporaries.

The popular violence and iconoclasm which accompanied some of these panics, as they have been described by Professor Manning and Dr Hunt, were scarcely the products of indiscriminate hooliganism. Rather, they were directed at what were taken to be ritually impure or threatening objects – either the possessions of known papists or the altar rails and images introduced into parish churches under Laudian rule and commonly associated with popery. As Hunt has shown, men and ministers who surely deserve the appellation Puritan were centrally involved in identifying those targets as popish and therefore objectionable. Nonetheless, it remains (at least) questionable whether all those involved in these disturbances would, under normal circumstances, have numbered themselves or been numbered by others among the godly. John Ayly, who, as Jim Sharpe has shown, played a central role in the destruction of the altar rails at Kelvedon, was a persistent offender in the local courts of a sort unlikely to have found a welcome in Puritan circles.[58]

That popular disturbances included both Puritan leadership and non-Puritan support illustrates rather neatly the relationship between Puritanism and anti-popery. For while anti-popery had never been anything like a Puritan monopoly, Puritanism had always enjoyed a peculiarly symbiotic relationship with popery. Popery, with its alleged preference for human as against divine authority in the Church, had always had a special part to play in the Puritan campaign to base the government and structure of the Church directly on the warrant of scripture and the divine authority it embodied. If Puritans were peculiarly sensitive to popish backsliding in matters of doctrine and ceremony, then the obverse side of that sensitivity had always been a rigorous concern for the personal and collective godliness and orthodoxy of the Christian community. The positive side of the rhetoric of Antichristian corruption was thus the rhetoric of edification and spiritual building. Moderate Puritans had always held that edification could take place within the rather imperfect structures of the national Church. But as the Laudian dominance of the Church, which Puritans regarded as the vanguard for popery, reduced those structures from morally neutral products of human reason and authority to corrupt, popish remnants (or innovations) Puritans came once again to associate edification with the total restructuring of Church government, along austerely scriptural lines. That position had, of course, underlain Elizabethan Presbyterianism and by the late 1620s the process of regression to that earlier position had already started amongst the real radicals. Alexander Leighton in 1628, and then, through the 1630s, Burton, Bastwick and Prynne, all turned their backs on episcopacy and espoused the cause of ecclesiastical reform. By the early 1640s others were joining them in droves.[59]

How far such avant-garde notions of further reformation commanded a genuinely popular following is open to question. While the example of the London artisan Nehemiah Wallington shows that relatively humble men could and did espouse that cause with vigour, we can hardly assume that the likes of John Ayly and his friends were proto-Presbyterians.[60] Yet the fact remains that the political and polemical circumstances of the late 1630s and early 1640s conspired to allow Puritans to lead bodies of opinion which in normal times could scarcely be called Puritan. In short, the 'fused group' of the godly, whose unity was based on a common apprehension of the truths of right doctrine and on a recognition of one another as properly godly saints of God, had been placed at the head of the 'serial group' of the non-popish, whose unity derived only from a common opposition to popery.[61] Since the grounds for and intensity of their opposition to popery might vary considerably from group to group and individual to individual this community of the non-popish was inherently likely to be short-lived. Any attempt to convert it into a politico-religious force over the long term would surely founder on those differences. And yet, as Anthony Fletcher has pointed out, in 1642 it was the short term which counted.

Once the war had started, both sides erected structures of command and coercion that were able to withstand the reduction, if not the disappearance of the popular passions of 1642.[62] They needed to, for during the 1640s and 1650s the coalition which had been created by applying the rhetoric of Antichrist to the Laudian church and the Caroline court gradually fell apart. Its popular support was eaten away, on the right, by the austerities of Puritan worship, the impact of civil war and the reformation of manners. On the left, the coalition fell victim to the inherently fissiparous nature of the Puritan search for first a scriptural and then a spiritual authenticity of belief and practice. This first disrupted the unity of the godly and then, by enlisting some of the hitherto unregenerate populace to the cause of spiritual enthusiasm, created a brand new cause for moral panic in the sects and the Quakers.[63] In the process, contemporaries, like Prynne, alarmed by the drift of events, developed new ideal types of deviance and spiritual degeneracy to control the forces and anxieties unleashed by these changes. It should not surprise us, in these circumstances, to find the old anti-type of popery put to new uses; as phenomena as disparate as the regicide and the rise of the Quakers were attributed to some Jesuit plot to divide and rule.[64] Along with many other fixed points on the polemical map of pre-war politics, anti-popery was transformed by the turmoil of the interregnum and thus made available as a free-floating term of opprobrium. Even so, that should not blind us to the fact that before 1642 popery had a limited meaning to contemporaries as a polemical signifier or label, defined by its place in a longstanding ideological code.

It has been argued here that that code was itself a product of a dialectical process. Populist elements in the conventional Protestant image of true religion and the struggle against popish tyranny and ignorance prompted a political, theological and cultural reaction which reached its apogee in the Laudian church and the Caroline court. The seemingly popish nature of that reaction in turn strengthened the radical populist strain in English protestantism which it was designed to suppress. In the resulting turmoil anti-popery did not simply determine political attitudes, still less allegiances in the civil war. It was and always had been more than possible, with Archbishop Abbot or Lord Montague, to oppose both popery and popularity.[65] During the 1630s, however, to many outside the court the threat from the former must have seemed rather greater than that from the latter. But once the many-headed monster was loosed in massed demonstrations and petitions, once the principles of hierarchy and degree, enshrined in episcopacy, were called into question, things might look very different. For many, the choice between the King and Parliament may have devolved into a choice between popery or a populist Puritanism as the greater threat to order. Certainly much of the propaganda put out by the king and Parliament seems to have been predicated on that assumption.[66] And yet in that choice we have travelled a long way from an irrational panic or knee-jerk response to a non-existent popish threat. Rather, we are confronted with a choice between two competing sets of social and political, as well as religious, priorities and values.

That choice may not often have been approached in a spirit of rational detachment, but that need not surprise us given what was at stake. Certainly anti-popery appealed to people's emotions. It did so because it incorporated deeply held beliefs and values and it helped to dramatize and exorcize the fears and anxieties produced when those values came under threat. But that, surely, is what political ideologies do, and it is from their capacity to do it that they derive their ability to motivate and mobilize large numbers of people. It is, of course, always tempting to overestimate the 'rational' element in our own choices and to write off the ideologies of others as irrational. It is particularly easy when, as in the case of anti-popery, most of the carriers of that ideology are either dead or in Northern Ireland. If, however, we wish to understand a central strand in the political and religious history of seventeenth-century England it is a temptation we must resist.

Notes and References

1. A. J. Fletcher, *The Outbreak of the English Civil War* (London, 1981), pp. 407–19; K. Sharpe, 'Archbishop Laud', *History Today*, 33 (1983) 26–30; M. Finlayson, *Historians, Puritanism and the English Revolution* (Toronto, 1983), *passim*; J. S. Morrill, 'The religious context of the English civil war', *TRHS*, 5th ser., 35 (1985), 135–57; for Professor Lamont's opinion see his review of Caroline Hibbard's *Charles I and the Popish Plot* (Chapel Hill, 1983) in the *London Review of Books* (21 July–3 Aug. 1983).

2. This paragraph represents a perhaps rather crude pastiche of the views put forward in C. S. R. Russell, *Parliaments and English Politics, 1621–9* (Oxford, 1979) and J. S. Morrill, *The Revolt of the Provinces* (London, 1976).

3. C. S. R. Russell, *The Origins of the English Civil War* (London, 1973), pp. 24–6.

4. See S. Clark, 'Inversion, misrule and the meaning of witchcraft', *P&P*, 87 (1980). Also see P. Burke, *Popular Culture in Early Modern Europe* (London, 1978), esp. 185–91. For the use of inversion in popular religious propaganda see R. W. Scribner, *For the Sake of the Simple Folk* (Cambridge, 1981).

5. On the currency of the belief that the pope was Antichrist see C. Hill, *Antichrist in the Seventeenth Century* (Oxford, 1971). By far the best discussion of the theological issues involved is R. J. Bauckham, *Tudor Apocalypse* (Abingdon, 1978). For popery as devil worship see W. Fulke, *The Text of the New Testament* (Cambridge, 1589), p. 881; 'they that worship Antichrist worship the devil not in their intent (for Antichrist boasteth himself to be God) but because they worship him who hath the power of the devil and serveth the devil in deceiving the world'. On popery as worse than paganism, Islam or Judaism see J. Bridges, *The Supremacy of Christian Princes* (London, 1573), pp. 952–3; on Antichrist's gradual rise to power in the church see W. Whitaker *An Answer to the Ten Reasons of Campion the Jesuit*, translated from the original Latin by Richard Stock (London, 1606), p. 172. On the deceit involved, see Whitaker, *A Disputation of Holy Scripture*, (Cambridge, 1849), pp. 20–1.

6. What follows is based on a variety of sources, but especial attention has been paid to one particular genre – the true confessions of Catholic renegades, converted or reconverted to Protestantism. Designed for a fairly low-brow audience, these pamphlets represent rather crude exercises in inversion and thus afford a view of the stock Protestant attitudes to Rome. This procedure has been borrowed from Dr Robin Clifton. See his article in Russell (ed.), *Origins of the English Civil War*, pp. 148–9. The renegade tracts used here are J. Gee, *The Foot out of the Snare* (London, 1624); Thomas Abernathy *Abjuration of Popery* (Edinburgh, 1638); J. Wadsworth, *The English Spanish Pilgrim* (London, 1630); R. Sheldon, *The Motives of Richard Sheldon Priest for his Just, Voluntary and Free Renunciation of Communion with the Bishop of Rome* (London, 1612) and *A Survey of the Miracles of the Church of Rome* (London, 1616).

7. Idolatry was central to the Protestant vision of popish corruption. Perhaps the basic text is the homily on idolatry in *Certain Sermons Appointed by the Queen's Majesty* (Cambridge, 1850), pp. 167–272. Also see Bridges, *Supremacy*, pp. 476–495; Sheldon, *A Survey*, p. 76, for the notion of 'bread worship', pp. 91–3; Sheldon, *The Motives of Richard Sheldon*, pp. 80–1, 85. On papists as idolators, *Works of Richard Sibbes*, ed. A. B. Grosart, 7 vols (1862–4), vol. 2, pp. 379–81; W. Perkins, *Works* (Cambridge, 1626) vol. 1, pp. 400, 676–94.

8. W. Whitaker, *Ad Nicolai Sanderi Demonstrationes . . .* (London, 1583), pp. 112–14; for Bridges the papists' doctrines of salvation by works not faith infringed the liberty and glory of God and led to popish doubtfulness; it stood, in fact, as a type for their wider preference for human rather than divine authority. See his *A Sermon Preached at Paul's Cross on the Monday in Whitsun Week, 1571* (London, 1573), pp. 36–7; also see W. Perkins, *Works* (Cambridge, 1626), vol. 1, 397–8. On hypocrisy based on the priestly power of absolution, see Gee, *Snare*, pp. 9–10; Wadsworth, *The English Spanish Pilgrim*, p. 28; Sheldon, *A Survey*, pp. 51–3.

9. W. Perkins, *Works* (Cambridge, 1626), vol. 1, p. 401; on sexual looseness as a peculiarly popish trait particularly in 'monkish cells' see J. Bridges, *Supremacy*, pp. 302–3; R. Sheldon, *A Survey*, pp. 17, 51–3, 134–7, 141, 192; R. Sheldon, *The Motives of Richard Sheldon*, pp. 85, 151, 155–6, 159.

10. According to Bridges in his Paul's Cross sermon (9), the papists had invented purgatory 'for lucre'; J. Gee, *Snare*, pp. 49–53; R. Sheldon, *A Survey*, pp. 51–2; R. Sheldon, *The Motives of Richard Sheldon* 77–83; W. Perkins, *Works*, vol. 1, p. 401. For the quotation about the carnal man, see W. Charke, *An Answer to a Jesuit* (London, 1580), sig, B8; see also R. Sibbes, *Works*, vol. 4, p. 357; on popish magic and enchantment, see J. Gee, *Snare*, pp. 41, 49–53, 62, 72; J. Wadsworth, *The English/Spanish Pilgrim*, pp. 76–7; see also Reginald Scott, *The Discovery of Witchcraft* (Wakefield, 1973), pp. 365–80; on the fit between popish doctrine and corrupt human nature, see W. Perkins, *Works*, vol. 1, pp. 398–9; T. Scott, *The Highways of God and the King* (London, 1623), pp. 13–15; John Bridges agreed that the papists' rejection of the orthodox Calvinist doctrine of predestination showed typical popish presumption in making the will of God (expressed in election) subject to the will of man (expressed in the presence or absence of human merit) and thus appealed to human vainglory. *A Sermon*, 30–1, 36–7, 76–7, 81. See also Bridges, *Supremacy*, p. 517.

11. Bridges saw the presumption inherent in popish attitudes to justification and election as typical of a wider presumption which expressed itself in the usurpation of God's power over the Church and an aspiration 'to be equal to kings'. *A Sermon*, pp. 37, 127–30. For the pope's tyranny, defined as the denial or usurpation of the prince's powers, see Bridges, *Supremacy*, pp. 65, 228, 592, 765; see also T. Bilson, *The True Difference between Christian Subjection and UnChristian Rebellion* (Oxford, 1585), pp. 68, 349, 437; Perkins, *Works*, vol. 1, p. 399; R. Sheldon, *A Survey*, p. 186; R. Sheldon, *The Motives of Richard Sheldon*, 'To the Christian reader'. The pope's claim to supremacy

and infallibility in the church and his power to depose princes were at the centre of Sheldon's reasons for turning against Rome.

12. J. Bridges, *Supremacy*, pp. 455–7, where the papists' oppression of the church with superstitious ceremonies is compared to that of the pharisees. Also see ibid, p. 476 and R. Sheldon, *The Motives of Richard Sheldon*, p. 140; the tyranny of the pope is here defined in terms of the deprivation of the people of a saving knowledge of scripture.

13. J. Bridges, *Supremacy*, pp. 160–70, describes popery as a clerical conspiracy to keep the prince and people in ignorance; ibid. p. 396 notes the refusal of the papists to explain the sacrament to the people through the reading of scripture. Perkins, *Works*, vol. 1, p. 399; J. Gee, *Snare*, p. 84, describes the papists as 'blind guides and lovers of darkness more than the light' who (ibid. pp. 36–7, 41) used a 'foreign idol gull composed of palpable fiction and diabolical fascination, whose enchanted chalice of heathenish drugs and Lamian superstition hath the power of . . . Medea's cup to metamorpise men into bayards and asses' in order to 'gull, terrify and amaze the simple, ignorant people' into 'admiration of their priesthood, the sanctity of their attire and the divine potency of their sacrifice'. Richard Sheldon likewise saw the papists' reliance on false miracles to convert the people as rooted in the paucity of scriptural backing for their faith (*A Survey*, preface to the reader). They were 'children of darkness' who deal 'covertly and will not come to the light because they fear reproving'. The glory of the mass in particular was based on popular ignorance, as was the rise to power of the pope. See R. Sheldon, *The Motives of Richard Sheldon*, pp. 65–6, 129–31, 140.

14. For John Foxe see N. V. Olsen, *John Foxe and the Elizabethan Church*, Berkeley, 1973) and for the eschatological framework within which these attitudes were developed, see Bauckham, *Tudor Apocalypse*. For the belief that 'as ice melteth at the rays of the clear sun' so popish error would be dispelled by the gospel, see J. Bridges, *Supremacy*, 459. Such optimism was not confined to conformists; a group of puritan ministers gathered together in 1589 concluded that the downfall of Antichrist, prophesied in scripture, was already taking place 'in the hearts and consciences of men' through the preaching of the word. (See Cambridge University Library MSS Hh. VI 10 fo. 21 f.) Even Josias Nichols who, as a parish minister of long standing, knew the difficulties of converting ignorant papists and atheists, was convinced that where a learned minister was assiduous in 'preaching and private conferring' with the people the gospel would triumph; a point he made by comparing the progress of the relatively well-taught south with the ignorance and popery of the untutored north. See J. Nichols, *The Plea of the Innocent* (1602), pp. 219–25. As I have observed elsewhere, the Protestant attitude to popery contained a nice balance between optimism and pessimism. Isolated quotation of the pessimistic statements of Protestants about the prospects of the gospel cannot be used to 'prove' the 'failure' of protestant evangelism.

15. Thus Protestant criticisms of popery revolved around the juxtaposition of the merely human authority of the Church and the divine authority of scripture. For a very clear statement of that position, see

W. Whitaker, *Disputation of Holy Scripture*, pp. 415, 440–50; for popery as contradictory see Perkins, *Works*, vol. 1, pp. 402–4; to this can be added the constant Protestant allegations that the appeal of popery consisted in magic, enchantment, illusion, all of which contributed to a vision of popery as 'irrational'. See note 13 above for references.

16. Matthew Hutton, *A Sermon Preached at York before Henry Huntingdon* (London, 1579), 4r–6r; Thomas Scott, *The Highways of God and the King*, p. 13.

17. This summarizes the argument of Jane Facey, 'John Foxe and the defence of the English church' in M. Dowling and P. Lake (eds), *Protestantism and the national church* (London, 1987).

18. J. Whitgift, *The Works of John Whitgift* (Cambridge, Parker Society, 1851–53), vol. 1, pp. 405–6.

19. See Facey, 'John Foxe' and J. Bridges, *Supremacy*, pp. 657, 784, 806.

20. J. Bridges, *A defence of the government established in the church of England for ecclesiastical matters* (London, 1587), pp. 763, 765. Such arguments were not limited to conformists and anti-Presbyterian polemicists like Bridges. Robert Some, an erstwhile puritan, made the same points against the separatists. See R. Some, *A godly treatise containing and deciding certain questions moved of late in London and other places touching the ministry, sacraments . . .* (London, 1588), pp. 17–18 and *A defence of such points in Robert Some's last treatise as Mr Penry hath dealt against* (London, 1588), pp. 58–9.

21. On popish disloyalty, see J. Bridges, *Supremacy*, pp. 70–1, 74; T. Bilson, *The True Difference*, pp. 101, 109; Thomas Scott (the elder), *Christ's Politician and Saloman's Puritan* (London, 1616), pp. 24–5; J. Wadsworth, *The English-Spanish pilgrim*, pp. 72–3; R. Sheldon, *A Survey*, p. 267. for the 'abominable regicides, rebellions, treasons, civil commotions, prophanations of churches, ruin of kingdoms' produced by popery; for the identification of Spanish monarchy and tyranny as the equivalent and concomitant of the tyranny in the Church of the pope, see Thomas Scott, *Vox populi or news from Spain*, sig. A3–B3; for the black legend, see W. Maltby, *The Black Legend in England* (Durham, North Carolina, 1971), *passim*. For popish theories of resistance, see P. Holmes, *Resistance and Compromise* (Cambridge, 1982); for the increasingly absolutist response of English polemicists to this challenge, see J. Sommerville 'Jacobean political thought and the controversy over the oath of allegiance', Ph.D thesis, University of Cambridge, 1981.

22. For moderate puritans, see P. Lake, *Moderate Puritans and the Elizabethan Church* (Cambridge, 1982), pp. 55–76; also see J. Nichols *The Plea of the Innocent*, pp. 148–87; for moderate conformists, see P. Lake, 'Matthew Hutton; a puritan bishop?', *History*, 64 (1979) and J. Bridges, *A Defence*, pp. 172, 1336. Hard line conformists, however, sought to assimilate Presbyterian clericalism to that of the papists, see R. Bancroft, *Dangerous Positions* (London, 1593), pp. 2–3. For the Presbyterian use of the popish threat and the notion of the discipline as the natural culmination in the realm of outward government of a reformation already complete in terms of doctrine see, for instance, *An humble motion with submission unto the right honourable lords of her*

majesty's privy council (1590) sig. C4ᵛ and F3ʳ. On the argument that Protestant preaching, even by Puritans, was a bastion of order in the face of popular irreligion and popery, see D. Zaret, *The Heavenly Contract* (Chicago, 1985), pp. 81–9.

23. See Tom Cogswell's essay in this volume and C. Hibbard, *Charles I and the Popish Plot* (Chapel Hill, 1983).

24. K. Erikson, *Wayward puritans* (New York, 1966); J. Bossy, *Christianity in the West, 1400–1700* (Oxford, 1985); for another anti-type, developed to express and control anxiety about certain types of belief and behaviour, see M. C. W. Hunter, 'The problem of atheism in early modern England', *TRHS*, 5th ser., 35 (1985). Interestingly some contemporaries lumped papists and atheists together as threats to the cause of true religion, see, for instance, J. Nichols, *The Plea of the Innocent*, pp. 218–22.

25. On popular conservatism, see C. Haigh 'The continuity of Catholicism in the English Reformation', *P&P*, 93, (1981); see also C. Hill, 'Puritans and the dark corners of the land', *TRHS*, 5th ser., 13 (1962).

26. For the introduction of the 'reformation of manners' as an organizing concept in the study of English Protestantism and society, see C. Hill, *Society and Puritanism in Pre-revolutionary England* (London, 1964); for more recent repetitions and refinements of Hill's position, see K. Wrightson, *English Society, 1580–1680* (London, 1982), esp. chs 6 and 7, and D. Underdown, *Revel, Riot and Rebellion* (Oxford, 1985).

27. C. S. R. Russell, *Parliaments and English Politics 1621–9* (Oxford, 1979), esp. ch. 1; see also M. Kishlansky, 'The emergence of adversary politics in the Long Parliament', *JMH*, 99 (1977); see also his *Parliamentary Selection* (Cambridge, 1986).

28. J. P. Sommerville, *Politics and Ideology in England, 1603–40* (London, 1985); Russell, *Parliaments and English Politics*, pp. 49–53, 64–84; see also the introduction above pp. 17–21.

29. P. Lake, 'The significance of the Elizabethan identification of the pope as Antichrist', *JEH*, 31 (1980); 'William Bradshaw, Antichrist and the community of the godly', *JEH*, 36, (1985).

30. On the 'elect nation', see Bauckham, *Tudor Apocalypse*, pp. 70–3, 86–8.

31. J-P. Sartre, *Anti-semite and Jew*, transl. G. J. Becker (New York, 1948).

32. R. Clifton, 'Fear of popery', in C. Russell (ed.), *The Origins of the English Civil War*; and 'The popular fear of catholics during the English revolution', *P&P*, 52 (1971).

33. L. A. Knafla, *Law and Politics in Jacobean England* (Cambridge, 1977), pp. 186, 254–62; *H.M.C. Report on the Mss of the Marquess of Salisbury (at Hatfield House)*, vol. 21 (1970), p. 266; J. R. Tanner, *Constitutional Documents of the Reign of James I* (London, 1930), p. 279. I owe these last two references to the kindness of Richard Cust.

34. Knafla, *Law and Politics*, pp. 54–5; K. C. Fincham and P. Lake, 'The ecclesiastical policy of James I', *JBS*, 24 (1985).

35. 'To his sacred majesty ab ignoto' in *Cabala sive scrinia sacra*, 3rd edn (London, 1691), pp. 255–7; *The Works of William Laud*, eds W. Scott and J. Bliss, 7 vols (Oxford, 1847–60), vol. I, pp. 63–89, esp. pp. 82–3; R. Montague, *A Gagg for the New Gospel? No: a New Gagg for an Old Goose* (London, 1624) and *Appello Caesarem* (London,

1625). For detailed references see note 37 below. For Elizabethan anti-Puritan and anti-Presbyterian polemic see my *Puritans and Anglicans? Presbyterianism and English Conformist Thought from Whitgift to Hooker* (London, 1987).

36. *Works of Laud*, vol. 6, pp. 244–6, Laud, John Howson and John Buckeridge to Buckingham, 2 Aug. 1625; see also ibid., p. 249, Montaigne, Neile Andrewes, Buckeridge and Laud to Buckingham, 16 Jan. 1626; on the role of the fear of popularity in the genesis of the forced loan, see Richard Cust, *The Forced Loan and English Politics, 1626–1628* (Oxford, 1987), pp. 13–30, 39–51.

37. For the identification of the doctrine of predestination with Puritanism and of Puritanism with popularity and Presbyterianism, see Montague, *Appello Caesarem*, pp. 7, 23, 39, 42, 43, 60, 72, 111, 114, 118, 182, 213, 320; for the equation of order and reverence in the Church with order and reverence in the state and the argument that the word-based Puritan style of religion was inherently irreverent and disordered, see M. Wren, *A sermon preached before the king's majesty on Sunday 17 February last at Whitehall*, (Cambridge, 1627); see also Isaac Bargrave, *A sermon preached before King Charles March 27, 1627* (London, 1627) *passim* and esp. pp. 4–5, 14; *The Works of William Laud*, vol. 1, pp. 63–89; for Laud's conviction that there was a populist Puritan plot on foot during the 1630s, see S. Foster, *Notes from the Caroline Underground* (Hamden, Conn., 1978), and for the same assumptions applied on the local level by Robert Sibthorpe, see V. Stater, 'The Lord Lieutenancy on the eve of the civil wars: the impressment of George Plowright' *HJ*, 29 (1986). For Laudian changes in the internal arrangements of churches in Cambridge and the opposition it aroused, see D. Hoyle, 'A commons investigation of Arminianism and popery in Cambridge on the eve of the civil war', *HJ*, 29 (1986).

38. See, for instance, C. S. R. Russell, *Parliaments and English Politics*, pp. 26–34 or P. Collinson, *The Religion of Protestants* (Oxford, 1982), *passim*. Such claims are, of course, in many ways quite justified and certainly to be preferred to the assumption of an inherent Puritan radicalism.

39. R. Cust and P. Lake, 'Sir Richard Grosvenor and the rhetoric of magistracy', *BIHR*, 54 (1981).

40. For Burton, see B. S. Capp, 'The political dimension of apocalyptic thought', in C. A. Patrides (ed.), *The Apocalypse in English Renaissance Thought and Literature*, (Manchester, 1984). For Baxter, see W. Lamont, *Richard Baxter and the Millenium*, (London, 1979), pp. 76–119.

41. K. C. Fincham, 'Archbishop Abbot and the defence of protestant orthodoxy', *HR* 61 (1988), 36–64. I should like to thank Dr Fincham for letting me see this article in advance of publication.

42. Fincham, 'Archbishop Abbot'; P. Lake, 'Constitutional consensus and puritan opposition in the 1620s: Thomas Scott and the Spanish match', *HJ*, 25 (1982); for John Preston, see C. Hill, 'The political sermons of John Preston', in *Puritanism and Revolution* (London, 1958) and I. Morgan, *Prince Charles' Puritan Chaplain* (London, 1957). See Cogswell (Ch. 4 in this volume).

43. Fincham and Lake, 'Ecclesiastical policy of James I'; P. Clark *English Provincial Society from the Reformation to the Revolution: Religion, Politics and Society in Kent, 1500–1640* (London, 1977), p. 316; T. Scott, *Philomythologie* (London, 1622); Chester city record office MSS CR 63/2/19, fo. 9ʳ; L. L. Peck, *Northampton*, (London, 1982), p. 210.

44. R. P. Cust, 'News and politics in early seventeenth century England', *P&P*, 112, (1986); Chester city record office MSS CR 63/2/19, fos 2ʳ–14ᵛ for the Overbury scandal; fos 14ᵛ–18ʳ, on the fate of Raleigh; fos 24ʳ–25ᵛ, 27ᵛ–28ʳ, 35ʳ for the Spanish match; fos 43ʳ–59ᵛ for the impeachment of Buckingham. Throughout, Davenport associated evil counsel with popish plotting.

45. Lake, 'Thomas Scott' and Cust and Lake, 'Sir Richard Grosvenor'. See also Richard Cust (Ch. 5) in this volume.

46. S. White, *Sir Edward Coke and the Grievances of the Commonweal*, (Manchester, 1979), pp. 38–9; Lake, 'Thomas Scott'.

47. Lake, 'Thomas Scott'; Fincham, 'George Abbot'; for Abbot's dislike of the Low Countries, see PRO SP 105/95, fos 4ᵛ–5ʳ, Abbot to Dudley Carleton, March 22, 1617/18; for Scott's very different estimation of the Dutch, see in particular his *The Belgic Pismire* (1622).

48. It is perhaps worth noting that there was a conceptually necessary vacancy in the attitudes of many contemporaries for crypto-popish evil counsellors, a vacancy which the Arminians were exceptionally well qualified to fill. See note 44 above. As early as 1616 Richard Sheldon had complained of the activities of 'hypocrite clergy . . . which being neither hot nor cold God doth cast out of his mouth and would God this church had or could spew them out'. (See Sheldon, *A Survey*, 'Preface to the reader').

49. C. S. R. Russell, *Parliaments and English Politics*, pp. 406–8; N. R. N. Tyacke *English Anti-Calvinism* (Oxford, 1987). See also Dr Tyacke's review of Caroline Hibbard's *Charles I and the Popish Plot* in *Albion*, 16 (1984), 49–50.

50. Fincham, 'George Abbot'.

51. C. S. R. Russell, 'Arguments for religious unity in England, 1530–1650', *JEH*, 28 (1967); 'The parliamentary career of John Pym, 1621–29', in P. Clark and N. R. N. Tyacke (eds) *The English Commonwealth* (Leicester, 1979); J. P. Sommerville, *Politics and Ideology*; see also his contribution to this volume (Ch. 2).

52. C. Hibbard, *Charles I and the Popish Plot*, p. 95; Cust, *The Forced Loan*, ch. i, conclusion. John Fielding in a forthcoming article in *HJ* on Robert Woodford, the Puritan steward of Northampton, has identified fears of a popish plot in 1637; I should like to thank John Fielding for letting me read and cite his paper on Woodford and Richard Cust for showing me an unpublished paper on the role of the fear of popularity in Charles' relations with Parliament both in the 1620s and in 1640.

53. S. R. Gardiner, *Constitutional Documents of the Puritan Revolution* (Oxford, 1951), pp. 206–7, 216.

54. B. Manning, *The English People and the English Revolution* (London, 1976), pp. 33–59; W. Hunt, *The Puritan Moment* (Cambridge, Mass.,

1983), ch. 11; R. Clifton, 'Fear of popery' and 'The popular fear of popery'.

55. M. McDonald, 'Religion, social change and psychological healing in England, 1600–1800', in W. J. Sheils (ed.), *Studies in Church History*, vol. 19, 1982; C. Holmes, 'Popular culture? Witches, magistrates and divines in early modern England', in S. Kaplan (ed.), *Understanding Popular Culture* (New York, 1985); E. Duffy, 'The godly and the multitude in Stuart England', *Seventeenth century*, 1 (1986).

56. R. Sheldon, *Survey*, pp. 39–40; see also W. Whitaker, *Praelectiones . . . de ecclesia* (Cambridge, 1599), p. 348 and *Ad Nicolai Sanderi demonstrationes*, pp. 168–171.

57. R. Clifton, 'Fear of popery' and 'The popular fear of popery'; Cust, 'News and politics'.

58. Manning, *English People*, pp. 189–96; and Hunt, *Puritan Moment*, ch. 11; J. Sharpe, 'Crime and delinquency in an Essex parish', in J. S. Cockburn, *Crime in England, 1550–1800* (London, 1977).

59. P. Lake, 'Identification of the pope as Antichrist'; P. Christianson, *Reformers and Babylon* (Toronto, 1977), chs 4 and 5; see also Capp, 'The political dimension of apocalyptic thought' and W. Lamont, *Marginal Prynne* (London, 1963), pp. 11–84.

60. P. Seaver, *Wallington's World* (London, 1985), ch. 6; that there were also respectable supporters of 'further reformation' amongst Ayly's Essex neighbours is clear from J. Sharpe, 'Scandalous and malignant priests in Essex; the impact of grassroots puritanism', C. Jones, M. Newitt and S. Roberts (eds), *Politics and People in Revolutionary England* (Oxford, 1986).

61. J-P. Sartre, in his *Critique of Dialectical Reason*, distinguished fused groups, those united by a common world-view or political or emotional project from serial groups, those united only by their relation to an external object (like the members of a bus queue, united only by their relation to the approaching bus). Opposition to popery clearly evoked stronger emotions than waiting for a bus and yet the community of the non-popish scarcely fulfilled the criteria of the fused group. The different conceptions of and attitudes to the popish threat operative in the early 1640s prevented that common sediment of agreement from providing the basis for a genuinely fused group, united by a positive religio-political programme and a common core of spiritual experience.

62. A. Fletcher, *Outbreak of the English Civil War*, Conclusion; R. Hutton, *The Royalist War Effort* (London, 1982), pp. 201–3; A. Hughes, 'The king, the parliament and the localities during the English civil war', *JBS*, 24 (1985).

63. J. S. Morrill (ed.), *Reactions to the English Civil War* (London, 1982), pp. 89–114; for the splintering effect on the left see C. Hill, *The World Turned Upside Down* (London, 1972); and F. McGregor and B. Reay (eds), *Radical Religion in the English Revolution* (Oxford, 1984).

64. On the emergence of the stereotype of the quaker as populist incendiary and anti-nomian threat to order, see B. Reay, *The Quakers and the English Revolution* (London, 1985), ch. 5; see also J. C. Davis *Fear, Myth and History: the Ranters and the Historians* (Cambridge, 1986),

which argues that the ranters were, in effect, a polemical invention, produced to label and control the threat posed to order by the sectarian left. For the role of the reworked version of the popish threat in all this see W. Lamont, *Marginal Prynne*, ch. 6 and *Richard Baxter*, pp. 109–13. See also I. Thackray, 'Zion undermined; the protestant belief in the popish plot during the English Interregnum', *History Workshop Journal*, 18 (1984) and S. A. Kent, 'The papist charges against the interregnum quakers', *Journal of Religious History*, 2 (1982–3).

65. For Montague see Esther Cope, *The Life of a Public Man: Edward, First Baron Montagu of Boughton*, 1562–1644 (Philadelphia, 1981).

66. Manning, *English People*, pp. 59–83, 249–58; D. Hirst, 'The defection of Sir Edward Dering', *HJ*, 15 (1972); B. H. G. Wormald, *Clarendon; Politics, History and Religion* (Cambridge, 1952). For an example of the royalist propaganda, predicated on the existence of a populist Puritan and Presbyterian threat to order see Sir Thomas Aston *Remonstrance against Presbytery* (London, 1641).

4 England and the Spanish Match

Thomas Cogswell

I

Mr Wiats, a publican in Godalming, welcomed a group of prominent travellers who had stopped to refresh themselves early in the evening of 5 October 1623. The fact that such a distinguished party insisted on riding through the night to London was indeed singular, and the visitors' evasive replies to polite inquiries about their travels only further aroused suspicion. Eventually the identity and journey of the travellers became apparent when they paid their bill – in Spanish coin. In the ensuing excitement, the publican's wife repeatedly kissed the leader of the group while an old woman clung to his hand refusing to let go until he promised never to repeat his journey.[1]

The man was Prince Charles who had arrived earlier in the day at Southampton after a half year in Spain, and the scene in the tavern gave him a taste of the pandemonium his arrival would cause in the capital. Although a light drizzle was falling when the Prince reached the Thames early in the following morning, the city was ready to receive him. The bells of the metropolis, the guns of the Tower, and the drums and horns in every street produced a deafening din. Amid the noise, the main concern of the citizens was the creation and maintenance of the largest possible bonfires, and thanks to the rain and the size of some fires (one began with 14 cartloads of wood), this was no mean feat. Once the firewood ran out, the revellers fed anything combustible to the flames – refuse, fat, washtubs and furniture. A few jubilant watermen and coachmen even broke up their boats and carriages. In fact the fires became so dense on the major thoroughfares that when the Prince left the

Strand for Royston, he had to swing around rather than through the City. From Whitehall to Temple Bar alone, one contemporary counted no less than 335 bonfires.[2]

To be sure the high spirits owed much to the generosity of those who opened their cellars. 'The salutations of joy' convinced Secretary Conway that there was not 'a sober head betweene Southampton and ... '; at first he wrote Royston, then added Cambridge and finally settled on 'God knowes where to fynde one'. Little wonder then that one poet found in the carnival atmosphere the appropriate image to commemorate the occasion. Just as 5 November lent itself to rhymes about 'remember', so too 5 October naturally rhymed with 'sober', as in

on the 5th day of October
it will be treason to be sober.[3]

The ample liquor helped transform the excitement into mass hysteria whenever Charles appeared. A throng eager for a glimpse of the prince quickly surrounded Yorkhouse where he rested for a few hours. Consequently prominent officials had a great deal of trouble slipping in, and when Charles went out, his coach had to be carried in places through the mass. Since 'the peoples harts did burn to see him', Charles 'leaned his body out of the coach, with his hatt in the hand and gave thancks to them all for their loves'. In response some shouted 'God save your Highnes and the Lord of Heaven preserve you', and others, 'we have him ... we have our prince again'. Afterwards 'the people for joy and gladnes ran up and down like madde men and none of what condition soever would work upon that day'.[4]

The festivities were not confined to the capital. In Great Yarmouth old men wandered the streets 'with droppes of joy trickling along their cheekes acknowledging that such triumphanting they did never behold'. In Oxford the city celebrated with its largest single expenditure of the year, and in Coventry, the bells rang for two nights while the members of the Corporation treated themselves to drinks. In the Irish Plantations the settlers expressed their joy through a mass review of the militia; and in Aberdeen the magistrates led the men of the town in an extended procession through the streets.[5] The memory of the event moreover was not shortlived. At least two chapels, one in rural Kent and the other at Exeter College, Oxford, were later dedicated to commemorate Charles's return. Poets, both popular and courtly, continued to perpetuate the recollection of that day, and at St Margaret's,

Westminster, the bells continued to toll on 5 October until the outbreak of the Civil War.[6]

Similar details can be produced in almost overwhelming abundance, but they would only confirm what should already be obvious; the popular response to the return of the Prince in 1623 was one of the most impressive displays of popular emotion in the entire seventeenth century and certainly the most impressive in James' reign. The most remarkable of the many contemporaries to support this verdict was Bishop Laud; he recorded in his diary on 6 October that he had just witnessed 'the greatest expression of joy by all sorts of people that ever I saw'.[7]

The obvious question is why all the fuss? Unfortunately for students of Stuart England, the scene in October 1623 is much easier to describe than it is to explain. What initially seems simply an early manifestation of the popular interest in the 'royals' becomes more complicated once it is appreciated that the crowds were celebrating the fact that Charles was *not* going to marry an attractive princess. The crowds plainly were reacting to the long-planned Anglo-Spanish dynastic match, but precisely what they thought about the match has been little studied. Notwithstanding the obvious importance of the Spanish match in early Stuart politics, it has attracted surprisingly scant historiographical attention, and what little work that has been done has centred on diplomacy and particularly on the trip to Madrid in 1623.[8] Swashbuckling episodes in which the naturally phlegmatic heir-apparent vaulted walls to surprise his paramour have an understandable attraction, as do the equally theatrical manoeuvres between King James and Gondomar, the Spanish ambassador. Nonetheless to focus too narrowly on events at Whitehall and Madrid is to miss the equally dramatic tale of how a Spanish teenager managed to plunge the realm into a bitter controversy.

An examination of this hitherto overlooked episode pays handsome dividends. Not only does it explain the wild excitement over Charles' return, it also illuminates fundamental historiographical problems. Whether or not the Civil War was actually a Puritan Revolution, the fact remains that most contemporaries were intellectually unable to separate politics and religion, and there are few better examples of the way in which these two are inextricably bound up in the early-seventeenth-century *mentalité* than the reaction to the prospect of a Spanish queen. In fact the near ubiquity of contemporary comments about the Spanish match merits attention in its own right.

The mass of Englishmen outside Whitehall have been seen as being 'surprisingly ill-informed' about events at the centre. Yet the response to the Spanish match clearly reveals that this mass ignorance was not for lack of interest. When a sensational story like that of Charles and Maria came along, many made it their business to know the latest news; it was not their fault that they had to sift through a farrago of half-truths and outright fabrications. With some justice Gilbert Sheldon, the future Archbishop of Canterbury, complained that the reports about the match were 'more [than] I can either write or remember and many of them so improbable'.[9] Nevertheless this should not obscure the vital fact that many eagerly received and disseminated any information about the match, no matter how far-fetched.

Popular interest sufficient to sustain an 'underground' news network also underscores the problems inherent in allowing parliamentary history to pass for political history. Notwithstanding repeated pleas for broader contextual studies, almost all political studies of the decade, even those of 'revisionists', have rarely ventured outside the Palace of Westminster. Thus it is possible to use parliamentary diaries to construct a case, as Professor Russell has done, which holds that only late in the 1620s did contemporaries abandon the ideal of consensus for more aggressive, ideological confrontations and then only in response to the burdens of war.[10] Unfortunately a tight focus on Parliament overlooks much of the storm over Charles' bride which, as will be seen, opened the most dangerous gap between the political 'court' and 'country' in James's reign. And this early rise of ideological politics was due to the lack, not the burden, of war. Therefore the analysis of domestic politics between two particularly well-studied sessions in 1621 and 1624 amply supports the revisionist insistence on broader contextual studies and reveals the dangers of textual studies of Parliament, whether revisionist or Whiggish.

The pronounced polarization of the realm during the Spanish match furthermore was not a passing aberration in early Stuart politics; rather it became a model to which contemporaries reverted again and again in the years before the Civil War. For many Englishmen the memory of the tense months when they were awaiting the Infanta profoundly coloured their political perceptions of the military crisis later in the decade. Likewise Charles' 'Personal Rule' in the 1630s was in many ways a revival of his father's policies during the Anglo-Spanish negotiations; the stress on the blessings of peace, the tight episcopal control over preachers, the campaign against Puritans amid a *de facto* toleration of Catholics, and above all else the reliance on Spain, were hallmarks of the early 1620s as well as the 1630s. The names of those whom modern heirs-apparent have wooed and not wed slip all too easily from the modern memory; few contemporaries, however, found it as easy to forget Donna Marïa Anna of Spain.

II

Among the many controversial policies of James I, none provoked such heated debate as did his plan to marry his heir to a Spanish princess. The notion of an Anglo-Spanish dynastic alliance had arisen in 1614 as a Spanish alternative to an Anglo-French match, and since the proposed Spanish dowry was larger than the annual royal income, much less the French dowry, the proposal had obvious attractions for a monarch congenitally unable to balance the budget. Financial considerations aside, the paramount merit of a Spanish princess was her ability to balance the earlier marriage of James' daughter to the leading Calvinist prince of the Empire, Frederick V of the Palatinate. Consequently with prominent relatives in both confessional camps, the Stuart dynasty would stand as a potent safeguard against the revival of the religious wars which had racked the continent in the preceding century. In other words, a Spanish match coming on the heels of the Palatine alliance would provide a solid foundation to James' claim to be *Rex Pacificus*, the King of Peace. The chief obstacle to early nuptials was the fate of the English Catholics, and rather than risk immediate shipwreck, both sides agreed to place this vexatious issue at the end of the agenda. On this basis the discussions fitfully continued for several years.[11]

These extended negotiations afforded Englishmen ample time to brood over the projected marriage, and the longer some pondered the matter, the less they could follow James's logic. Admittedly, the recollection of the hard-fought fifteen-year war under Elizabeth I made an Anglo-Spanish marriage hard to swallow. Indeed after this struggle in which all Jacobean military experts had earned their laurels, it was very hard not to think of Spain as *the* enemy. NATO commanders would now find it just as difficult to think benevolent thoughts about their opposite numbers in the Warsaw Pact.

Solid political and religious reasons seconded this instinctive aversion to all things Spanish. The proposition that an Anglo-Spanish match would guarantee continental peace rested on the assumption that the Spaniards could be trusted since they shared James's desire for peace. Unfortunately the history of the Habsburg 'empire' did not support this vital assumption. The Prince would be marrying into no ordinary royal family. Since the days of Charles V, the Habsburg Kings of Spain had presided over a sprawling collection of family possessions on which, as one Englishman noted with awe, the sun never set. And since the days of Charles V, Europeans not under Habsburg control had been driven by the fear that the vast Habsburg 'empire' might very well soon get larger. Thanks to the combination of Spanish administrative talent and military prowess with Genoese banking skills and most importantly South American silver, the Kings of Spain periodically appeared poised to exceed the ancient Romans with their own 'universal monarchy'.[12]

Charles' prospective in-laws appeared even more ominous since it was well known that the House of Austria had achieved much of its greatness through timely marriage. Primogeniture only compounded these fears. Notwithstanding James' desire to use his children to maintain a balance between Catholics and Protestants, the old king allotted the heir of his three kingdoms to the Catholics. Hence a fecund Infanta could well draw England into the 'empire' just as earlier Habsburg princes had done in the Netherlands and in Spain itself. Thus many Englishmen in the 1610s found cold comfort in the recollection of the witticism which contemporaries a century earlier had coined about Maximilian I, the architect of Habsburg greatness: 'Bella gerunt alii, tu felix Austria nube [others may wage wars, but you, happy Austria, marry]'.

What seemed politically unwise also appeared religiously dangerous. Since the Reformation, marriages within royal families had strictly followed confessional lines; thus James was proposing the first exception to this rule. While some contemporaries were beginning to grasp the wide distinctions among Catholics, all understood that Spanish Catholics represented the most ardent supporters of the Counter-Reformation and the most implacable opponents of the Reformed creeds. Therefore the match would introduce into the royal bedchamber, not the modest devotions of James's Catholic consort, Queen Anne, but rather the most aggressive strain of contemporary Catholicism. And with this strain, godly Englishmen felt well acquainted; after all many of the grislier scenes in Foxe's *Book of Martyrs* occurred during the reign of a daughter of an earlier Anglo-Spanish marriage.

To be sure, the match might ensure peace; it might also bring the realm back to the old Roman faith. Reactionary though it now seems, Englishmen by and large felt it was futile and more importantly dangerous to seek a rational accommodation with Catholics. In the first place, such a settlement meant dealing with the Pope, whom many of the godly regarded as nothing less than the Antichrist, the Whore of Babylon. 'Have peace *from* Babylon?', Theophilius Higgons asked sceptically; 'you can have no peace *with* her.' Rather he reminded his audience that 'you are sent against Rome . . . to destroy it with fire and sword'. Equally axiomatic was the belief that Catholics would not be content with a limited toleration for the Infanta's household. As a Cheshire gentleman proclaimed, the Catholics will move from 'toleration' to 'equallitie' to 'superioritie . . . till they have used all plotts and practises for the quite extirpation of our religion'.[13] Hence the nobility of James's plans to secure peace through the Spanish match was not as apparent as its dangers were. Indeed many found it incomprehensible that James should gamble the hard-won gains of the Reformation on this novelty.

Thanks to the languid pace of negotiations, these apprehensions about the Spanish match remained unfocused, but in 1618 they were given ample substance when the Empire plunged into an extended religious war. By then the Bohemian Estates, dominated by Prot-estants, had become convinced that their monarch, Ferdinand II, a young Habsburg prince, was subverting religious toleration. In response, the Estates in an unusual constitutional move deposed Ferdinand II and in his place elected Frederick V. The Elector Palatine ignored his father-in-law's strenuous advice and accepted the crown.

This attempt to shuffle sovereigns was nothing less than a bid to alter the continental balance of power. If the Bohemian rebels succeeded, the Habsburgs would lose much more than wealthy provinces. They might lose control of the Imperial crown, for a Protestant elector in Prague would for the first time create a Protestant majority in the Electoral College. They might also forfeit central Europe for the Catholic Church; other Protestant popula-tions under Habsburg control attentively followed the Bohemian news and required little encouragement, as one German cartoon crudely put it, to castrate the Jesuits and the Pope.[14]

Some Englishmen, particularly among the godly, were eager to assist in this operation. News of the Bohemian revolt quickly became a marketable commodity in London and the provinces. One Londoner remarked that he could not 'passe the streets but I am continually stayed by one or other, to know what newes [from

Prague]'. In the excitement chiliastic hopes ran high: Archbishop Abbot predicted that the time had at last come when Catholic princes 'shall leave the Whore and leave /her desolate', and a Protestant astronomer saw in Halley's Comet astrological proof that 'the House of Austria cannot continue above the yeare 1623' and Rome 1646. In the circumstances the popular ballad of the day entitled 'Gallants to Bohemia' had much more than a snappy tune to recommend it.[15]

These glittering prospects, far from exciting James, terrified him. The justice of Frederick's quarrel with Ferdinand was not readily apparent to an advocate of the divine right of kings, and *realpolitik* also advised a wary English response to the crisis. A quick count of heads revealed which side had the larger battalions in central Europe where James could do little to tip the balance unless, as one wag quipped, 'his greate fleete could flie thether over land'. Given the long odds on Bohemian rebels, there seemed to be no reason for requesting awkward divine favours; 'god doth not in these dayes', one prince reportedly warned Frederick, 'send Prophets more to the Protestants than to others . . . to engage them into unnecessarie warres and combustion with theire Neighbours'. James could not have expressed his own views better. His solution was not war, but rather an expansion of the Anglo-Spanish marriage negotiations. Disavowing both the rebels and his son-in-law, the King pressed for a ceasefire and a return to the status quo ante bellum. The cement for the general peace was to be the marriage of Frederick's brother-in-law, Prince Charles, to the daughter of Ferdinand's chief paymaster, Philip III of Spain. As always James was flexible; once Spanish troops overran the Palatinate in 1620, he simply added it to the Infanta's dowry.[16] In short the Bohemian war transformed the Spanish match into a diplomatic instrument concluding the continental religious war and removing the pressure for English military intervention.

The flaw in James's plan was not lack of Spanish interest; Philip's ministers embraced the proposal neutralizing England with alacrity, and the Palatinate provided them with the necessary leverage to overcome the hitherto firm English opposition to a general Catholic toleration. The flaw was James' rancorous dissolution of the Parliament of 1621.

Parliament was essential in James's plan. Only the threat of English military intervention and a wider war could make the diplomatic restoration of the Palatinate and a general peace possible, and the noisiest sabre the impoverished king could rattle was a bellicose Parliament. For most of the year MPs were eager to play the part James cast for them. They broke precedent and promptly voted supply before passing other bills, and when James unexpectedly adjourned the first session, they found solace by publicly vowing to assist James in a war on behalf of Frederick and Elizabeth. Likewise when James recalled the Parliament men for an emergency session in November, they quickly agreed to underwrite mercenaries in defence of the Palatinate. Throughout both sessions, MPs had carefully avoided the delicate question of the Spanish match, but their true feelings became apparent when on 29 November 1621 the government seemingly gave the green light to an assault on the Spanish marriage. The result was a forthright petition begging James to make war on the King of Spain, not to marry into his family, and an equally swift royal dissolution of Parliament.[17]

James's reaction ensured, as some Englishmen bitterly remarked, that the Promised Land was the Palatinate, not Palestine. Without parliamentary assistance, the threat of English military intervention was farcical. Consequently in 1622–23 James could do little else than move closer to Spain in hopes his compliance would eventually lead to a restoration. The Defender of the Faith thus could only turn a deaf ear to the cries of persecuted Protestants whom Imperial troops introduced to Tridentine Catholicism. Indeed so helpless was James that when English volunteers were slaughtered defending the Palatinate in 1622, he did not dare interrupt the recruitment of his subjects into the same Spanish regiments which had earlier begun the reduction of the Palatine fortresses. With good reason the Spanish ambassador in London had hailed the dissolution of the 1621 Parliament as the best news in a century.[18]

The logic behind James' action and inaction, Sir Balthazar Gerbier recalled, eluded most of his subjects and resulted in a marked 'cooling of their affections towards theire Souveraigne'. This remarkable 'cooling' could be readily seen at the Exchange and St Pauls as well as in alehouses and parish churches across the kingdom. By 1622, the Infanta had come to represent much more than a bride for Prince Charles; she was as well a symbol of England's firm alignment within the Habsburg orbit at a time of religious war, and of the Crown's softening attitude towards Rome. Opposition to these policies is often associated with Thomas Scott whose polemical works were largely written in the uneasy period between the parliaments of 1621 and 1624. Unfortunately the sheer number and brilliance of his tracts has overshadowed the other contemporary commentators. Thus since this chapter seeks to establish the diversity of the debate over the Spanish match, it will consciously exclude his oeuvre in order to treat his less celebrated contemporaries at greater length.[19]

III

Rare indeed were the parishioners who managed to avoid on Sundays any mention of the religious conflict on the Continent. Ministers across the realm felt compelled to interpret the meaning of the war and to comment, if only obliquely, on James's foreign policy. In this weekly skirmishing between clerical boosters and critics of the King, the sharpest engagement centred on the recent Protestant martyrs whom both sides sought to claim as their own.

James himself sketched the royal line in his final address to the 1621 session. After dismissing the Commons' press for a Spanish war, James reminded the House of the adage, 'dulce bellum inexpertis [only to the inexperienced is war sweet]'; 'we rather expected you should have given us thanks for the long maintaining a setled Peace in all Dominions, when as all our neighbours about are in miserable combustion of War'. The keynote having been struck, a chorus of ministers regularly expounded on the blessings of peace and the horrors of war. Samuel Purchas for example assured his audience that they would not 'long for Warre, if we would but present to our imaginations the miseries of Warre'. To assist in this process he urged them to

> think what it is to see thy house fired; thy Goods seized; thy servants fled; thy wife ravished before your face and then hung up by the heels (modestie forbids the rest); thy daughter crying to thee for helpe in one corner while thy little Sonne is tost on another's Pike and the Sword at thine own throat.

Having rivetted his auditors Purchas reminded them of James's adage, and then referring to the rhetoric of divine-right monarchy, he begged them to repent their sins, 'none of the least' in 1622 was 'to be censorious of those whom God had called Gods [i.e. Kings]'.[20]

Unfortunately for the royal apologists, their insistence on maintaining peace at all costs overlooked the possibility of a just war, and at this point royal critics found ample entrée as Thomas Jackson, a minister in Kent, illustrated. After reviewing the suffering of the Continental brethren, Jackson asked 'Why doth the Church of God suffer so much evill?' The answer doubtless discomfited many in Whitehall: 'because Gods faithful servants give way and doe not stand in the breach for her'. He then reminded his congregation of 'a curse, yea a bitter curse, laid upon the inhabitants of Meroz'. When they had refused to honour their obligation to assist the Israelites in a crisis, God diverted the disaster threatening Israel to Meroz. Lest his listeners think this a Biblical oddity, Jackson pointed out 'no lesse curse doth lie on the Inhabitants of any Place and Country' that failed to assist the godly. This chilling threat suddenly made the plight of the Continental brethren a clarion call to arms, a call which other preachers echoed. Meroz's fate thus allowed critics to scorn those who cried 'peace, peace when there was no peace'.[21] The horrors of war could be used to question as well as to support the royal quest for peace through the Spanish match.

Questions about dissent and obedience soon led to questions about who represented a greater threat – Catholics or Puritans? Those who defended James's policy from attacks within the Church of England somewhat naturally found the answer to be the Puritans or, as Richard Gardiner dubbed them, 'the brainsicke undisciplin'd Disciplinarians'. On the other hand those who pressed for a tougher response against Catholic aggression on the Continent equally naturally took a hard line on the domestic Catholics; Thomas Taylor could not leave a fairly standard account of 'how insatiable she [Rome] hath alwaies been . . . of English Blood' without a timely application; given Rome's implacable hatred, 'I cannot thinke we can be so inconsiderate as to dreame of any toleration.'[22]

Although toleration was far from a dream in 1622, still others insisted that grave reservations about royal policy notwithstanding, all loyal Protestants were obliged to trust in James's judgment. Robert Harris was certainly no critic of the godly, and yet he begged his listeners that instead of 'pratling and enterdealing in State businesse, doe thou pray, pray for thy Souvereigne'. Foreign affairs, he insisted, must be left to James; 'it is not for us to sit upon Crownes and Thrones and to turne Statemen'. James himself endorsed this position in a remarkable poetic apology entitled 'The wiper of the Peoples teares, the dryer upp of doubts and feares'. In 170 lines of doggerel verse he exhorted his subjects to

> hold your pratling, spare your penn
> Bee honest and obedient men.

National security, if not the divine right of kings, required the dogged defence of the *arcana imperii*; otherwise

> to noe use were Councill tables
> If state affaires were publique bables.

The poem makes clear that of all the recent criticism the reports of his imminent conversion to the Infanta's faith stung him the most. He pleaded with those

> that knowe me all soe well
> Why doe you pushe me downe to hell
> By making me an infidell?[23]

James' work and that of his clerical apologists reveal that acceptance of the Spanish match and James's non-interventionist policy had become the litmus test of loyalty, a test which many, notwithstanding their own best efforts, failed. The extent of this failure became publicly apparent in April 1622 when a young Oxford scholar, John Knight, defended the subject's right to rebel 'in case of religion'. Although Knight based his case in part on James's recent aid to French Protestants, his sermon was especially provocative amid persistent rumours of the royal family's conversion to Rome. It certainly elicited a swift response from James. He imprisoned Knight indefinitely, and he commanded all divinity students in the future to stick to the Scripture and the Church Fathers, and to avoid modern theologians who 'live in Churches and States, which are not so settled as it hath pleased God these are'.[24]

Knight's case illustrates the dangerous propositions to which anti-Spanish agitation might lead, and in 'The wiper' James had warned that if his repeated proclamations against public discussions of foreign policy continued to be ignored,

> be warr what may befall
> I must do more
> . . . to keepe all in obedience.

By August 1622 James had lost all patience. On the 2nd, Bishop Williams, the Lord Keeper, ordered the wholesale suspension of the penal laws against Catholics. Two days later, to stifle clerical dissent, Archbishop Abbot issued new Directions on Preaching. Bishops and deans – and then only on feast days – retained free rein in their sermons; all others had to avoid in their morning sermons all mention of Predestination, 'bitter invectives and railing speeches' against the Church of Rome, and all 'matters of State'. Even severer were the restrictions on afternoon preaching which limited ministers to reading one of the set sermons in the Book of Homilies; and to close any loopholes, James ordered the first reprinting of this Elizabethan standard in thirty years. Clergymen who found this an unappealing way of spending the afternoon were advised to examine the local 'Children in their Catechisme'.[25]

Later in the year James extended the crack-down to the centres of secular dissent in the metropolis. Admittedly there were respectable Elizabethan precedents for ordering the aristocracy and gentry to retire to their rural estates, but the timing of James's action suggested that his motives extended well beyond the rural poor. His action, one observer noted, was aimed at those in London who 'being together and often meeting . . . one revealing discontents to another and soe in time grow to some head'. James's interest in breaking up centres of dissent found ample confirmation in the uncharacteristic energy with which he enforced the proclamation; after a 'diligent survey' of the metropolitian area, he prosecuted those who ignored the proclamation. Given the king's mood, Salvetti judged 'very fewe will venter the kings displeasure at this tyme'.[26]

Controversial though James's actions were, they at least allowed him to tighten royal control and to ride out a potentially alarming storm of popular criticism in 1622. 'No man can now mutter a word in the Pulpit', Buckingham boasted to Gondomar, 'but he is presently catched and set in straight prison'. To be sure, some oblique protest continued largely by drawing attention to the new royal restrictions; one minister preached on St Paul's rebuke to apostates only to end abruptly without the customary application of the text, announcing simply 'he was not ambitious of lying in prison'. Nonetheless by the end of the year the new repression began to yield results. John Donne, whose sermons in this period regularly stressed the importance of obedience, judged that 'the people are flat'; they had at last learned to trust 'in the King's Way'.[27]

Such an unpopular campaign was not without psychological costs. The ghost of John Buchanan, the formidable Calvinist who had tutored the king, reportedly troubled James's sleep in 1622. But the best illustration of the mental costs of the Spanish match was the first thought that came to James's mind on being awoken over the Christmas holidays. Students at the Inns of Court testified to their devotion to Elizabeth of Bohemia by touching off a cannon whose report echoed across the sleeping city. When James heard the noise he started out of bed crying 'treason, treason'.[28]

IV

Early in 1623 John Chamberlain, one of the inveterate news-gatherers of the capital, confessed that he was no longer 'greatly inquisitive after news'; 'the continual bad-tidings hath taken away my taste'. Unfortunately for him even worse news lay ahead. In 1623 the German conflict came to a halt with Ferdinand II in undisturbed possession of Bohemia and the Palatinate. The vanquished Palatine couple could only splutter with rage from the safety of the Dutch Republic as their last battered army melted away. Little wonder that many of the godly came to believe that the millenium was at hand. Thomas Gataker could only interpret the recent Protestant debacle as firm evidence that 'the last houre is now running. And we are those on whom the end of the world are fallen.'[29]

Further confirmation came in February 1623 when Charles and the Marquis of Buckingham slipped out of England and rode for Spain. This unexpected development left most Englishmen in 'a deade dumpe'; with Charles in the hands of Philip IV, the only question was not if the marriage would take place, but rather at what cost. Consequently contemporaries spent much of the year in grim speculation on the terms the Spaniards would 'extort'. 'If I was with you', John Beaulieu wrote to a relative in Brussels, 'I could tell you such things as would make your haires stand at an end. God have mercie on us for we are in a deplorable condition.'[30]

An almanac prediction held that in 1623 'shall Religion be scoft at', and for many Protestants, this prophecy was all too accurate. While the Directions gagged godly ministers, the absence of prosecutions for recusancy allowed Catholic clerics to flourish; indeed in the West Midlands the Bishop of Chalcedon reportedly paraded about in full episcopal attire. Once given free rein, Catholics garnered a rich harvest of converts, the most notable being Buckingham's mother and wife, while at Court an aristocratic 'catholic party' emerged. Not surprisingly a later chronicle of the decade labelled 1623 as the year 'the Romish Foxes came out of their Holes'. In case any Protestants overlooked these sudden changes, some Catholics openly gloated over the fact that the tables might soon be turned completely if either James or more likely Charles converted. In fact the tendency of some 'impetuous, unbounded, unlimited' Catholics to broadcast 'dangerous and fearefull positions, insolently intimating what a golden time they now shall have' embarrassed some supporters of the Spanish match.[31]

Equally unsettling to loyal adherents of the Church of England was the discovery within their ranks of 'Hollow Hearts who swamme with the tide'. With the imminent rapprochement with Spain came a more ecumenical stance. No less than three Englishmen, among them Francis Bacon, worked on treatises urging all Christians to exchange their doctrinal differences for a common holy war against the Turks. In John Stradling's view, rival theologians were venal careerists who feathered their own nests by obscuring the basic point that 'w'are Christians all', and a little bloodletting in the Near East could only lead to the wider acceptance of this point.[32] Sir Henry Goodere launched a more direct attack on doctrinal nicety. If fanatics on both sides could be silenced, it could be easily proven Rome and Geneva 'are not directly opposite as North and South Poles'. The fanatics who interested Goodere most, however, were the Calvinists who 'through transported zeal' insisted that 'the present Church of Rome is not part of Gods Church'. Instead he praised

> waxen hearts with pure and simple zeale
> they soften and they fit them for heavens weale.[33]

Given this background, the reason for Richard Sheldon's violent attack on 'Our Luke-warm Laodiceanizers . . . gaping after performents' becomes eminently understandable. Much to the government's embarrassment, Sheldon, hitherto a royal favourite, used the opportunity to preach at Paul's Cross to denounce 'Neutralists . . . such as dare secretly mutter . . . Rome and the Reformed Churches agree in the substance of Religion'. The height of the Anglo-Spanish negotiations therefore revealed that a Catholic revival was only part of the problem; the other was that 'a cardinal's hat' would 'make many a scholar in England beat his braines to reconcile the Church of Rome and England'.[34]

While some sought to meet Rome half-way, others prepared for the worst; after all, as one popular poem reported,

> true Religion's buried in the Dust
> The popes Bulls breath and crosses be adorned.

In this gloomy atmosphere 'when so much cause of sorrow', Gataker thought his congregation did not need his customary chastisements; instead they had 'more need of cheering up'.[35] Alternatively Dr DuMoulin attempted to steel his flock for the trials their continental brethren were already suffering; and Simonds D'Ewes received in April a divine message 'to arme my selfe for preparation against worser times'. Drastic though these preparations might now appear, they were only logical in a year which promised 'much alteration shall happen in religion'.[36]

Even those indifferent to religion could not regard the Spanish match with complete equanimity. The sudden appearance of Anglo-Spanish grammars and dictionaries in London bookshops in 1623 promised much more than a new language for aspiring courtiers to master. Plainly the popular tales of Elizabethan exploits against the Dons were due for retirement. Samuel Ward had discovered this a year earlier when he issued a thoroughly ordinary cartoon celebrating divine intervention against the Armada and the Gunpowder Plot. In any other period of James' reign, Ward's cartoon would have been unexceptional; during the Spanish match, however, it earned Ward a stint in prison.[37] Goodere pleaded with his countrymen to appreciate the 'change of time and state' and to shed their traditional Hispanophobia just as they had their earlier 'French and Scottish hates'. To assist in this task Michael DuVal reinterpreted English history; the Armada for example was 'provoked by Grievous and Intolerable Iniuries', the most heinous of which was Elizabeth's aid 'to the Rebellious Hollanders'.[38]

DuVal's slighting reference to the Dutch Republic revealed other important changes to which Englishmen would have to become accustomed; the flipside of the Anglo-Spanish entente was a hostile attitude to the Dutch and to representative assemblies, whether in London or The Hague. A dynastic alliance with the Habsburgs would naturally dissolve England's longstanding political and religious links with the King of Spain's 'disobedient' provinces; as one popular poet exulted over the imminent marriage of Charles and Maria, now 'the Dutchmen must pay'. Equally outdated was Parliament; the Spaniards rather obviously had little time for either parliamentary privileges or anti-Catholicism. DuVal openly ridiculed the parliamentary aversion to a strong monarch; instead of a 'Royal Cedar' or 'Palmes of Caesars', MPs longed for a 'Hedge-Bramble' as their sovereign. More importantly, since the Infanta's dowry would provide more gold 'than London can hold/ were the walls built as high as heaven', Parliament might well go the way of the Elizabethan protectorate of the Dutch.[39]

In response to these fears, supporters of the match continued the stress on obedience and the blessings of peace. Thomas Myriell asked his listeners 'may we not heare some weary of ease and wishing for warre?'; with these he pleaded 'take heed, be not weary of peace'. Likewise John Hayward's mediation on Christ's prayer, 'Father forgive them, for they know not what they doe', had a timely application in 1623; given James' willingness to forgive direct slights against his daughter, the king's handling of the German crisis obviously followed the doctrine of Christ, 'a perfect peacemaker'. The readily apparent wisdom of James's policy made Edmund Garrard pray that 'the people might not so much expostulate of our Prince's Royal Match and the Affaires of State as now they doe'. The domestic expostulations, however, became so loud that they prompted another royal poem. While granting that the recent departure of 'Jacke and Thom . . . afflicts Arcadia soe', James urged the 'kinde Sheappeardes . . . bee not soe rash in Censuring wronge'. Rather they should

> remitt the Care to Royall Pan
> of Jacke his sonne and Tom his man.[40]

In normal circumstances few would have had trouble following James's advice, but in 1623 some simply could not hold their peace. Bishop Montaigne, for example, sought to head off excessive lamentations by ordering his clergy to pray for the prince's safety 'and no more'; one minister quickly reappeared before his bishop for praying for Charles's return 'and no more'. Others with powerful court patrons could dare to be more direct; thus Joseph Hall (with the Earl of Pembroke's assistance) startled those who had rationalized a *de facto* toleration with a sermon on the text, 'buy the truth and sell it not'. Yet while patrons could save audacious ministers from serious harm, they had much more trouble getting controversial sermons into print. Nehemiah Rogers (with the Earl of Warwick's assistance) was one of the fortunate few. In *A Strange Vineyard in Palaestrina* he applauded the Directions on Preaching only to ignore them. The great taboo subject during the Spanish negotiations was the pronounced Catholic revival, and yet Rogers begged the local magistrates to enforce the penal laws and to 'let neither young nor old bee spared'. Next Rogers calmly advanced into the *arcana imperii*. 'It is lawfull', he pointed out, 'for Catholic princes to make leagues with Protestants only for their owne advantage.' The perfidy of this policy led him to ask 'whether it be safe then to suffer such [in treaties]' when the Spaniards could so easily evade 'their promises, oathes, vowes at their pleasure'.[41]

Equally impassioned efforts reached the public but only in manuscript which circulated in the channels that newsletter-writers had developed for their reportage. One of these tracts, an emotional open letter to Buckingham from Thomas Alured, reviewed all earlier Anglo-Spanish marriages in order to illustrate 'how little God hath blest [them]'. His conclusion was predictable; the match was neither 'safe for the Kings person nor good for the Church and Commonwealth'. Another tract, a spurious letter from Archbishop Abbot to James, rebuked the king for attempting to 'set up that most damnable and heretical Doctrine, the Whore of Babylon'. A third was Simonds D'Ewes's first literary work, a dramatic account of the scene on 20 July when James reportedly trembled uncontrollably when he heard the terms of the marriage treaty.[42]

The most direct and scurrilous exchanges over the match took place in poetry, not prose. James himself contributed to the battle of the couplets with his own upbeat piece on Charles' pursuit of the 'golden fleece'. In less skilful hands, double entendre often gave way to graphic descriptions of Charles and Maria spending their first night together.[43] Likewise the death of one of Charles's attendants, hounded in his final hours by priests and ultimately denied burial, was the subject of no less than three poems all denouncing Spain and Catholicism; as one concluded it must be

> counted for a greate mishappe
to see Spaine anywhere but in a mapp.[44]

Perhaps the best illustration of the bitterness of these exchanges was the fact that Dr Corbett's adulatory verses on the trip to Madrid prompted two sharp replies. One attributed Corbett's clerical rise to his sycophantic 'ballads more than merit' and to his ability to 'down white, canary and sherry', while another questioned his faith; if Corbett was a Christian, the poet would rather turn Turk.[45]

As the poems became more abusive, their focus narrowed on Buckingham, who was widely credited with having used his

> best tricks with Catholicks
to bring our Prince to Spaine.

Not surprisingly a common prayer in 1623 was

> God send our Charles well home againe
And lett his Worshipp [Buckingham] tarry.

The favourite's close identification with the Spanish match certainly accounted for the scandalous fashion with which one poet proved 'they get the divell and all/ that swive the kindred' of Buckingham. In the poet's hands, the friendship between Buckingham's mother, a recent convert to Catholicism, and Lord Keeper Williams, one of the mainstays of the Spanish party, became a torrid amour. Then one prominent Spanish supporter, the Earl of Arundel, put cuckold's horns on another, Lord Treasurer Middlesex. Yet the poet's supreme insult to the favourite's family was his descriptive account of Sir Anthony Ashley sodomizing one of Buckingham's kinswomen. These squibs understandably struck home, and late

124

in 1622 Buckingham offered a £1,000 reward for the author of one song.[46] No royal favourite could expect widespread popular applause, but the remarkable level of abuse directed at Buckingham during the Spanish match seems due much more to the policies he advocated than to the speed of his elevation.

Evidence of the mounting popular opposition could also be found in the streets of London. Londoners earlier in the decade had greeted the Spanish envoys and their entourage with 'many Insolencies of rude and savage barbarisme'. By 1623 the ambassador formally protested that they were 'beseeged' in their residence and 'dares scarce go abroade' because 'the people throwes stones at them and abuseth them in their Coaches'. The running battles along the Strand finally resulted in a fatality in September when a brawl in Drury Lane left a baker dead. At this point, fearful of vigilante reprisals the Privy Council ordered a strong guard around the embassy.[47] Popular hispanophobia nonetheless remained high; a highwayman went to the gallows a folk-hero for his insistence that hatred of the Spanish match, not avarice, had driven him to rob a Spanish courier, and a Spanish envoy was shocked one day to see 'an apparent Gentleman in a grey sute' across the street who 'did with actions of his hands and Jackanape tricks with his face seeme to scorne him much'.[48]

The crisis reached its climax a few weeks before Charles's tumultuous welcome in early October. Once king and Council approved the marriage terms on 20 July, Beaulieu noted with horror that 'we account him as good as married'; indeed 'he may lye if he please with his Mistres'. Well might the recusants 'not expresse small exultations'. D'Ewes spent the next few days on his knees praying 'for and hoping the best', and answer came from an unlikely corner.[49] While James and Philip IV had agreed on terms, Urban VIII had not; thus one song celebrated the fact that the Pope

> will not alowe
> King James to bee her dady.

Even better news quickly followed; exasperated with the delays Charles announced he would leave with or without the Infanta. Although Charles remained formally espoused and both sides spoke of a spring wedding, it was clear in August that the best chance to conclude the match had passed. Hence the situation in July was reversed two months later; now 'the publicke joye . . . doth ring lowed' while the recusants 'are silent and much dasht in their countenances'. The unexpected reversal of the seemingly inexorable progress towards the match delighted many Englishmen. Even the long list of expensive gifts to Spanish grandees could not dampen one contemporary's high spirits; 'so wee have him safe, lett our honour doe what it will, in bringing no Mistress wee have an incomparable recompense for our losse'.[50]

V

The pandemonium over Charles's return, once set in context, assumes a much different, almost cathartic nature, exorcizing the dark fears which had haunted many about the Infanta's impact on England and Europe. To be sure, the crowds were celebrating the Prince's safe deliverance from the foreign perils, but they were also celebrating their own deliverance from Spain. The prospect of another Queen Mary had sharply divided the kingdom, and the repeated royal stress on obedience only drew attention to the gaping fissure between the King and many of his people. Quite understandably several ambassadors perceived a nation on the verge of rebellion.[51] Foreign visitors of course always tend to extreme verdicts, but in this instance, several natives concurred. As Charles and Maria neared the altar, the recollection of Mary and Philip II became ominous indeed; the earlier Anglo-Spanish marriage, *Tom Tell-troath* recalled, 'was so discontenting to the people that it caused Wyatt's Rebellion'.[52] Advocates of the match did nothing to relieve this anxiety with their eagerness to label their opponents as those who sought 'to raise sedition in the Commonwealth', and their success can be seen in the first thought which came to James on waking to the sound of gunfire early in 1623. Thus someone as prim as Simonds D'Ewes was willing to excuse the 'great excess and drunkennes' on 6 October: the wild display of the 'abundant and true loves of his people to himselfe' refuted 'the forged popish persuasion . . . that subjects loved not him nor his sonn'.[53]

For all but the politically inept therefore Charles's return from Madrid a bachelor symbolized the end of Anglo-Spanish dynastic plans, and as the prospect of the Infanta receded so too the fissure within the political nation closed. Yet it is vital to remember that a new consensus emerged because many saw the passing of the Anglo-Spanish alliance as the advent of an Anglo-Spanish war;

the return of the Prince, Sir Benjamin Rudyerd observed, was 'the turn of Christendom'. Admittedly there were, as Russell has observed, some contemporaries for whom 'the desire to have no truck with the Spaniards did not imply a desire to fight them'. Yet, as we have seen, the debate over the Infanta concerned much more than the appropriate bride for the prince; she represented as well a precise response to the European crisis in which Protestants and James's daughter had hitherto suffered devastating setbacks. In this polarized atmosphere there seemed only two choices – either marriage or intervention. Thus to have had no truck and yet no war with Spain was to consign the Reformed religion and national liberties to the Jesuits and 'the universal monarchy'. Hence some revellers on 5–6 October were heralding a more aggressive military response to the continental war. After all 'now let us to the warres again', the tune contemporaries heard in the streets, may not have been an entirely random musical selection for that day.[54]

Future campaigns moreover would not be confined to the continent. Many English adherents of the old faith reportedly were fellow-travellers, if not actual agents, of the Most Catholic King of Spain; even the sedulous efforts of Tillières, the long-time French Ambassador in London, could not woo many from their confirmed hispanophilia. War against the Habsburgs therefore would necessarily imply a vigorous offensive against these fifth columnists who had flourished during the recent toleration. Moreover the repression of 1621–23 had not convinced many Protestants of toleration's virtues. Charles had scarcely returned before Samuel Ward, a vocal critic of the match who had spent a good deal of time in and out of confinement, began to rhapsodize over 'the pretious balme of reproofe'; only this time the same ecclesiastical authorities who had harried Ward could now be employed in the 'dispelling of the AEgyptian [i.e. Catholic] fogs'.[55]

The clearest example of the anti-Catholic backlash could be seen later in October when the Catholic chapel in Tillières's house collapsed killing nearly 100 recusants. When a Catholic girl was pulled half dead from the wreckage, a crowd attacked, eager to finish the job, and Tillières, fearful of another incident, ordered the victims buried on the embassy grounds rather than attempt to remove the corpses.[56] As one poem reveals, the disaster brought out the tensions of the Spanish match as much as ritual anti-Catholicism; the 'sons of antichrist' were 'rebellious multitudes' that

Praye for Queen Maryes dayes that sword and fire
may make professors feele of your ire.

But the real culprit was the power which had manipulated the
recusants, 'proud Spaine, great Brittaines enemy' whose punishment 'doth wait, though yet delayde'.[57] It was this expectation of
a belated counter-blow both on the continent and in England that
accounts for much of the frenzy over Charles' return.

Once we have a clearer understanding of the exuberant welcome,
we can assess the legacy of the Spanish match. First and foremost the
Infanta left behind her a generation made keenly aware of political
trends and quite able to gather information in spite of the Crown's
best efforts to leave them, as Sir Thomas Wentworth observed, 'in
the Suds'. Political reportage, which is often now taken for granted,
was essential in the seventeenth century if contemporaries and their
parliamentary representatives aspired to a political role higher than
that of rubber-stamps. The German war and the Spanish match
focused the attention of a generation on diplomacy and politics, and
this intense interest led to the development of a fairly sophisticated
system for circulating information outside of Whitehall's control.[58]
As Charles I was to learn to his cost, however much royal apologists
might exhort their contemporaries to be obedient subjects, the habit
of scrutinizing and criticizing royal actions was almost impossible
to break. In the circumstances, it is perfectly logical than when
Englishmen later in the century sought to understand the Great
Rebellion, they began their inquiries with the crisis over the
Spanish match.[59]

These earlier historians also turned to the Spanish match because
the furore over the Infanta established a certain political pattern
which was to recur in subsequent years. Until recently the willingness
of seventeenth-century Englishmen to believe tales of Catholic
plots has not generally struck responsive chords among modern
historians; except for the Gunpowder Plot, the reports seem
half-baked, if not ludicrous. Yet Caroline Hibbard has recently
shown that the Popish plot which Pym employed in the Long
Parliament rested on a solid foundation of fact.[60] Admittedly the
situation twenty years earlier had not deteriorated to the point where
Arminian bishops harrassing the godly and Papal agents at Charles
I's elbow all seemed part of a larger plan. Nevertheless there were
ample grounds for grave concern in the early 1620s. Therefore
if we count the opposition to the Spanish match as a serious
anti-Catholic scare roughly equal to those of 1605 and 1638–42,

Englishmen of Pym's generation would have reckoned Laud and Con as at least the third attempt to subvert the Church of England in their lifetime.

The controversy over the Infanta, moreover, was a Catholic scare with an important difference; for the first time the monarch was involved. In the preceding half-century, it would have required a vivid imagination to suggest that the sovereign was plotting to subvert the Reformed religion; in 1605 for example, in order to eradicate the Protestant élite, James would have to have been willing to blow himself up. But as the Spanish match matured, with the silencing of godly ministers, the toleration of Catholics, and persistent rumours of James's conversion, the idea of a threat from above became much harder to dismiss. And as the fears of royal involvement grew, so too blind loyalty from James's Protestant subjects became questionable. John Knight's sermon on resistance in 1622 was sensational precisely because he had dared answer a question which had come to trouble many others. After all, four years later, when a common man was asked 'whether he would be for the king or the Country', he did not object to choosing between the two; rather he simply replied that 'hee had bin asked that question, before'.[61] With the Spanish match, this question became all too natural. Thus Charles I's subsequent tolerance of Catholics and his patronage of Arminian clerics were all simply variations on a theme with which far too many of his subjects had become acquainted in the early 1620s. With good reason Gerbier dated the 'cooling of their affections towards theire Souveraigne' from the Spanish match.

Conspiracy theories of course were not a monopoly of the godly. During the Anglo-Spanish negotiations, the King became troubled by fears that the religious criticism of his foreign policy might easily lead to disorder and even rebellion. Admittedly the idea of a Puritan plot to subvert the monarchy was a hardy perennial which James had carried south from Edinburgh. Yet in the early 1620s it became thoroughly domesticated to the English political climate. Forceful criticism of royal foreign policy allowed all those who disliked Parliament, the moderate Calvinist consensus, the Dutch Republic, indeed the entire Elizabethan inheritance, to speak out not simply with impunity but also with a certainty of royal favour; for the criticism provided them with excellent material to pander to James's well-developed sense of regal authority and his absolutist tendencies. James, apprehensive of potential Calvinist extremists, then took a series of counter-measures which simply lent credence to fears about his religious and political reliability. Thus during the domestic crisis over Charles's Spanish bride, devotees of one conspiracy theory succeeded in confirming the other's worst fears.

It is important to remember, however, that the aftermath of the Spanish match was not general civil war; rather it was a general rapprochement, or, as some contemporaries termed it, a revolution in which the political nation fell into line behind the King in the European conflict. Nevertheless the quarrel over the Spanish match had already poisoned the political atmosphere; even the greatest optimism and enthusiasm could not fully excise the memory of 1621–23. Consequently when the expectations about an active war against Spain abroad and Catholics at home were not immediately fulfilled, it was only natural that contemporaries should revert to the political pattern which had developed earlier in the decade. Less than three years after his rapturous return, Charles dug in his heels over Buckingham's impeachment in order to stop what he perceived as an assault on his authority; and in the mean time the situation in the provinces became so polarized that one Suffolk minister was convinced an inadvertent comment would produce reports that 'the whole state were revolting'.[62] Likewise when renewed popular and parliamentary turbulence forced Charles I to withdraw from the war, it was only natural that he should withdraw into his court just as his father had done in the early 1620s. Royal apologists could then rebuke the people for their disobedience and praise the wisdom of royal counter-measures which were consistently misunderstood by the 'obdurant people'. Yet the clearest expression of his debt to his father's domestic experiment during the Spanish match came when he unleashed Archbishop Laud on the Puritan 'dissidents'. The result was almost predictable to any veteran of the early 1620s; the King's ministers, Clarendon lamented, 'improved the faults and infirmities of the court to the people; and again, as much as in them lay, rendered the people suspected, if not odious to the king'.[63]

The Spanish match, in short, did not nearly provoke widespread armed conflict. Nor was it the entry ramp onto the highway toward inevitable civil war. Yet it did introduce a generation to a potentially dangerous brand of polarized politics. It also revealed the contours of a political fault-line which could in the right circumstances open to engulf a kingdom.

Notes and References

I would like to thank Richard Cust, Ann Hughes, Peter Lake, and the members of the Early Modern England Seminar at the Institute of Historical Research for many helpful comments on this paper.

1. *The Diary of Simonds D'Ewes* (Paris, 1974), p. 162.
2. *The Joyfull Returne of the Most Illustrious Charles* (1623), p. 42; John Taylor, *Prince Charles His Welcome* (1623), pp. 101–4; BRO, Trumbull MSS, VII/131; *Chamberlain*, II, p. 515; and D'Ewes, pp. 162–3.
3. SP 94/28/147; and Yale U., Osborn b 197, p. 63.
4. BRO, Trumbull MSS, XLVIII/104; and Thomas Reeves, *Mephiboseths Hearts Joy* (1624), p. 31.
5. *Oxford Council Acts, 1583–1626* (Oxford, 1928), pp. 322–3 and 420–1; *Coventry: Records of Early English Drama* (Toronto, 1981), p. 417; Stephen Jerome, *Irelands Jubilee* (Dublin, 1624), dedication; Reeves, *Mephiboseths Hearts Joy* p. 37; and *Extracts from the Council Register of . . . Aberdeen* (Aberdeen, 1848), pp. 389–90.
6. John Newman, *West Kent and the Weald* (1969), pp. 296–7; John Prideaux, *A Sermon Preached on the Fifth Day of October 1624* (Oxford, 1625), dedication; and Westminster City Library, Archives, EP3, [p. 4].
7. Laud, III, p. 143.
8. See the Suggested Readings for this chapter.
9. WCRO, CR 136 [Newdigate MSS] B480; J. S. Morrill, *The Revolt of the Provinces* (1976), p. 22; and R. P. Cust, 'News and politics in early seventeenth-century England', *P&P*, 112 (1986), pp. 60–90.
10. Russell, *Parliaments*, pp. 417–33 and *passim*.
11. Gardiner, II, pp. 216–58 and 314–369, and III, pp. 37–106.
12. Add. MS 28,326, p. 35. See also *The New Cambridge Modern History* (1958), II, pp. 301–33; and J. Lynch, *Spain under the Habsburgs* (New York, 1981), I, pp. 74–108.
13. Theophilius Higgons, *Mystical Babylon* (1624), I, pp. 137–8 and II, p. 78; and R. P. Cust and P. G. Lake, 'Sir Richard Grosvenor and the rhetoric of magistracy', *BIHR*, LIV (1981), p. 44.
14. *Propaganda in Germany*, E. A. Beller (ed.), (Princeton, 1940), pp. 21–3; and Geoffrey Parker, *The Thirty Years War*, pp. 48–61.
15. Inner Temple Library, Petyt MSS 538, v.19, f.33ᵛ; Rushworth, I, p. 12; Taylor, *Taylors Travels to Prague* ([1620]), p. 90; and *Gallants to Bohemia* (1620?).
16. Add. MS 4181, fos 14–16; and A. W. White, 'Suspension of arms: Anglo-Spanish mediation, 1621–1625' (Ph.D, Tulane, 1978), pp. 132–300.
17. Robert Zaller, *The Parliament of 1621* (Berkeley, 1970); and Conrad Russell, 'The foreign policy debate in the House of Commons in 1621', *HJ* (1977), pp. 289–309.
18. Gardiner, IV, pp. 266; and *APC*, XXXVII, pp. 240, 271 and 315.
19. Add. MS 4181, fos 17–17ᵛ. On Scott, see Peter Lake, 'Constitutional consensus and Puritan opposition in the 1620s: Thomas Scott and the Spanish Match', *HJ*, XXV (1982), pp. 805–25; and Simon Adams,

'Captain Thomas Gainsford, the "Vox Spiritus" and the *Vox Populi*', *BIHR*, XLIX (1976), pp. 141–4.

20. Samuel Purchas, *The Kings Towre* (1623), pp. 101–2; and Rushworth, I, p. 48.
21. Thomas Jackson, *Judah Must into Captivitie* (1622), pp. 41, 60, and 84–5.
22. Richard Gardiner, *A Sermon Preached at St. Mary's Oxford* (1622), p. 23; and Thomas Taylor, *A Mappe of Rome* (1620), p. 2.
23. Robert Harris, *Peter's Enlargement* (1624, 3rd edn, 'To the Reader'; and *The Poems of James VI and I* (Edinburgh, 1958), pp. 182–91.
24. Anthony á Wood, *The History . . . of Oxford* (Oxford, 1797), pp. 341–5.
25. Thomas Fuller, *The Church History* (1655), pp. 101 and 109–10; and *Certayne Sermons or Homilies* (1623).
26. *Stuart Royal Proclamations*, I, pp. 561–2; *APC*, XXXVII, pp. 413; PRO C115/N8485; and D'Ewes, p. 162.
27. *Cabala* (1663), I, p. 242; Edmund Gosse, *The Life and Letters of John Donne* (1899), II, p. 168; *C. and T. Jas I*, II, p. 335.
28. *C. and T. Jas I*, II, pp. 301 and 359–60.
29. Thomas Gataker, *A Sparke toward the Kindling of Sorrow* (1621), dedication to T. Crewe; and *Chamberlain*, II, 475. On the German conflict, see Parker, pp. 61–71.
30. HMC Kellie and Mar, II, p. 155; and BRO. Trumbull MSS, VII/98 and 106.
31. Jacke Dawe, *Vox Graculi* (1623), p. 42; John Vicars, *Englands Hallelujah* (1631), stanza 40; and Edmund Garrard, *The Countrie Gentleman Moderator* (1624), p. 54.
32. *The Works of Francis Bacon* (1861), VII, pp. 1–36; John Stradling, *Beati Pacifici* (1623), pp. 20–2; Michael DuVal, *Rosa Hispani-Anglica* (1623?), p. 73; and Vicars, stanza 40.
33. SP 14/145/12A.
34. Richard Sheldon, *A Sermon . . . at Paules Crosse* (1625), pp. 30 and 49; and *C. and T. Jas. I*, II, p. 392.
35. FSL, V.a. 275, pp. 11–12; and Thomas Gataker, *The Joy of the Just* (1623), pp. 1 and 28.
36. Pierre DuMoulin, *A Preparation to Suffer* (1623); Yale, Osborn b 197, p. 189; and D'Ewes, p. 130.
37. *C. and T. Jas. I*, II, 226. See also John Minsheu, *Pleasant and delightful dialogues* (1623) and Richard Percyvall, *A Spanish Grammar* (1623) and *A Dictionnarie* (1623).
38. DuVal, p. 54; and SP 14/145/12A.
39. Yale, Osborn, b 197, pp. 110–11; and DuVal, 'To James'. On the polarity between the Dutch Republic and Spain, see Simon Adams, 'Spain or the Netherlands?' in H. Tomlinson (ed.), *Before the Civil War* (1983), pp. 79–101.
40. Thomas Myriell, *The Christians Comfort* (1623), pp. 57–8; John Hayward, *Christs Prayer* (1623), pp. 113 and 117–18; Garrard, 'To the Reader'; and *The Poems of James VI and I*, pp. 192–3.
41. Nehemiah Rogers *A Strange Vineyard* (1623), dedication to Warwick and pp. 116–18; and *C. and T. Jas. I*, II, pp. 375 and 418–20.

42. FSL, V.a. 402, Fos 57–62; Yale, Osborn fb 57, p. 125; and Longleat House, Whitelocke Papers, II, fos 101–2ᵛ.
43. *Poems of James VI and I*, pp. 192–3. See also FSL, V.a. 162, f. 48v; and Yale, Osborn, b 197, pp. 110–11.
44. Yale, Osborn b 197, pp. 170–2. See also FSL, V.b. 43, f.3; and V.a. 345, pp. 101–2.
45. *The Poems of Richard Corbett* (Oxford, 1955), pp. 76–9; NRO, IL 4278; and FSL, V.a. 345, pp. 133–4.
46. Add. MS 5832, f. 206ᵛ; Yale, Osborn b 197, pp. 222–3; and D'Ewes, pp. 112–3.
47. *Stuart Royal Proclamations*, I, pp. 508–11; SP 14/152/4 and 40; and BRO, Trumbull MSS, VII/129.
48. Add. MS 36,446, f. 104–4ᵛ; BRO, Trumbull MSS, XVIII/101; and SP 14/160/17.
49. BRO, Trumbull MSS, VII/120 and 121; and D'Ewes, p. 148.
50. Yale, Osborn b 197, pp. 186–8; BRO, Trumbull MSS, VII/129 and 130, and XVIII/103 and 104.
51. See *CSPV*, XVII, p. 397; and *Stuart Royal Proclamations*, I, pp. 495, n. 1, and 562, n. 2.
52. *Somers Tracts*, II, p. 474. See also Rushworth, I, p. 92; and P. Clarke, 'Thomas Scott and the growth of urban opposition', *HJ* (1978), pp. 1–26.
53. DuVal, p. 69; and D'Ewes, pp. 163–4.
54. Lockyer, *Buckingham*, p. 168; Russell, *Parliaments*, p. 165; and Add. MS 389, f. 360.
55. Samuel Ward, *A Peace-Offring to God* (1623), pp. 43 and 45; and PRO 31/3/57, fo. 257.
56. BRO, Trumbull MSS, VII/134 and XVIII/105; PRO 31/3/57, fos 260–60ᵛ; and *CSPV*, XVIII, p. 147.
57. FSL, V.a. 345, pp. 117–18.
58. *The Earl of Strafford's Letters and Dispatches* (London, 1739), I, p. 24. See also Richard Cust, 'News and politics in early seventeenth-century England', *P&P* (1987), pp. 60–90.
59. See for example Rushworth's *Historical Collections*, Clarendon's *History of the Rebellion*, and the *Cabala* which all begin their studies of the Civil War with the Spanish match.
60. Caroline Hibbard, *Charles I and the Popish Plot* (Chapel Hill, 1983).
61. SP 16/39/41.
62. *The Diary of John Rous* (1856), p. 17. On the 'revolution', see Beaulieu to Trumbull, BRO, Trumbull MSS, VII/151.
63. Sir William Davenant quoted in Roy Strong, *Van Dyck: Charles I on Horseback* (1972), p. 86; and Earl of Clarendon, *The History of the Rebellion* (Oxford, 1843), p. 2.

5 Politics and the Electorate in the 1620s

Richard Cust

I

Until recently early Stuart historians were in broad agreement about the nature of parliamentary elections. There were differences of emphasis – particularly, as we shall see, on the question of how far voters were politically aware – but most were content to accept the account of J. H. Plumb and Derek Hirst. This presented elections as relatively 'open', providing opportunities for the 'middling sort', and even the 'lower orders', to participate and exercise some degree of political choice.[1]

Plumb and Hirst stressed that from the 1580s onwards there was considerable growth in the size of the electorate, as a result of inflation – which devalued the 40s-freehold qualification – and the adoption of a broad freeman franchise in many larger towns. Crowds at elections could run into thousands, and procedures for their conduct were extremely haphazard. This, they argued, made it difficult for the gentry to control elections, particularly as they lacked experience of management techniques, such as use of pollbooks or large-scale 'treating'. As a result candidates came more and more to appeal directly to the electors, in terms of political issues. Speeches at the hustings and circular letters which resembled manifestoes became a regular feature of elections; and there was a growing expectation that once MPs reached Westminster they would keep constituents informed about their actions. In the process the electorate became better educated and more politically aware.[2]

At the same time the number of contested elections was increasing: from only 13 in 1604, to between 20 and 40 at each election in the 1620s, then up to 62 in the spring of 1640 and 86 in the autumn. Since a high proportion of these took place in county or large borough seats they affected large numbers of electors and enabled them to exercise some degree of choice. Thus in the elections of 1640 one can see developments over the previous fifty years reaching some sort of maturity, with vigorous campaigning, discussion of issues such as ship-money, religion and the influence of the court, and large numbers of voters being asked to take sides.[3]

As this last conclusion indicates, the prevailing view of elections has been whiggish. The divisions of 1642 are traced back over a long period and there is a general assumption that elections were becoming more 'open', more democratic and more modern. This approach has been challenged by Mark Kishlansky in his book *Parliamentary Selection*.[4] He takes as his starting point the evidence that before 1640 the overwhelming majority of elections were uncontested. This had been noted by Hirst and others, but they failed to appreciate its significance. For Kishlansky it demonstrates that early Stuart elections were more akin to selections. In most cases leading gentry and aldermen simply presented electors with a *fait accompli*, and asked them to acclaim their selections rather than choose between rival candidates. Polling of individual voters was resorted to only rarely and elaborate measures were taken to avoid contests. In the shires preliminary discussions and rota systems generally ensured that there were no more than two candidates on election day. In the boroughs normal practice was to accept the nominee of a local patron or select those who emerged from the *cursus honorum*. Ideological considerations were largely excluded since selection was based on wealth, lineage, social status and community service.

Kishlansky sees this system as solidifying during the 1620s, but then falling apart in 1640 and thereafter. What held it together was a fear of factiousness and disunity, and a sense that selection was a matter of personal worth and honour. Winning a contested election was much less honourable than enjoying the undivided assent of one's community; and the shame attached to losing was a deterrent to anyone uncertain of success. Thus contests before 1640 were, according to Kishlansky, largely unintended – the result of misunderstanding or a breakdown in communications. After 1640 circumstances changed, with Parliament growing in influence and ideological divisions becoming too open and clear-cut to be excluded from elections. This led to more intense competition for places in Parliament and the depersonalization of electoral politics. Candidates were now expected to represent particular religious and political views, and gained honour and credit from standing for a cause rather than securing undivided assent. The numbers of contests rose dramatically, electioneering became more sophisticated, regular polling procedures were developed and ideological issues became a central element in many campaigns. Out of this, Kishlansky argues, there emerged two-party politics and the beginnings of a participatory democracy.

Kishlansky's general thesis – that the conduct of elections can be treated as a paradigm of the processes which transformed political assumptions during the seventeenth century – is very persuasive. It helps us to understand the striving for unity and consensus which characterizes a good deal of political activity in the early period. It also reveals some of the dynamics of the transition whereby the 'social' and the 'political' become separated, and 'politics' emerged as a sphere apart in public life. However the electoral shift which Kishlansky proposes is surely too sharp to be plausible. What he presents us with is a sort of inverted whiggery, in which the changelessness of pre-1640 is played up to emphasize the extent of change in 1640 and thereafter. We are asked to believe that a system which was stable, and almost universally acceptable suddenly fell apart as a consequence of external developments which are never very clearly established. Given the magnitude of the transition which he is arguing for, it seems rational to look again at the period before 1640 for signs of a more gradual transformation. In the process we might hope to uncover more evidence about the role and influence of electors.

To give this investigation coherence we will explore two separate, but related, problems. The first of these is the question of who mattered in electoral politics, who wielded the decisive power. Was it – as Kishlansky argues – confined to the leading gentry and magnates; or – as others would have it – were the 'middling sort' and the 'lower orders' coming to participate in their own right?

Linked to this is the second, more complex, question of how far the outcome of elections was influenced by broad political issues. Were gentry and freeholders simply concerned with bread-and-butter local matters – feuds and personal conflicts, the effect of taxes on their pockets and the regulation of the local economy – or is it possible to detect a wider concern with religious and political principle? Kishlansky has little to say about this, assuming that considerations of status and local unity overrode all others. Amongst other historians, however, there is a significant divide. Those with a more whiggish outlook, such as Plumb and Christopher Hill, have tended to argue that by the 1620s electors were concerned about the broad political stance of candidates, taking note of their religious views, whether or not they were linked with the court and above all whether they would speak out in defence of the subjects' liberties.[5] In the absence of really consistent positive evidence revisionsists have been more cautious and have largely followed Hirst in arguing that it is local concerns which come first. Even in 1640, when broader issues were certainly aired at election time, Hirst stresses that 'the political cries raised normally concerned the local manifestations of court policies rather than those policies themselves'.[6]

This emphasis has been particularly important because it underpins Russell's revision of the parliamentary history of the 1620s. Accepting Hirst's thesis that MPs were increasingly answerable to their constituents, particularly over taxation, Russell argues that it is this which explains obstructiveness towards the Crown's requests for supply. MPs were fearful of facing electors if they had granted away their money without securing redress of local grievances. Hence they were reluctant to confront the great issues of war and peace and concentrated instead on legislation which would bring immediate local benefit.[7] Through Russell's work, then, the electorate has been integrated into national politics; but not, perhaps, in the way one might expect. It is their insularity rather than their attachment to principle which is seen as significant.

II

To understand electoral politics we need first of all to investigate the concerns and assumptions which structured the behaviour of the electorate. This is by no means straightforward because different aspects have been stressed by different historians. For Kishlansky, and other revisionists, the most important elements are the sense of hierarchy and deference, and the concern for unity, which pervaded this, and other areas of contemporary politics. Their emphasis has been amply documented, notably in Kishlansky's perceptive analysis of the rhetoric of election contests, which shows that participants repeatedly subscribed to the notion that unified selection was the most desirable outcome.[8] However to concentrate on this aspect to the exclusion of others would be misleading. As Whig historians have argued, there was also a strong contemporary emphasis on individual choice.

This can be illustrated by looking at the speech delivered by Sir Richard Grosvenor, as sheriff, before the Cheshire election of 1624. Kishlansky argues that this was a model of how parliamentary selection and consensus decision-making operated, with Grosvenor inviting his audience of freeholders to approve the two candidates recommended to them by the Justices sitting beside him. So in a sense it was. But it was also much more than this. For Grosvenor made it abundantly clear to his audience that the main reason why they should accept the recommendation was because these candidates were staunch Protestants, 'ripe in judgement, untaynted in their religion . . . without feare to utter their countrye's just complaintes and grievances'. Had they been otherwise – popish fellow-travellers perhaps – then he insisted that the freeholders should cast aside any notions of deference or concern for maintaining unity and veto the selection. As he argued, the main safeguards in the electoral system, the elements which ensured the purity and effectiveness of parliament, were the freeholders' willingness to elect according to his conscience and his right to an independent voice. 'Freedom of voice', he explained, 'is your inheritance and one of the greatest prerogatives of the subject, which ought by all meanes to bee kept inviolate and cannot be taken from you by any command whatsoever.'[9]

This is a good example of the ideas about representation which were gaining ground in the early-seventeenth century. Whilst not exclusively Puritan, they were nevertheless expressed most often and most clearly by godly spokesmen like Grosvenor. Implicit in such ideas was the belief that electors should act as individuals and where necessary place considerations of religion and political principle before the maintenance of unity. John Preston, one of the most influential of Puritan preachers, insisted that electors 'ought to keep their minds single and free from all respects, so that when they come to choose, they might choose him whom in their own consciences . . . they think fittest for the place'. Thomas Scott, the godly author of *Vox Populi*, echoed this in a Norwich assize sermon. He urged freeholders at election time to 'conferre together and (neglecting both their landlords or great neighbours or the Lord Lieutenants themselves) look upon the wisest, stoutest and most religious persons . . . for he that is religious will stand for the countrie's good'. Many gentry were conscious of these ideals and, as a result, sometimes found themselves pulled in different directions. This can be seen, for example, in a letter written by a former pupil of Preston's, Sir John Pickering, during the run up to the Northamptonshire election of 1626. Applauding the efforts of leading gentry to arrange an accommodation whereby the county might be spared a contest, he was nevertheless insistent that this be concealed, 'lest the freeholders whose birthright it is to elect should take it ill, conceivinge themselves concluded thereby'.[10]

Not all gentry, however, shared this concern to uphold the freeholders' right to individual choice. Some saw it as further evidence of the 'popular/puritan' threat to hierarchy and order which was a marked feature of contemporary rhetoric. The best-known expression of this is the protest by the Arminian Lord Maynard in Essex in 1640. Having experienced an election dominated by the Earl of Warwick and his Puritan allies he declared his abhorrence of such 'popular assemblies where fellowes without shirts challenge as good a voice as myselfe'. Maynard was not alone. Sir Thomas Wentworth, amongst others, was prepared to argue that the quality of votes cast in elections mattered as much as the quantity; in other words that the votes of the gentry counted for more than those of others. As we shall see, Wentworth was also preoccupied with the 'popular' nature of the support enjoyed by his opponent in Yorkshire during the 1620s, Sir John Savile.[11]

Complaints like these were themselves a measure of the extent to which ideas about individual choice and active participation were gaining ground. At a theoretical level those ideas were clearly in conflict with older notions of hierarchy and unified assent; but, in practice, conflict was often avoided through what Kishlansky calls self-correcting mechanisms in the electoral process. These could operate in various ways. They might involve a subterfuge of the sort envisaged by Pickering, whereby the gentry settled matters, but the appearance of electoral choice was preserved. They might encourage the gentry to select candidates who were acceptable anyway to the broad body of the freeholders. This appears to have happened in Cheshire in 1624. Or they might provide a deterrent which dissuaded candidates from putting themselves forward if they were likely to meet popular antagonism. As we shall see, this probably happened in 1628. These various sorts of accommodation made it possible to avoid contests and maintain unity without necessarily depriving electors of their veto or excluding political considerations from the election. Where the gentry were prepared to be flexible – as they usually were – the different priorities could be reconciled.

But if there was scope for freeholders to bring their political concerns into the choice of MPs what form did these concerns take? Here again the answer is far from straightforward. Sources for the views of electors are very scanty and this has led revisionists to emphasize more local concerns, whilst Whigs assume a preoccupation with broader issues. It would be anticipating the main argument of this article to try to answer the question at this stage. But it is appropriate to offer some general suggestions about political consciousness amongst electors.

The key to understanding what the local gentry and freeholders thought about politics is provided by investigating the various meanings attached to the word 'country'. Time and again in the correspondence of the gentry, the reports of local gossip and rumour and the public addresses delivered before local audiences, 'country' was used to sum up everything which people held most dear. It conveyed a sense of loyalty and respect which they felt towards something which was at the same time concrete and abstract, representing kin, neighbours, the local community, the English nation and also a vision of the social order, purified and reformed by the removal of all forms of corruption. These various meanings have been discussed in the introduction and in Ann Hughes' article.[12] Here we should concentrate on the associations between 'country' and Parliament. Parliament was seen as representing the various social and geographical entities which made up the 'country', and also as embodying the ideals and values which it stood for. This had important implications when electors came to decide who was suitable to be returned.

The fullest evidence for the electors' perception of Parliament is contained in the news reports which filtered back to the localities. These took the form either of newsletters and 'separates' (containing transcriptions of parliamentary speeches and debates) – which tended to be restricted to the literate gentry and 'middling sort' – or verbal reports by MPs and general gossip and rumour – which reached all levels of society. One might argue that an examination of news tells us more about the information on which opinion was based than opinion itself. But when combined with direct evidence about electors' concerns it provides a reasonably coherent picture.[13]

One of the most pervasive images in the news is of a Parliament which blended together the local and the national. There were occasions when it was seen as functioning to meet exclusively local interests; but by and large it was implied that through Parliament these were subsumed within the national interest. Sir William Heyricke's report to the Leicester Aldermen, whilst acting as MP in 1621, illustrates this. He assured them that he had delivered their petition of grievances – probably relating to purveyance – but explained that 'it is a generall grievance all England over; as yet there is no time for the regulatinge of yt. . .'. He then proceeded to relate the circumstances of the Commons' declaration of support for the King over Bohemia, and enclosed a copy for the information of the Aldermen. Heyricke's attitude was shared by other MPs, both in towns and in the shires. For example, in an address to the West Riding subsidy assessors, which took the form of a report to constituents on his work as MP, Sir Thomas Wentworth described various bills with local implications, but above all stressed the general benefits of the punishment inflicted on the patentee Sir Giles Mompesson, 'being of more safety to the commonwealth in the example than 6 of the best lawes that have been made in 6 of the last Parliaments'.[14]

Such attitudes on the part of MPs were hardly surprising. After all they chimed in with what Sir Edward Coke saw as the rightful role of the MP: 'though he be chosen for one particular county or borough, yet when he is returned and sit in parliaments he serveth for the whole realm; for the end of his coming thither, as in his writ of election appeareth, is generall'. What is perhaps more noteworthy is the evidence that these views were shared by constituents. The East Anglian diarist, John Rous, commented in 1626, that what caused most 'griefe in the country' was the exclusion from Parliament of Sir Edward Coke and the imprisonment of the Earl of Arundel. Both men had local connections, but in the minds of Rous' neighbours their fate was linked with a general threat to popular liberties, 'making way as was thought for the utter bringing under of parliament power and the jealousie betwixt the King's prerogative and the freedom of the country'. Responses like these reflected a habit of mind becoming more and more deeply ingrained in this period. Local people could readily set their immediate interests in a broader context; and the House of Commons, and the publicity surrounding its activities had helped to reinforce this. In the words of Robert Ashton, it was 'the agency of a subtle alchemy whereby MPs who came up to Westminster armed with the grievances of their constitutents came, via a process of shared experience, to contribute to the emergence of a national or 'country' attitude'.[15]

This association of Parliament with 'the Country' also served to reinforce more overtly ideological images in the minds of electors. Naturally enough news of Parliament tended to focus on the headline material, on the broad concerns which affected the assembly as a whole rather than the 'little businesses' of individual MPs. In the process Parliament, and in particular the Commons, was frequently seen as standing for a purified Protestant commonwealth and the defence of liberties against the corruption and tyranny sometimes associated with 'the Court'. A good example is provided in the news from the first session of the 1621 Parliament. Much of this concerned the Commons' attack on Mompesson, seen as the archetype of 'the evil projector'. Newsletters kept track of proceedings and stressed the King's support for the Commons actions. This was also confirmed in a Proclamation on 30 March banishing Mompesson. Popular verses denouncing him circulated in London. A printed cartoon appeared – one of the earliest relating to Parliament to survive – which drew comparisons with Empson and Dudley and celebrated the way in which 'Parliament once call'd then Giles was brought/Unto account contrary to his thought.' Finally a 'separate' from later in the 1620s, recalling 'some memorable matters done by Parliament', set his punishment alongside the destruction of 'the Pope's power' and the impeachment of Piers Gaveston, Empson and Dudley, Lionel Cranfield and other 'caterpillars' and 'polers [*sic*] of the commonwealth'. The whole episode was presented as a model of the way Parliament operated, in conjunction with the King, to strike at the root of the evils which afflicted 'the country', both locally and nationally. It was precisely the sort of event which did so much to enhance its reputation as the 'Representative of the People'.[16]

The Mompesson episode was not alone. Parliament's role in prosecuting corrupt courtiers and evil counsellors was again prominent in 1624 – with reports of the impeachment of Cranfield – and in 1626 and 1628 – with lengthy accounts of the proceedings against Buckingham. It was significant that when local inhabitants at Honiton in Devon quizzed Sir John Eliot during his journey home from the 1628 Parliament, it was about the fate of Buckingham that they wanted to be informed. Eliot had to declare regretfully 'that the Duke shall lose many of his offices is more than hee doth conceive'.[17] Another prominent theme was the Commons' role in combating popery in its various guises. Heyricke reported the Commons declaration on Bohemia in 1621 with the comment that it was 'a rejoysinge to all true affected in religion and a blow to all recusants and remise papists'. Similar views were conveyed back to Hull and Exeter at the same time by their MPs. And in 1624 Grosvenor made the threat from popery, and the measures which parliament could take to counter this, the main theme of his address to the Cheshire freeholders.[18] The other topic which attracted particular attention in the news was Parliament's struggle to contain the royal prerogative. In 1621 there were extensive reports on the debates over freedom of speech, in 1626 on the imprisonment of MPs opposed to the Duke and, of course, in 1628 on the protracted negotiations over the Petition of Right. In this latter Parliament public interest reached unprecedented heights, with a heavy demand for newsletters and 'separates', evidence of day-to-day discussion amongst the gentry and 'middling sort' and widespread lighting of bonfires and ringing of church bells when the King's final assent to the Petition was announced.[19] This underlined very clearly Parliament's status in the eyes of 'the country', as the main upholder of the values which 'the country' was taken to represent.

III

Contested elections provide the readiest means of investigating how the assumptions and concerns of electors applied in practice. This is not because they are of statistical significance – as Kishlansky argues the incidence of contests did not necessarily relate to political awareness or broad electoral involvement – but rather because they tend to yield the most evidence.[20] They therefore allow us to explore in detail the various forces –political, personal and ideological – which shaped electoral politics at this time.

Perhaps the most fully documented elections during the 1620s are those for Yorkshire. The first of these, in December 1620, involved a fierce struggle between Sir Thomas Wentworth and Sir George Calvert, Secretary of State, on one side and Sir John Savile on the other. Wentworth made the early running in a campaign which began well over a month before the election was due to take place. He saw the election partly as a means of obtaining advancement at Court – through 'managing' the return of a leading councillor – but, perhaps more importantly, as a way of consolidating his standing in the shire, which had been threatened in 1617 when Savile had tried to force him to surrender the post of *custos-rotulorum*. As Wentworth acknowledged, 'if the old knight should but endanger it, faith we might be reputed men of small power in the country'. His first priority, then, was to win over the county leaders. He took care to observe the customary proprieties, disclaiming any personal ambition and offering himself as the candidate who could maintain unity and amity amongst the county families. He used his influence at Court, offering his supporters the prospect of an introduction to Calvert when next in London. And where necessary he was prepared to invoke the spectre of popular unrest, nudging Lord Scrope with the reflection that victory for Savile would represent 'such a carriage of the Commons . . . it might breed ill blood in the example and imbolden them more that wer fitt for this government'.[21]

Wentworth left little to chance and aimed to deter Savile from standing by building up a strong head of support. He took care to secure control of the election writ and sounded out the sheriff to ensure that he was 'by his faithful promise deeply engaged' for Calvert. He also made extensive preparations for entertaining his supporters, securing the use of Sir Arthur Ingram's house in York to provide a grand dinner on the election day and arranging a rendezvous at Tadcaster the day before so that his party could ride into York in unison and impress waverers. Essentially he was relying on the influence of the magnates and their ability to carry their tenants with them; but he was careful to back this up by interviewing some of the high constables and pressing them to see that the parish constables supported Calvert and himself and publicized their candidature in local churches. In some cases he went further and instructed them to draw up lists of freeholders who had promised him support 'as a testimony of their good affections'. This was a highly dubious tactic because, as was pointed out in the protest against the election in the 1621 Parliament, it also enabled Wentworth to identify those who had not supported him. His readiness to resort to it was perhaps an indication of his uncertainty. Although he had pledges of support from most of the leading magnates in the North and West Ridings, and was confident of freeholder support in Hallamshire, Osgoodcross and Staincross – where his own influence was greatest – success was still far from assured.[22]

It had been predicted by one of Wentworth's allies that when Sir John Savile understood 'his friends' and neighbours' engagements, he will think it more wisdom and safety for his reputation to go to the grave with that honour the country hath already cast upon him, than to hazard the loss of all at a farewell'. In spite of this Savile remained determined to force a contest. This was in keeping with his character, typifying the mixture of stubborness and bloody-mindedness which had long been evident in his relations with the Yorkshire gentry. But it must also have been based on the calculation that he had enough support to ensure a reasonable chance of winning. Even Savile would not relish the personal shame accompanying a heavy defeat. Significantly this support came not from county magnates, but from some of the lesser local gentry, the two leading godly ministers in the West Riding – Dr Favour of Halifax and Alexander Cooke of Leeds – and, above all, from the thousands of freeholders inhabiting the clothing area, bounded by Leeds, Wakefield and Halifax. Similar forces had carried the day for him in the last contested shire election in 1597. Then he had entered the fray at the last moment and defeated two candidates backed by most of the leading shire gentry. He had based his appeal to electors on the fact that he was a leading employer amongst the clothiers, with a reputation for defending their interests, whereas his opponents were both outsiders.[23] This was again his approach in 1620; but with an important addition.

According to Wentworth, Savile was 'by his instruments extremely busy intimating to the common sort underhand' that Secretary Calvert 'being not resiant in the county cannot by law by chosen and being his Majesty's Secretary and a stranger not safe to be trusted by the Country' . . . 'whereas himself is their Martyr having suffered for them, the Patron of the clothiers, of all others the fittest to be relied on'. The attempt to denigrate Calvert as an outsider, unaware of local interests and ineligible under the terms of the King's election Proclamation, was reinforced with the very significant observation that simply because he belonged to the court he was 'not safe to be trusted by the Country'. Savile then went on to demonstrate his own fitness to serve with a reference to his sufferings in the 1614 Parliament, when he had spoken out against impositions, 'alleging that he had warning from some of his neighbours not to give anything' that might confirm them. As a result he had been summoned by the Council and removed from the bench.[24] He was thus basing his appeal on a reputation which, in the early 1620s, was strong enough to obscure his own close connections with Buckingham. In 1622 Alexander Cooke, in the dedication to one of his numerous tracts against popery described Savile as 'a noble and worthy Patriot'; and the comments of John Chamberlain during the 1624 Parliament suggest he enjoyed a similar esteem nationally.[25] In invoking this Savile was clearly introducing an ideological element into the election.

The precise impact of this is, as always, hard to gauge. It appears that Wentworth and Calvert carried the election itself fairly comfortably, backed by the sheriff and the great phalanx of county governors who signed the return. But Savile still seems to have enjoyed considerable and committed support, with several witnesses testifying that 'about 1000 cried "A Savyle!"', and over 350 signing his petition of protest.[26] Wentworth's reaction to his campaign was also revealing. To counteract Savile's influence he changed the running order of his side so that he rather than Calvert would be contesting the first seat against Savile. He also suggested that Calvert procure a letter from the Lord Chancellor ordering Savile to stand down, a course which was not pursued presumably because it smacked of electoral 'undertaking'. Finally he responded to Savile's insinuations by sending out his own letter to at least one of the high constables, vindicating Calvert's candidacy.[27] This is worth examining because it showed a clear recognition that broader issues were influencing the electorate.

Wentworth attempted briefly to deflect the charge that Calvert was an outsider, but concentrated mainly on the allegation that he was unfit to serve 'the country'. He seems to have sensed a general desire to keep courtiers out of the Commons and argued rather unconvincingly that it was ultimately pointless to oppose Calvert since 'assuredly he will be of the House though the countrie not chuse him'. He then set out to demonstrate the positive aspect of choosing a councillor, that it was 'an honour to our countrie' and that 'they can have none that for any matter concerning any Parliament of our countrie or the good of any private men therein . . . can soe effectually deale for them both with his majestie and the parliament house'. This was an argument which seems to have carried considerable weight in the late sixteenth century, but it was apparently less effective in the 1620s.[28] However Wentworth returned to the same arguments in his address to the subsidy assessors during the recess, showing that Calvert had used his influence to promote a bill against informers and vindicating him against 'such as indeavoured to persuade you the chusing of this noble gentleman to be little better than a betraying of the country'.[29] Notions of 'court' and 'country', and the values associated with each, then, were a consistent theme in this election. The final result was probably determined by the territorial influence of the leading gentry, which remained strong, particularly outside the manufacturing areas. But both Savile and Wentworth seemed to recognize that broadly political considerations could influence a significant minority amongst the voters. The rather thinner evidence for Yorkshire elections later in the 1620s suggests that this continued to be the case.

In 1624 Sir John Savile and his son, Sir Thomas, were returned unopposed for the county. Again Sir John's stance on the broad issues was an important factor. In Yorkshire, as elsewhere in the aftermath of the Spanish Match, the main concern was to elect candidates who would take a firm stand against popery. Wentworth himself, who was no Puritan and if anything a supporter of the Match, reflected the mood when he suggested the election for Pontefract be declared void because 'it had been procured by a popish faction'. In these circumstances Sir John, with his reputation as an opponent of papists and patron of godly ministers came into his own. Even Wentworth gave his blessing to the return, acknowledging that 'the father and son are men whose soundness in religion' is 'well approved by us all'.[30]

This concern to elect loyal protestants went hand-in-hand with a continuing sense that MPs had an obligation to serve 'the Country'. Immediately after the election, when the leading gentry were gathered in Castle Hall at York, Sir Francis Wortley tried to pick a fight with Sir Thomas Savile by insisting that since 'trust was laid upon him by the country he would look to have an account of his doings'. Sir Thomas responded with understandable aggravation 'that the country had laid other businesses upon him therefore he would not'. This exchange was to lead to a lengthy feud between the two men, resulting in a duel; but its most interesting aspect was as an indication that both clearly accepted that MPs had 'a trust' laid on them by 'the Country'. Wortley saw this as sufficiently strong to be able to belabour Savile with it; he in turn believed it was flexible enough to free him from any need to give Wortley a report.[31] These themes were to re-emerge in 1625.

There were in fact two shire elections in this year. The first was declared invalid when Sir John Savile appealed successfully against the return of Wentworth and Sir Thomas Fairfax of Denton, and the whole contest had to be refought at the start of August. Apart from this the basic pattern was similar to 1620. Wentworth and Fairfax relied on the influence of the leading gentry and devoted their preparations to ensuring that their tenants remained loyal, particularly after some had abandoned the cause at the first election when it looked as if there might be a lengthy poll. Savile and his son again appealed directly to the freeholders. This time, because none of the candidates had obvious court connections, they focused on the threat of popery which was continuing to cause rumour and alarm in Yorkshire. Savile's curate, Anthony Nutter, a preacher at the Halifax lecture, circulated what Fairfax described as a 'scandalous and seducing letter' directed against a fifth candidate William Mallory, who was suspected of Catholic sympathies. 'By these meanes', Fairfax predicted, 'as if the state of religion did lie upon the stake, they will no doubt accumulate such a multitude of people in those well disposed towns of trades as they will be powerful.' Wentworth and Fairfax's response to this, particularly in the second election, was to emphasize the popular nature of Savile's support and suggest once more that this was a threat to the gentry and the preservation of order. One of their allies, Sir Richard Beaumont, described the first contest as more like 'a rebellion than an election', because of the way Savile's supporters – many of them supposedly non-freeholders – had thronged the castle yard. And Wentworth built on this by urging Fairfax that 'it should be handsomely infused into the gentry how much it concerns them to maintain their own act', lest 'Sir John be able to carry it against you and me' and 'all the gentlemen too besides'.[32]

This approach paid dividends. At the first election support for the two sides was apparently even, and Wentworth and Fairfax won largely because the sheriff suspended the poll and simply declared them winners. Afterwards Savile was able to obtain 1,400 signatures for a petition to overturn it.[33] The second time around, however, there is no sign of sharp practice and Savile apparently allowed the result to stand. This was testimony to the continuing influence of the leading gentry when they were roused; but it should not be taken to imply that Wentworth was simply appealing to a narrow social élite. He had seemingly learnt from his experiences in 1620 when his confident assertions of backing at court had come close to being counter-productive. In 1625 he was much readier to invoke 'the Country'. Hardly a letter from him survives during this campaign in which he did not mention his readiness 'to serve the country' or refer to his recognition of the 'trust' conferred on him.[34] He was generally emphasizing a different aspect of 'the Country' from Savile, identifying it with the gentry and reputable freeholders more than loyal Protestants. But he was just as evidently trying to appropriate to himself the values which it represented.

The 1626 election was again contested; however evidence relating to the campaign is limited to one letter from Wentworth reflecting gloomily on the difficulties of preventing Savile's return. Wentworth himself was disqualified from standing, after being 'pricked' as sheriff in November 1625, and this he thought would leave the way open for Sir John to secure a clear majority of freeholders in the West Riding. Again the main issue was probably religion, with great concern about the activities of Lord Scrope, president of the Council of the North, who was alleged to be encouraging the spread of popery. Wentworth believed that Savile's reported readiness to investigate Scrope in Parliament would ensure that 'except Sir William Constable stand, a great part of the East Riding will voice with him'. In the event both Savile and Constable were returned.[35]

Savile's reputation as a spokesman for 'the Country' was probably at its height at this time. But during 1626 there is evidence that it began to diminish. Initially this was because it at last became clear how closely he was associated with Buckingham. During the Parliament a letter in his name was circulating around Yorkshire which detailed the efforts he had made to secure a hearing for the clothiers, but also observed that the Commons 'are so resolutely bent . . . upon the pursuit of a great man as rather than they will fail or surcease they are resolved to hazard the whole estate of the common-wealth'. The House investigated this as an attempt to obstruct their impeachment proceedings and news of the episode was relayed back to the shire. Observers drew the obvious conclusion, with one of Wentworth's Yorkshire correspondents commenting on all Savile's 'devyses of advancing the Duke's desygnes in parlement'.[36] In the following months Sir John's dependence on Buckingham became more and more obvious. Wentworth was removed from the bench and Savile secured a series of grants which made him the most powerful man in Yorkshire. He tried to use this power to secure concessions to 'gratifie the country' and offset any suspicion that he had abandoned it. But the tactic does not appear to have worked. His scheme for compounding with recusants won him admirers amongst the Catholic gentry, but at the cost of damaging his reputation as a loyal Protestant; and his securing the incorporation of Leeds in 1626 aroused hostility from the smaller clothiers. By September 1627, Wentworth's friend Christopher Wandesford could observe, with certain qualifications, that 'Sir John hath lost many by his harsh carradge of things in the cuntry'. The resulting damage was perhaps most clearly reflected in the decision of a group of freeholders from the clothing towns to adopt Sir John's enemy, and Wentworth's friend, Sir Henry Savile, for the county by-election in 1629.[37]

Meanwhile Wentworth had done much to bolster his standing in the eyes of 'the Country'. His suffering at the hands of the Duke, when he was 'pricked' as sheriff in 1625, led some of his fellow gentry for the first time to number him amongst the 'Parliament-Men' who were standing out against the prerogative. This view was reinforced by his resistance to the forced loan in 1627. Savile was said to have hoped that if he was forced to pay this would 'lessen' him 'in the Country'. However after thinking long and hard about it Wentworth decided to resist. On doing so he received a stream of supportive letters from his Yorkshire neighbours, several reflecting the views of his friend Sir Arthur Ingram, that 'to be committed in cause of this matter doth so much redound to your honour . . . that your friends should rather be glad of itt then otherwise'. Now it was Wentworth who was being seen as the 'Patriot' and 'Martyr'.[38]

The effects of this for the 1628 county election are, however, difficult to assess. Clearly it did not guarantee his victory. A few months before the poll Wandesford was gloomily reflecting on the apathy of his neighbours in Richmondshire, when it came to defending their liberties. He also stressed that for Wentworth to have any chance in a coming election he would have to ally with the pro-Catholic Sir Henry Bellasis who wielded considerable influence in the North Riding. Wentworth's preparations as before were directed largely to securing gentry support, and in particular to reassuring those who disliked him standing with Bellasis. However as the election approached in early March the mood seems to have changed with the spread of news that loan refusers were being elected in several shires. Joseph Mead, one of the best-informed contemporary commentators, believed that Yorkshire would follow suit; and James Howell, who sat for the borough of Richmond, observed that 'there is much murmuring about the restraint of those that would not conform to the loan moneys'. Confirmation of this is perhaps provided by the clear-cut nature of Wentworth and Bellasis' victory, with even Savile acknowledging in his petition against the return that they 'had most voices'.[39] However if Wentworth had indeed gained from a newly acquired reputation as a 'Patriot', this was not to last. When he accepted a peerage in July 1628 this was immediately interpreted by his neighbours as a defection from 'the Country', 'the common opinion', according to Wandesford, 'passing you nowe under Sir John Savile's character, and that there is a Thomas as well as a John for the King'.[40]

This analysis has attempted to show that such considerations did matter to the electorate. Running through these elections as a consistent theme was the concern to return candidates associated with 'the Country'. It was this which introduced an ideological element into the elections. As both Savile and Wentworth had come to recognize, standing for 'the Country' did not just mean representing the immediate interests of the gentry or other local groupings, it also meant standing for Protestantism and the liberties of the subject. It was on these issues above all that electors seem to have judged the elusive quality of trust. This suggests that historians like Hirst and Peter Salt are mistaken when they argue that throughout the 1620s local issues took priority in the minds of the electors. The distinction which they draw between local and national is in itself misleading, since through Parliament the two were often seen as interlinked. But beyond this one can point to the evidence that again and again Yorkshire electors responded quickly and sensitively to what they knew of the broader sympathies of their candidates.

The other feature which clearly emerges is the 'openness' of Yorkshire elections in this period. The recent expansion in numbers had produced an electorate of different shades and complexions, ranging from the rural tenants of the large landlords in the North and West Ridings, whom Wentworth could treat almost as a block vote, to the freeholders in the clothing towns, who had to be wooed with political arguments. It also led to very large crowds assembling on election day, with estimates as high as 10,000 in 1628.[41] This made electioneering very uncertain. Wentworth had the support of nearly all the leading Yorkshire gentry which according to Kishlansky's model should have guaranteed success. But Savile always seems to have felt he had a chance of winning; and, to judge by some of his more desperate campaigning techniques, Wentworth himself shared this view. There was also some scope for freeholders to take the initiative. In the 1629 by-election, when there was no candidate acceptable to the smaller clothiers, they took it on themselves to approach Sir Henry Savile and eventually helped to secure his return.[42]

Yorkshire, then, during the 1620s displayed many of the features which electoral historians have associated with later periods. The obvious question is how typical was it? Clearly it was unusual in facing bitter factional divisions and six contests in nine years. No doubt this helped to develop the habit of contested elections and also the political awareness of electors. But it can be argued that these were developing anyway, since even in 1620 there is evidence of a concern with issues of principle and a willingness to override the conventions inhibiting contests. Yorkshire may have been precocious: but similar developments can be traced elsewhere, particularly if we examine the electorate's concern with broad issues.

IV

The issue of principle which surfaced most frequently in elections was religion, and in particular anti-popery. This had been a source of concern to electors back into Elizabeth's reign. It helps to explain

151

the bitter contests in normally quiescent shires such as Rutland, in 1601, and Worcestershire, in 1604. This concern reached new heights, however, in the 1620s, notably in 1624 in the aftermath of the Spanish Match. Grosvenor in his address to the Cheshire freeholders voiced what seems to have been a common fear, that in the coming Parliament the papists might 'procure a partie . . . fittinge to their purpose'. In Norfolk freeholders took the initiative in pressing the staunchly Protestant Sir Roger Townsend to stand against Sir Thomas Holland. Holland was a client of the Earl of Arundel who was widely suspected of popish sympathies. In Kent supporters of Sir Edwin Sandys branded one of his opponents in the shire election as 'a Papist'; while Sandys himself assisted his friend Thomas Scott in the Canterbury election by suggesting that his main rival was 'a dangerous man', since he had been seen to cross himself before the Spanish ambassador.[43] Such smears were relatively commonplace in this period; but they have often been seen simply as the expression of negative and irrational prejudice. As Lake shows in his article, this is to misunderstand the positive implications of anti-popery.

Contemporaries linked popery with many of the corruptions which they saw as undermining the political system. In the context of elections it was sometimes associated with interference in the exercise of individual choice. Thomas Scott of Canterbury was greatly concerned with this problem and wrote a series of treatises analysing its effect on Kentish elections between 1614 and 1628. As far as he was concerned, the 'undertaking' in these elections – by deputy lieutenants and courtiers, such as the Duke of Buckingham – could be traced back ultimately to popery, the source of 'all our diseases'. In Kent at least, his views seem to have been shared by others. During the debate on 'undertaking' in the 1614 Parliament his neighbour, Sir Dudley Digges, described the origins of the problem in very similar terms: 'It was thought that particular men went to the Kinge and in hope to merit favour to betraye their countrye; and therefore thought to come from a corrupted roote: Papistes.'[44]

Popery, then, was for many a 'disease' with political implications; and as such demanded political remedies. For Scott the most effective of these involved freeholders and freemen exercising their rights in 'free indifferent and reasonable' elections, to return MPs like his friends, Sir Dudley Digges and Sir Edwin Sandys, 'men of redoubted courage and grounded in the love of god and their countrye'. This was the common solution amongst the godly, shared by the likes of John Preston, Thomas Scott, author of *Vox Populi*, and Sir Richard Grosvenor. Grosvenor, indeed, was prepared to carry the process even further and urged the Cheshire freeholders not only to exercise their right of individual choice, but also to 'command your knights that if there bee occasion offered they shall in the name of the country make publique protestacion against a tolleracion of religion or the repealing of laws formerli made against recusants'.[45] The threat from popery, then, underwrote a dynamic view of Parliament and the whole process of election; and many of those subscribing to anti-papist slogans and supporting candidates with an anti-papist platform must have been aware of the positive implications of what they were doing. The same can be said for those expressing hostility to courtiers.

This can be traced back at least as far as the 1614 elections, when Sir Henry Neville observed that 'there is exception to all those that have any way dependence on his majesty'. Similar comments can be found during the 1620s; and in some cases, as with Calvert, this hostility was explicitly linked to a suspicion about the ultimate loyalties of those associated with 'the Court'. In 1625 when Sir John Suckling stood for Great Yarmouth one of the aldermen observed that 'itt would bee a question whether Sir John should inclyne rather to the King than to the subject'. And when John Winthrop pressed Sir Robert Naunton's candidacy for Suffolk in 1626 – on the grounds that he was well placed to help the clothiers and had given proof of his loyalties by undergoing imprisonment for resisting the Spanish Match – he was told by the Common Councilmen of Bury St Edmunds that Naunton 'was tyed in so partikular an obligation to his majesty as if ther was occasion to speake for the Cuntry he would be silent, and in generale they would give no voise to anye Cortier espetially at this time'. Concerns like these may well explain the reaction in boroughs against the nominees of great patrons like the Duke of Buckingham, which J. K. Gruenfelder has traced to the late 1620s. Certainly they seem to account for the fate of Sir Edwin Sandys once it became clear in 1626 that he had aligned himself with the Duke. Having formerly been assured of a seat in Kent, through his reputation as a popular patriot, he was reduced to seeking election for a Cornish borough on a blank indenture.[46]

Anti-court sentiment undoubtedly existed; but it is often difficult to document. There are relatively few examples of open denunciations of courtiers during the 1620s – certainly in comparison with the 1640 elections, when anti-court slogans were rife. This has prompted Hirst to argue that it was not of great significance for ordinary electors. However against this it should be recognized that for much of the period anti-court slogans only tended to surface when a councillor or royal official was standing; and, as D. H. Willson has demonstrated, such candidates were generally deterred from seeking seats in the shires or large boroughs because they expected a difficult passage. In 1640 the situation was rather different, with the Crown making a particularly concerted effort to get its nominees into Parliament almost regardless of the difficulties.[47]

By 1640 it also appears that electors were able to recognize that local gentry who did the bidding of 'the Court', as well as those directly connected with it, might be tainted by association. This important notion was still developing during the 1620s and, as we have seen, much of the time Savile and Wentworth were able to conceal from the electors the implications of their court connections. However this was certainly becoming more difficult. John Poulett evidently felt that the Somerset electors in 1624 could grasp the complexities of the situation when, 'upon design to withdraw the good opinion of the country', he spread the rumour that Sir Robert Phelips 'had forsaken the country and was turned courtier': this after the circulation of news that Phelips was acting as Buckingham's spokesman in the Commons. Similarly, earlier in the same year, Sandys' supporters had smeared his Kent rival Digges as 'a royalist', again in the wake of news of his closer links with the Court. Such ideas became more firmly established after 1626, when certain local governors were clearly seen as doing the bidding of 'the Court' in collecting the forced loan or supporting the activities of Buckingham. Thus in the Canterbury election of 1628 Sir John Finch, the City Recorder and former MP, could be described as 'altogether a Dukeist, or Duckling, as some call them, a Buckinghamist'.[48] Instances like these, although infrequent, are surely significant, suggesting that some electors could view national politics almost in terms of two sides – for or against the interests of the subject. This impression is strengthened if we look at the reverse of the coin, the way in which some candidates came to be highly regarded as spokesmen for 'the Country'. Once more this indicates a set of ideologically based criteria by which electors assessed their candidates.

The classic study of this sort of politician is Barnes' account of Sir Robert Phelips, who assiduously cultivated his fellow gentry, made himself the main spokesman for the grievances of ordinary freeholders and repeatedly denounced the burden laid on local tax-payers. What Barnes does not perhaps stress sufficiently, however, is that Phelips consistently spoke up on a whole range of broader ideological concerns. Although no Puritan, he was one of those MPs who most vigorously trumpeted a concern with popery on the floor of the Commons. He repeatedly drew attention to impositions; and when remaining silent on the issue in 1624 sought to cover himself by drafting a Protestation that in doing so he was not waiving the subject's rights. He was also prominent in opposing the unparliamentary benevolences of 1614 and 1626, and carefully weighed the options before avoiding a decision on the forced loan. Finally one suspects that his prominence in the attack on Buckingham in the 1625 Parliament was not entirely unconnected with the local allegations that he had 'turned courtier' in 1624.[49] Like Wentworth and Savile, Phelips was an intensely ambitious opportunist. Given his flexible principles, and his acute sensitivity to his standing amongst his neighbours, his willingness to take a stand on broad principles surely suggests that such things mattered to local freeholders.

These three men were not alone in seeking to cultivate a reputation for standing for 'the Country'. Most shires could boast at least one local politician of this sort. In Northamptonshire there was Sir Edward Montague, whose willingness to stand up for the godly ministers deprived in 1605 was said to have 'won and wedded to him such honour and esteem that what he said ordinarily went for current and that he was alwayes chosen by the better sort to be one of the knightes of Parliament'. In Cheshire Grosvenor earned the epithet of 'father of his county' largely because of his efforts to support the godly and hammer the papists. And in Buckinghamshire Sir Francis Goodwin – of Goodwin *v.* Fortescue fame – again closely associated with the godly, was still being described in the mid-1620s as the 'most popular man' in the upland part of the shire. Similar reputations were enjoyed by Sir Francis Barrington in Essex, Richard Knightley in Northamptonshire, Sir Thomas Lucy in Warwickshire and Sir Henry Wallop in Hampshire. In each case this was clearly an electoral asset. Montague was elected knight of the shire for each Parliament until he became a peer in 1621; Barrington and Lucy were knights of their shire for all five of the Parliaments of the 1620s, Knightley for the four for which he was eligible – since he was 'pricked' as sheriff in 1625 – and Goodwin, Grosvenor, Phelips and Wallop for three each. In every instance they represented their county more often than any other local gentleman during the decade.[50] What distinguished them from those of similar status and ambition was their reputation as 'patriots'.

In most cases these candidates were returned without a contest, after the sort of preliminary conferences and meetings described by Kishlansky.[51] This implies that even in such circumstances some account was taken of the broad preferences of the lesser gentry and freeholders. The county leaders might select the candidates, but at some stage the electors had to approve their choice. If the magnates got it wrong this could lead to a contest of the sort which occurred in Norfolk in 1624. To avoid embarrassment and preserve unity they had to take some notice of electors' preferences. This imposed an important constraint on the county leaders, and meant, for example, that it was very hazardous to try to select a candidate suspected of popery.

The significance of the widely held concern that candidates should adhere to the principles of 'the country' was shown most clearly in the elections of 1628. Hirst has argued that in common with the earlier elections of the 1620s these show little evidence of a concern with anything other than local issues. However, on closer examination, it appears that in the shires and large boroughs, at least, a crucial determinant was often a candidate's response to the forced loan. Because this had seemed to many to offer a direct threat to the subject's liberties and the future existence of Parliament, it was widely regarded as a crucial test of an individual's ultimate loyalties. The effect of this at election time was indicated in a letter from Joseph Mead:

> You heare what work the Londoners have made in choosing their 4 burgesses, that they passed by their Recorder and all their Knights and have chosen 2 Aldermen who were never Mayors, Moulson and Clethro, and 2 of their Commons, one Captain Waller and Bunce a linnen draper lately in prison for the loane. They were very unruly, not onely passing by their Recorder and others, but disgracing them with public outcrye . . . They are generally of this strange humour in their elections. In Lyncolnshire they have chosen Sir John Wray and Sir William Ermin, both loan recusants. In Yorkshire they are about to chuse Sir Thomas Wentworth . . . At Coventry they have done as at London, admitted 2 gentlemen recusants of the country to be of their Corporation that they might chuse them and passe by against their custom all their owne, as being not that way qualified. They were I heard in the like fury in Northampton, refusing Sir Richard Spenser to whom they have bin much beholding onely because he came off to the loane, and would chuse Sir Erasmus Dryden whether he would or no . . . [52]

Hirst suggests that this report and others like it were based on a false impression. He argues that many of those elected as knights of the shire would have been chosen anyway and that the relatively small number of contests in this year – 33 compared with 62 and 86 in 1640 – reveals a lack of political arousal amongst electors.[53] This sort of evidence, however, can be read more than one way. Several of the regular knights of the shire were themselves loan refusers, and alongside these there were several refusers being elected for the first and only time. Perhaps the latter were encouraged by the mood of the moment. The relative lack of contests can also be variously interpreted. It might be taken to indicate lack of excitement, but it could just as readily suggest that feelings were running so high that some prospective candidates were deterred from standing – particularly those who had made themselves unpopular over the loan – in which case the appearance of unanimity would be preserved. Positive evidence is not easy to come by in 1628, because there were relatively few contests; but what there is tends to confirm Mead's impression.

Each of the four counties where resistance to the loan had been heaviest – Essex, Gloucestershire, Lincolnshire and Northamptonshire – returned two refusers as their candidates. Where there was no loan refuser suitable to stand, a county often plumped for men who had deliberately refrained from involving themselves in the service. Buckinghamshire, Hampshire, Hertfordshire and Warwickshire all responded in this way, and elsewhere Phelips and Sir Roger Townsend gained county seats after distancing themselves from the service in a particularly calculating way. In fact out of 42 county MPs whose response to the loan is known, 18 were refusers, 13 either abstained or were uninvolved in the service and only 11 were active as commissioners.[54] These returns, then, suggest that over quite a wide range of shires gentry and freeholders were conscious of the way in which parliamentary candidates had responded to the loan. The implications of this were illustrated in Essex and Cornwall.

In Essex several of the local gentry who had been involved in collection of the loan collaborated with members of the Council to block the election of the loan refusers, Sir Francis Barrington and Sir Harbottle Grimstone. However they were thwarted by the influence of the Earl of Warwick and the apparently spontaneous support for those whom one local freeholder described as having 'suffered for their country'. When the Council's allies tried to spring a snap election at Stratford, it was reported that 'the freeholders to a number of 1000 or 1200 repaired presently thither to have hindered that choice and to have named Sir Francis Barrington and Sir Harbottle Grimstone in their place'; and when the return was finally made at Chelmsford the two refusers were said to have had 'all the voices of 15,000 men, those who say least and were there 10,000 freeholders'.[55]

The response in Cornwall was even more significant since here there had been little evidence of open resistance to the loan. Again two refusers, Sir John Eliot and William Coryton, were opposed by leading gentry with backing at Court who sought to overcome opposition with the local militia and threats of the King's disfavour. Eliot and Coryton responded with a popular campaign. They had previously published their opposition to the loan through 'separates' which one of their local opponents had found 'wandring amongst the subjects'. Coryton built on this foundation. First 'he laboured over the whole country, by means of himself and his friends, divulging amongst the vulgar that he had suffered for his country'. Then he had notes sent around to the local clergy, reminding 40s freeholders of their right to vote and the date of the election. And finally 'it was proclaimed in parish churches that Sir John Eliot and Mr Coryton desired all the freeholders to give their voices at the county court to make them Knights of the shire'. This carried the day. Their opponents absented themselves from the election and, as one of them observed, 'by report there were 4000 to 5000 persons present that gave their voices for them. Their pretence of suffering for their country had stolen away the harts of the people'.[56]

This sort of unambiguous display of popular support suggests that where there was a clear choice and issues were widely aired, the sympathy for the stand taken by the loan refusers was often crucial. Of course, in some cases this did not happen and other influences cut across the issues of principle. This helps to explain Wentworth's initial difficulties in Yorkshire and the return elsewhere of gentry who had supported the loan.[57] Nevertheless what remains striking about the 1628 elections is the positive evidence that the loan was often an issue which transcended localism and which for many freeholders offered a touchstone by which to judge the fitness of candidates to serve 'the country'.

V

This article has demonstrated that freeholders during the 1620s were not simply voting fodder for the leading gentry. Many of them had opportunities at election time to make their own views felt. Moreover these views were not simply confined to local matters. They reflected the full range of concerns attached to the notion of 'country'. This is not to imply that elections in this period were fully politicized. As Kishlansky has amply demonstrated, the general desire for unity and consensus prevented contests in a majority of constituencies before 1640. Where there was no contest public debate and choice between candidates was inevitably more restricted, although, as we have seen, it was not removed altogether. The leading gentry also continued to set the agenda in elections. Their support was still the most important factor determining success and failure for a candidate, as was demonstrated by the return of Calvert and Naunton in spite of popular disquiet about their associations with the court. However the leading gentry were no longer able to count on the unquestioning assent and support of tenants and freeholders, if indeed they ever had been. In this, as in other respects, there are already indications of the transformation in electoral politics which Kishlansky dates to the period after 1640.

This transformation is most visible in a county like Yorkshire, where the character and ambitions of the leading gentry led them to ignore or override the conventions inhibiting contests elsewhere. It was Savile's stubborness in 1621 and Wentworth's ambition to relaunch his political career in 1625 which led each to challenge their well-entrenched opponent.[58] In the last analysis it was often the personalities of the leading politicians which determined whether or not a constituency was contested in this period. However there were other factors, more deeply rooted in the system, which were coming to encourage individuals to press their candidature in spite of the shame attached to a defeat. This article has revealed two in particular: the uncertainties created by an expanding electorate and the ideological purchase afforded by securing the reputation of a 'patriot'. Again these are most visible in a contested shire such as Yorkshire: however this should not be taken to imply that they were absent elsewhere. After all Cornwall would appear almost entirely quiescent in electoral terms were it not for the conflicts of 1628, which revealed a large body of politically informed electors.

This article has been concerned almost entirely with county elections – because these are often more fully documented and involved the largest numbers of electors – but a similar transformation may be traceable in some of the larger boroughs. There were different combinations of forces at work here; but again during the 1620s one sees the constraints on contesting being overridden, electors disregarding the wishes of their social superiors and ideology influencing the choice of candidate. Canterbury, in 1626 and

1628, provides perhaps the best evidence, largely because of the remarkable accounts written by Thomas Scott. As a Puritan, Scott tended to heighten the impression of conflict; but, even when this is allowed for, there is ample evidence of electoral development. Scott himself insisted that he was reluctant to stand, and tried to avoid a contest through an accommodation with the aldermen. However local pressures and tensions made this unworkable. These included a long-standing struggle between the city oligarchs and the common councilmen, who prevailed on Scott to stand; religious divisions between Puritans and conformists; and a marked antipathy towards any candidate who was not a Canterbury man, which in 1628 involved denunciations of those connected with Buckingham. The ensuing campaigns were intense and well organized. The city oligarchs used a primitive poll book and applied every possible form of pressure to individual voters; Scott's allies rallied support through sermons and through his reputation as a spokesman for the godly; and Scott himself pressed for the election to be decided on a poll.[59]

Contests like these were not the result of misunderstanding or accident. Nor can they be attributed to the external influences which Kishlansky invokes after 1640, such as growth in the power of Parliament or the divisions accompanying civil war. The Civil War would help to fix in place processes which institutionalized conflict and division; but, in the case of elections, these processes were already emerging, as a result of changing ideas about representation and the role of MPs, and, at a deeper level, as a consequence of social and economic development.

In this context it is worth noting that electoral transformation was often a feature of those areas experiencing rapid economic change. This can be demonstrated by a rudimentary investigation of electoral geography. In the open-field areas, where change was relatively gradual and vertical social ties remained strongest, the gentry often appear to have been able to turn out tenants and freeholders in large numbers and in a relatively organized fashion. This is perhaps one of the reasons why Dr Hassell Smith has found that in shires such as Norfolk and Suffolk, and Somerset and Wiltshire, a preponderance of knights of the shire came from such areas.[60] However in the semi-urbanized, semi-industrialized parts of England, where population was expanding rapidly and the 'middling sort' enjoyed considerable economic independence, electoral management was much more difficult. This could lead to such areas being under-represented, which, as Ann Hughes shows, was the case for north Warwickshire; or it could lead to efforts to secure freeholder support on the basis of political issues. This was the pattern in Yorkshire where Savile directed his appeal to the West Riding cloth towns. It also applied in Kent in 1625, where Sandys and Edward Scott, the candidates who presented themselves as spokesmen for the 'country', drew strong backing from clothing towns like Cranbrook; in Essex, where the election indentures returning Sir Francis Barrington were signed by a preponderance of clothiers and minor gentry from areas such as Dedham and Braintree; and in Gloucestershire in 1640, where the freeholders from the Cotswold clothing towns rallied behind the Puritan ship-money refuser Nathaniel Stephens.[61]

These were also the areas where lay Puritanism was at its strongest. This is not a coincidence. As we have seen – and as Peter Lake shows in his article – Puritan emphasis on 'active citizenship' and the threat from popery tended to feed into a concern for freely elected Parliaments. It was godly spokesmen who were most insistent that, where necessary, freeholders should set aside considerations of unity and hierarchy and choose their MPs on the basis of individual conscience; and some of the earliest instances of electors following this course – in the Suffolk election of 1584, for example – can be traced back to contests where religion was a prominent issue.[62]

The gentry's response to such developments was mixed. As we have seen, some regarded them as a further manifestation of a 'popular/Puritan' threat to order and hierarchy. However for the most part they accepted the situation and adjusted their stance accordingly. Morrill and Walter imply that there was not yet the rooted hostility to political action on the part of the 'lower orders' which was to develop out of the Civil War.[63] So even Wentworth, who was otherwise hostile to 'popular' pretensions, was prepared to act in ways calculated to appeal to ordinary electors. Thus county elections can be seen as illustrating the essentially reciprocal nature of the relationship between leading gentry and those below them. There were obligations and expectations on both sides. Reports sent back from Parliament, speeches at the hustings and manifestoes helped to arouse and educate electors, often in ways which would benefit the candidate who had imparted the information. But having helped to promote certain views and establish certain expectations the candidate was then under pressure to respond to them. In the process 'politics' was emerging as a separate sphere in public life. Many gentry could no longer rely for electoral support on their economic power as landlords; increasingly this had to be reinforced by a political role and a reputation as a 'patriot' and 'parliament-man'.

This had important consequences for Parliament itself. Hirst and Russell have rightly emphasized that the involvement of ordinary electors created additional pressures for MPs.[64] But whereas the pressures they identify were mainly of a local nature – towards resisting taxation and securing local bills – this article suggests that they could involve much broader concerns. In itself parliamentary taxation was not necessarily a grievance. Freeholders were able to distinguish the legitimacy of different types of taxation and accept that if they were to obtain beneficial legislation they were expected to meet the King's necessities as well.[65] What alarmed them was the prospect of their money being misspent or grievances going unredressed; and redress could involve a whole variety of concerns, ranging well beyond the purely local. In 1625 John Delbridge expressed the belief that 'the country' – and, perhaps, in particular his Barnstaple constituents – would be disappointed not only by 'the interruption of fishing' and 'losses by pirates', but also by 'pardons to Jesuits' and 'the news from Rochelle', where the French Huguenots were losing their fight for survival. In 1626 Thomas Scott insisted that Sir Edwin Sandys lost the support of Kent electors, not because he had agreed too readily to granting taxes – as Hirst suggests – but because he had failed to defend their electoral freehold against the court and the deputy lieutenants. And in 1628, when Sir Roger Townsend returned to East Anglia at the end of the session, the news he imparted to freeholders was of the measures taken against Buckingham.[66]

This evidence should help us to understand more clearly the behaviour of politicians in Parliament, and in particular their readiness to confront the Crown over certain issues. When non-Puritan MPs such as Phelips and Sandys spoke out against popery; or backbench MPs voted to impeach Buckingham, in spite of dire warnings from the King; or MPs set aside local bills to push through the Petition of Right, they were acting, in part, in response to the expectations of the electorate. The processes at work became more visible in the Long Parliament, when, as Anthony Fletcher has shown, petitioning campaigns and addresses to MPs influenced the pattern of debate and strengthened the hand of the Crown's critics.[67] But here again we can see the developments of the 1640s being anticipated in the 1620s.

Notes and References

This article has benefited greatly from the comments of Peter Lake and Ann Hughes.

1. J. H. Plumb, 'The growth of the electorate in England from 1600 to 1715', *P&P*, 45 (1969), 90–116; D. M. Hirst, *The Representative of the People?* (Cambridge, 1975); C. Hill, 'Parliament and people in seventeenth century England', *P&P*, 92 (1981), 100–24; A. J. Fletcher and C. Hill, 'Debate: Parliament and people in seventeenth century England', *P&P*, 98 (1983), 151–8; S. P. Salt, 'Sir Thomas Wentworth and the parliamentary representation of Yorkshire, 1614–1628', *NH*, XVI (1980), 130–68; J. K. Gruenfelder, *Influence in Early Stuart Elections 1604–1640* (Columbus, Ohio, 1981).
2. These developments are described most fully in Hirst, *Representative of the People*.
3. Ibid., pp. 132–57, 216–22; Plumb, 'Growth of the electorate', 104–7.
4. M. Kishlansky, *Parliamentary Selection* (Cambridge, 1986). It should be noted, however, that Kishlansky has a narrower definition of 'contest' than other historians, allowing as contests only those elections contested on polling day.
5. Plumb, 'Growth of the electorate', 94–5, 97, 104–7; Hill, 'Parliament and People', 107–18.
6. Hirst, *Representative of the People*, p. 148; J. S. Morrill, *The Revolt of the Provinces* (London, 1976) pp. 13–31; Salt, 'Sir Thomas Wentworth and the parliamentary representation in Yorkshire', 145–7.
7. C. S. R. Russell, *Parliaments and English Politics 1621–1629* (Oxford 1979).
8. Kishlansky, *Parliamentary Selection*, chs 3 and 4.
9. Ibid., p. 57; Eaton Hall, Cheshire, MS. no. 25 (I am grateful to His Grace the Duke of Westminster for permission to quote from this); R. P. Cust and P. G. Lake, 'Sir Richard Grosvenor and the rhetoric of magistracy', *BIHR*, LIV (1981), 43–5.
10. M. Walzer, *The Revolution of the Saints* (London, 1966), p. 259; P. G. Lake, 'Constitutional consensus and puritan opposition in the 1620s: Thomas Scott and the Spanish Match', *HJ*, XXV (1982), 815–17; HMC, *Duke of Buccleuch and Queensberry MSS*, III (1926), pp. 258–9.
11. Plumb. 'Growth of the electorate', 107; C. Holmes, *The Eastern Association in the English Civil War* (Cambridge, 1974), pp. 21–2; N. R. N. Tyacke, *Anti-Calvinists* (Oxford, 1987), pp. 192–4; Hirst, *Representative of the People*, p. 14.
12. For further discussion of 'the country' see: P. Zagorin, *The Court and the Country* (London, 1969), pp. 33–9; L. Stone, *The Causes of the English Revolution 1529–1642* (London, 1972), pp. 105–8; R. P. Cust, 'News and politics in early seventeenth century England', *P&P*, 112 (1986), 75–9; Lake, 'Constitutional consensus and puritan opposition', 805–25.
13. Cust, 'News and politics', 60–90; Hirst, *Representative of the People*, pp. 178–81; Russell, *Parliaments and English Politics*, pp. 19– 22, 388–9.

14. H. Stocks (ed.), *Records of the Borough of Leicester 1603–1688* (Cambridge, 1923), pp. 195–6; *Wentworth Papers*, pp. 152–7.

15. Cited in Hirst, *Representative of the People*, p. 159; *The Diary of John Rous*, ed. M. A. Everett Green (Camden Soc. 1st ser. lxvi, 1856), pp. 2–3; R. Ashton, *The English Civil War* (London, 1978), p. 70.

16. *C and T Jas I*, ii, 216, 233–40; *Chamberlain*, ii, 350–1; *Proclamations*, i, 499–500, 502–3; BL, Satirical Prints, no. 91 (1621), 'The description of Giles Mompesson late Knight, censured by Parliament'; Chester City RO, CR 63/2/21.

17. *C and T Jas I*, ii, *passim; C and T Chas I*, i, *passim*; Chester City RO, CR 63/2/19; Cust, 'News and politics', 80–1; BL, Add. 35,331, fo. 21.

18. *Records of Leicester*, pp. 195–6; Hull RO, Corporation Letters, L. 168–71, 178–80; Devon RO, Exeter Corporation Letters, L.210; Cust and Lake, 'Sir Richard Grosvenor', 43–5.

19. *C and T Jas I*, ii, *passim; C and T Chas I*, i, *passim*; Russell, *Parliaments and English Politics*, p. 389; D. Underdown, *Revel, Riot and Rebellion* (Oxford, 1986), p. 71; Warwicks RO, DR 87/2, Churchwarden's Accounts for St Nicholas' Warwick. 1628–9. (I am grateful to Ann Hughes for this reference.)

20. Kishlansky, *Parliamentary Selection*.

21. *Strafforde Letters*, i, 8–13; *Wentworth Papers*, pp. 144–5; Guildford Muniment Room (hereafter GMR), Loseley MSS, LM 2014/109. (I am grateful to Major More Molyneux for permission to cite these MSS.)

22. *Strafforde Letters*, i, 9–13; *Wentworth Papers*, p. 145; Sheffield City Library, Wentworth Woodhouse Muniments, photocopy 2C; A Gooder, *The Parliamentary Representation of the County of York*, 2 vols (Yorks. Arch. Soc., xcvi, 1937), ii, 167; G. M. R., Loseley MSS, LM 1331/25; *CD 1621*, iv, 49; vi, 68–9; *CJ*, i, 556–7.

23. J. J. Cartwright, *Chapters in the History of Yorkshire* (Wakefield, 1872), pp. 20–2; *Strafforde Letters*, i, 10–13; G. M. R. Loseley MSS, More Corr. 4/44; Gooder, *Parliamentary Representation of Yorkshire*, ii, 168–9; R. Marchant, *Puritans and the Church Courts in the Diocese of York* (1960), pp. 30–4; *DNB*: Cooke, Alexander; Favour, John; P. W. Hasler (ed.), *The History of Parliament: The House of Commons 1558–1603*, 3 vols (1981), i, 281–3; 3, 352–3.

24. *Strafforde Letters*, i, 11, 13; *Proclamations*, i, 493–5; Gardiner, *History*, ii, 249; HMC, *Duke of Portland MSS*, vol. ix (1923), 138.

25. A. Cooke, *Yet More Worke for a Masse Priest* (1622), dedication; *Chamberlain*, ii, 549.

26. PRO, C.219/37/321; GMR, Loseley MSS, LM 1331/25–6; *CJ*, i, 556.

27. *Strafforde Letters*, ii, 10–11; Gooder, *Parliamentary Representation of Yorkshire*, ii, 168–9.

28. Hirst, *The Representative of the People*, p. 141.

29. Ibid., p. 175; *Wentworth Papers*, pp. 152–5.

30. R. E. Ruigh, *The Parliament of 1624* (Cambridge, Mass., 1971), pp. 104–5; *Wentworth Papers*, pp. 202–3.

31. BL, Add. MS, 24,470, fo. 30.

32.   *Strafforde Letters* i, 25–7; *Wentworth Papers,* pp. 231–2; G. W. Johnson (ed.), *The Fairfax Correspondence,* 2 vols (1848) i, 6–10; J. T. Cliffe, *The Yorkshire Gentry* (London, 1969), p. 200; Salt, 'Wentworth and the parliamentary representation of Yorkshire', 143; Marchant, *Puritans and the Church Courts,* pp. 42, 266.

33.   *Neg. Post.,* i, 96–7; HMC, House of Lords MSS, vol. ix (addenda 1514– 1714) (1962), 180.

34.   *Strafforde Letters,* i, 25–6; *Wentworth Papers,* pp. 231–2.

35.   *Strafforde Letters,* i, 32; Cambridge Univ. Library (hereafter CUL), Diary of Bulstrode Whitelocke Esq., Dd. xii, 20–2, 24 March 1626 (I am grateful to the Yale Center for parliamentary history for the opportunity to consult their transcript of this diary.)

36.   CUL, Whitelocke diary, 22 May and 8 June 1626; *Fairfax Correspondence,* i, 30–1; *Wentworth Papers,* p. 249.

37.   R. P. Cust, *The Forced Loan and English Politics 1626–1628* (Oxford, 1987), pp. 194–7; *Wentworth Papers,* pp. 254, 265, 313–14.

38.   *Strafforde Letters,* i, 28,31; *Wentworth Papers,* pp. 240, 259–69; *The Academy,* vii (1875), 582.

39.   *Wentworth Papers,* pp. 265, 268–9, 278, 283, 287; *Strafforde Letters,* i, 34 (Jackson's letter is misdated; it refers to 1628), 44; BL Harl. MS 390, fo. 356; James Howell, *Epistolae Ho Elianae: Familiar Letters,* ed. J. Jacobs (1890), p. 249; *P in P 1628,* ii, 507, 510, 513.

40.   *Wentworth Papers,* p. 301.

41.   Hirst, *The Representative of the People,* p. 226.

42.   *Wentworth Papers,* pp. 313–14.

43.   J. E. Neale, *The Elizabethan House of Commons* (1963 pbk edn), pp. 127–8; I. Grosvenor, 'Catholics and politics: the Worcestershire election of 1604', *Recusant History,* xxiv 149–62; (1977–78); Eaton Hall, Cheshire, MS no. 25; H. W. Saunders (ed.), *The Official Papers of Sir Nathaniel Bacon of Stiffkey, Norfolk* (Camden Soc., 3rd ser., xxvi, 1915), pp. 39–41; *Chamberlain,* ii, 540; PRO, SP 14/158/67.

44.   KAO, U.951/Z16/1; Bodl. L, Ballard MS 61, pos. 88–90; Canterbury Cathedral Library (hereafter CCL), Urry MS, U.66; *P in P 1628,* vi, 126–37; P. Clark, 'Thomas Scott and the Growth of urban opposition to the early Stuart regime', *HJ,* xxi (1978), 1–26; *CD 1621,* vii, 634.

45.   Eaton Hall, Cheshire, MS no. 25.

46.   W. Notestein, *The House of Commons 1604–10* (New Haven, 1971), p. 394; Hirst, p. 141; BRO, Trumbull MSS, alphabetical (Beaulieu), vii, 147–8 (I am grateful to Tom Cogswell for this reference); *The Winthrop Papers,* 4 vols (Massachusetts Historical Soc., 1929–43), ii, 326: Gruenfelder, *Influence in Early Stuart Elections,* ch. 3.

47.   Hirst, pp. 137–53; D. M. Willson, *Privy Councillors in the House of Commons 1604–1629* (Minneapolis, 1940), ch. 3; Gruenfelder, ch. 5.

48.   Hirst, p. 180; *Chamberlain,* i, 468, 540, 549; Clark, 'Thomas Scott and the growth of urban opposition', pp. 19–21.

49.   T. G. Barnes, *Somerset 1625–1640* (Oxford, 1961), p. 10; Russell, *Parliaments and English Politics,* pp. 55–6, 130, 136, 150–1, 154,

227–9, 230, 243; Cust, *The Forced Loan and English Politics*, pp. 106–8, 153–4.

50. NRO, Montague MSS, vol. 186, unpaginated. (I am grateful to Esther Cope for this reference); Cust and Lake, 'Sir Richard Grosvenor', 51; L. L. Peck, 'Goodwin v Fortescue: the local context of parliamentary controversy', *Parliamentary History*, vol. 3. (1984), 33–56; PRO, SP 16/34/69; A. Searle (ed.), *Barrington Family Letters 1628–32* (Camden Soc., 4th ser., xxviii, 1983), pp. 7–9; HMC, *Montague of Beaulieu MSS* (1900), p. 106; *C and T Chas I*, i, 249; A. L. Hughes, *Politics, Society and Civil War in Warwickshire 1620–1660* (London, 1987), p. 50; *Sir Henry Whitehead's Letter Book*, vol. 1, 1601–14 (Hampshire Records Series, 1976), p. 113; *Returns of Names of Every Members Returned to Serve in Each Parliament* (1878) i, 450–79. For similar comments about the representative of a large corporation see the endorsement of Henry Sherfield at Southampton in 1624: Hampshire RO, Jervoise of Herriard MSS, 44M 69, xxxix/8 (I am grateful to Tom Cogswell for this reference).

51. Kishlansky, *Parliamentary Selection*, pp. 25–31.

52. Hirst, *Representative of the People*, pp. 140, 145; BL, Harl. MS 390, fo. 356. The 1628 elections are discussed more fully in Cust, *The Forced Loan and English Politics*, pp. 307–15.

53. Hirst, *Representative of the People*, pp. 39–40, app. iv.

54. *Names of Members Returned to Serve in Parliament*, i, 450–79. These returns are analysed more fully in R. P. Cust, 'The Forced Loan and English Politics 1626–1628' (University of London, Ph.D thesis, 1984), app. iv.

55. B. W. Quintrell, 'Gentry factions and the Witham affray 1628', *Essex Archaeology and History*, vol. 10 (1978), 122–3: *Holles*, ii, 377; *C and T Chas I*, i, 323, 329.

56. PRO, SP 16/87/11; 96/36,48; 106/14.14i; 471/69; *P in P 1628*, ii, 33; *C and T Chas I*, i, 332.

57. Cust, *The Forced Loan and English Politics*, pp. 314–15.

58. Wentworth's pursuit of preferment at Court and election to Parliament had been interrupted by near-fatal illnesses in 1622 and 1623: *Strafforde Letters*, i, 16–17; ii, 430; *Wentworth Papers*, pp. 205, 323.

59. Clark, 'Thomas Scott and the growth of urban opposition', pp. 11–19; CCL, Urry MS U.66; *P in P 1628*, vi, 126–37.

60. A. Hassell Smith, 'Electoral geography 1585–1629' (Paper delivered at the CORAL conference on 'Relationships between local communities and the nation' at UEA September 1986). See also the essay by Ann Hughes in this volume.

61. KAO, U 1115/015/1–6; Scull, *Dorothea Scott*, pp. 142–3; PRO, C.219/37/ 98; 39/99; SP 16/448/79.

62. D. McCulloch, *Suffolk and the Tudors* (Oxford, 1986), pp. 333–7.

63. J. S. Morrill and J. Walter, 'Order and disorder in the English Revolution', in A. Fletcher and J. Stevenson (eds), *Order and Disorder in Early Modern England* (1985), pp. 137–65.

64. Hirst, *Representative of the People*, ch. 8; Russell, *Parliaments and English Politics, passim.*

65. Cust, *The Forced Loan and English Politics*, ch. 3 (see in particular the views of the Bedfordshire subsidymen cited on pp. 161– 2).
66. Russell, *Parliaments and English Politics*, p. 249; Scull, *Dorothea Scott*, pp. 132–43 (Scott's preoccupation with 'freehold' in the electoral sense is clearly indicated in his other treatises on this subject: KAO, U951/Z16/1; CCL Urry MS U.66; *P in P 1628*, vi, 126–37); *Diary of John Rous*, pp. 16–17.
67. A. Fletcher, *The Outbreak of the English Civil War* (London, 1981).

6 Court Politics and Parliamentary Conflict in 1625

Christopher Thompson

I

The accession of Charles I to the throne in March 1625 has traditionally been seen as one of the major turning-points in the political history of early seventeenth-century England. The new King, unlike his father who had fought only paper wars, was eager to play a full part in the European struggle against Spain and the Hapsburgs to secure the restoration of his brother-in-law, the Elector Frederick, to his hereditary dominions in the Palatinate. His favourite, the Duke of Buckingham, was equally anxious to display his genius in forging diplomatic coalitions and leading them to military victory. Unfortunately, Charles's first Parliament did not support the strategy by which it was proposed to achieve these objectives. The House of Commons favoured a naval rather than a continental war and declined to subsidize foreign allies. There were other, more pressing issues – over religion, taxation and, ultimately, over the role of Buckingham himself – that took priority. Eventually, the conflict between the King and the lower House became too acute and Parliament was dissolved. The dominant themes of the late 1620s, foreign war and domestic strife, were thus set in the first few months of Charles's reign.

The orthodox explanation of these events has been that Charles and Buckingham viewed Parliament as a simple tool to be used at their convenience to underwrite their continental adventures. They accordingly neglected to make the necessary electoral and legislative preparations for managing the assembly. Their lack of foresight and their incompetence were compounded by divisions at court and 'country' opposition. The King's unwillingness to bargain or to respond positively to the grievances of the subject made failure inevitable.[1] The 1625 Parliament can therefore be fitted neatly into a long-term view of a constitutional and religious struggle between the early Stuarts and their subjects.

Of course, the general argument and the particular grounds upon which this interpretation of proceedings in 1625 rest have recently been challenged. Conrad Russell has argued that Charles and Buckingham actually had a principled belief in the institution of Parliament which explains their efforts to work with them after 1625. He has maintained more specifically that the court was basically quiescent under the Duke's leadership until the autumn of that year and that clear Conciliar guidance was given to the lower House, particularly in the second 'session'. It was in the circumstances of the Parliament – the threat of the plague at Westminster and Oxford, the fears of MPs over the relaxation of the penal laws against recusancy and over the rise of Arminianism – and in the divided loyalties of members to their King and counties that the explanation for the breakdown lies.[2]

The contrast between these two lines of argument is so strong that there are good grounds for re-examining the evidence. The issues in dispute go to the heart of our understanding of the politics of the period. It is important to know exactly what the King's attitude to Parliament was and the terms upon which he sought to obtain supply. Was he or the Duke willing to bargain over the redress of grievances? Did their strategy command the support of the Privy Council? If it did not, if there were, in fact, divisions amongst the King's Councillors, what interplay, if any, was there between their discussions and the deliberations in the House of Commons? There are further questions about the connection between the attack on Buckingham in this Parliament and that in 1626 which naturally arise out of such an enquiry. The Parliament offers an opportunity to assess not only the orthodox and revisionist interpretations in detail but also the wider issues raised by the divergence between them.

II

The adoption of a war policy had been formally agreed in the Parliament of 1624. It was the result of the combined pressure brought on King James by Prince Charles, the Duke of Buckingham and a group of intermediaries in the House of Commons (including Sir Edward

Coke, Sir Dudley Digges, Sir Robert Phelips and Sir Edwin Sandys). An initial grant of three subsidies and three-fifteenths was voted towards the objectives of defending the realm, of securing Ireland, of setting out the navy and of assisting the Dutch as specified in the Subsidy Act. The money, which was under the control of parliamentary treasurers, was to be spent within a year of the repudiation of the Spanish treaties. This was clearly a defeat for the pro-Spanish group at Court: it was followed by the fall of the Lord Treasurer, the Earl of Middlesex, and the recall, in disgrace, of the Earl of Bristol, England's Ambassador in Spain. In return for this supply, the Prince and the Duke used their influence over the King to secure the passage of legislation dealing mainly with economic grievances. Even so, their success was only partial. Their Commons' allies had been strongly resisted by a group of 'country' members, including a strong northern element, led by Sir John Savile and Sir Francis Seymour, who were clearly sceptical about James's commitment to war. The old King's subsequent obstruction of a declaration of war against Spain, the unauthorized expenditure of the money granted on Count Mansfeldt's expedition to the Spanish Netherlands and, most seriously of all, the concession to the French in the negotiations for Prince Charles's marriage to Henrietta Maria – in clear breach of his promise to Parliament – not only of toleration for English Catholics, but also of aid to suppress the rebellious Huguenots, undermined the pillars on which the accord of 1624 rested. There had been no naval or privateering war of the kind envisaged in the House of Commons. None of the intermediaries had been promoted or restored to major office. In fact, it was not until James was dead that Charles and Buckingham were free to conclude the marriage negotiations with France, to promise Christian IV of Denmark £30,000 a month for intervening in the Empire and to press ahead with the assembly of the English fleet at Plymouth for a descent on the Spanish coast.

This reorientation of English foreign policy clearly affected alignments at court. It was widely believed that James had been disenchanted with Buckingham. The activities of the former supporters of the Spanish match continued to be of concern to the Prince and Duke. It was to frustrate them that the Earl of Arundel, Secretary of State Calvert and Lord Keeper Williams were dropped from the commission to negotiate with France in July, 1624. But neither Charles nor Buckingham formed any firm alliance with the leading Conciliar advocates of English intervention on the Continent, the Earl of Pembroke, Archbishop George Abbot, and the pro-French Scots, Lennox and Hamilton. Abbot was never admitted to the commission to negotiate with the French and Pembroke and Hamilton were dropped from it in December 1624, Dr Adams and Dr Sharpe have traced the course of both groups' estrangement from the Duke.[3] Arundel's resentment at his exclusion was openly expressed to the Prince in January 1625. Three months later, at the first Privy Council meeting of the new reign, he asked Charles to support the ancient nobility, to cease selling honours and offices and to 'let his Council share the things which he wishes to announce, publishing them as having been discussed with the Councillors'. The King was clearly displeased with this pointed criticism while Buckingham was angry enough to propose to drive Arundel out.[4] There is even clearer evidence of the personal animosity between the Duke and Lord Keeper Williams. Within three days of James' death, Buckingham was threatening 'to turn him out of his Office'.[5] A more conciliatory line was taken towards Pembroke: fears that he would lose his place as Lord Chamberlain under Charles were dispelled and he was appointed to the new Privy Council committee on foreign affairs. But Pembroke was still ready to advise Buckingham not to make unwarrantable concessions to the French at the end of May.[6] His support on foreign affairs was apparently conditional. So, even though Buckingham's position at Court was more secure after Charles's accession, there is evidence of resentment on the part of other members of the Privy Council at his monopoly of influence and of misgivings about his aims in the spring of 1625.

Admittedly, this is unlikely to have been of concern to the King or Duke at this stage. Charles's overriding aim was to pursue his foreign policy objectives for which parliamentary supply was essential. His initial intention was to recall the 1624 Parliament that had proved so accommodating until Lord Keeper Williams pointed out that his father's death had dissolved it. He therefore insisted on writs for a new one being sent out at once the day after James died. Williams's advice on canvassing the King's friends and servants first was ignored.[7] Indeed, the preoccupation of Charles and Buckingham with the burial of the old King, with diplomatic negotiations and military planning and with preparations for the reception of the new Queen, Henrietta Maria, seem to have precluded anything more than the most minimal consideration of parliamentary matters[8] over which the growing spectre of the plague in London increasingly hung. No attempt appears to have been made to re-engage the allies of 1624 or to prepare any legislative measures. It was apparently assumed that the problems of managing Parliament had disappeared.

Charles explained his position succinctly enough when he eventually opened Parliament on 18 June. It was on the advice of both Houses that the decision to recover the Palatinate by military means had been taken in 1624. He, like James, was bound in honour to proceed with the project – hence, the raising of forces in Germany and the preparation of his fleet. It was vital for his interests and their health that supply be granted quickly.[9] Lord Keeper Williams then asked the two Houses to remember that this was Charles' first Parliament and that they were jointly committed to the war. All the money granted in 1624 and much more of the King's revenue had been spent. Because affairs were so pressing, this would be a short meeting for supply only: domestic matters could be dealt with in the next session. If the normal method of contribution proved too slow, their advice on a more appropriate one would be welcome. Finally, it was essential to sustain the reputation of the King.[10] These were the themes, of honour and engagement, which were repeated to the Commons when Sir Thomas Crew, Speaker in 1624, was renominated.[11] When he came before Charles for approval on 20 June, Crew's speech contained a specific commitment to the Palatinate's recovery and a plea for the expulsion of Catholic priests and Jesuits and for the maintenance of true religion.[12] Lord Keeper Williams's reply significantly reserved the manner of executing the penal laws on religion to Charles alone.[13] The main elements of the King's strategy – immediate supply (by new means if thought appropriate), postponement of debate on domestic matters to the next session and the pre-emptive reservation of the emotive issue of the enforcement of the recusancy laws to the sovereign alone – were evident.

The Commons had its first chance to debate these priorites when it met to order its business on 21 June. Its initial proceedings – settling a communion and fast for itself, deciding to petition Charles for a public fast and appointing a committee of privileges to examine disputed election returns – were entirely customary. It was at this point that William Mallory, MP for Ripon, moved to petition the King for an adjournment until after Michaelmas because of the spread of the plague.[14] This was an openly obstructive move. He was supported, significantly, by Sir Robert Phelips, the Somerset member whose hopes for advancement after his alliance with Buckingham a year earlier had not been realized. His argument was that the commonwealth's business, particularly concerning religion and the examination of the accounts of the 1624 subsidies, was more important than giving supply now. But the threat of increasing sickness persuaded him to advocate adjournment.[15] So, too, did Sir Thomas Wentworth whose election for Yorkshire had just been challenged and who proposed the appointment of a committee to draft such a petition.[16] But neither Sir George More nor Alford wanted an immediate decision, preferring instead to discuss the proposal in committee on the 22nd.[17] Their reservations were reinforced by Solicitor General Heath who protested at the damage such action would do the King's reputation: he, too, wanted the House's business priorities determined by a committee.[18] His intervention proved decisive. Despite efforts by Wentworth's ally, Christopher Wandesford, to alter the proposal from adjournment to a new time to one for removal to another place, the House rejected the idea altogether.[19]

The defeat of this proposal was followed, however, by a motion on the 22nd from Mallory's partner for Ripon, Sir Thomas Hoby, for the appointment of a committee of grievances.[20] If adopted, it would have entailed a broad examination of the subject's complaints in direct contravention of the King's priorities. But it was met by an eloquent tribute from Pembroke's ally, Sir Benjamin Rudyerd, to Charles's personal virtues and to his role in reconciling James to Parliament in 1624. Rudyerd hoped his fellow members had come prepared to carry themselves 'in this first session with sweetnes, with duty, with confidence in and towards his Majestie' for which due recompense could be expected. He therefore proposed priority for urgent matters (i.e. supply) while more contentious issues, if raised, could be left until the next session.[21] Sir Edward Coke, that great legal oracle who, like Rudyerd, had been an undertaker for the Prince and Duke in 1624, also opposed the appointment of committees for grievances and the courts of justice because of the danger from the plague, the absence of grievances arising since Charles's accession and the fact that there had been no reply to the petition of grievances presented by the Commons in 1624: it was this reply that he suggested they now seek. In future, such petitions should be presented in time to ensure a response before Parliament broke up.[22] The key contribution, however, came from Sir Francis Seymour, one of the 'Country' leaders a year before, who linked the issue of supply to the more controversial topic of religion in general and the toleration of recusants in particular. He advocated a petition to Charles for enforcement of the laws against Catholic priests and to prevent any resort to mass at foreign ambassadors' houses. Seymour accordingly proposed a committee to consider religion and supply.[23] Phelips, however, was not keen on an immediate decision on this proposal: he had his own list of controversial matters – the collection of the new impositions, the disastrous decay of Crown revenues and the accounts of the 1624 subsidies – to propose for consideration.[24] It was eventually agreed to consider all these propositions the next morning. A decision was then made to adopt Seymour's proposal for a committee of the whole House to consider religion and supply, with religion having precedence.[25]

This tactical struggle over priorities is highly revealing. The mere expression of the King's wishes had not been enough to direct the House's procedural decisions. It was already evident that the group of undertakers who had co-operated with Charles and Buckingham in 1624 had broken up. Only Rudyerd was definitely playing an intermediary role but neither he nor Solicitor General Heath was persuasive enough to control the Commons. The precise attitude of Sir Edward Coke was unclear while neither Digges nor Sandys had yet spoken. Phelips, on the other hand, had clearly defected to the 'Northern' men who were being as obstructive as they had been a year before. The regional connection between Mallory, Hoby, Wentworth and Wandesford was evident: together, they threatened to raise not just the uncompleted business of 1624 but also to explore a number of unsettled parliamentary grievances of much longer standing. The obstructive nature of their tactics was noted by Sir John Eliot, the Vice-Admiral of Devon and client of Buckingham who was still in his confidence.[26] But it would be misleading to assume that Seymour's proposal was more moderate than theirs had been: on the contrary, it cut directly across the King's instructions and its adoption meant that Charles's priorities had been rejected. The initiative had passed into the House's hands.

For the next week, the House of Commons was preoccupied with the threat posed by the growth of recusancy and the preparation of a petition to Charles on religion. The King made no immediate response to this setback but there was certainly a hint of irritation on his part in the message delivered to the Commons by Solicitor General Heath on 28th June: his only desire, the message explained, was 'to take consideracion of the present state of Christendom, . . . [and] that were it not for urgent occasions, he would not hold us together'.[27] The King's priorities remained the same.

In fact, the completion of the first stage of the House's work on religion on 30 June gave Seymour the opportunity to spring a second and even more unwelcome surprise. Taking advantage of the absence of many court supporters, he raised the issue of supply in committee and proposed the grant of a single subsidy and one fifteenth, *c.* £100,000, to the King.[28] Such a sum was completely inadequate, as Rudyerd immediately pointed out in a prepared speech, to meet Charles's domestic charges quite apart from the £300,000 needed to dispatch the fleet and the additional resources required for the support of Mansfeldt's forces, the Dutch and the King of Denmark.[29] But he failed to specify a definite figure himself and, although a number of members were prepared to be more generous than Seymour, none, not even John Maynard's suggestion of three subsidies, would have met more than a fraction of these commitments.[30] The decisive speech, according to Eliot's later account, came from Phelips: he openly denied that there was an explicit engagement to supply Charles since no war had been declared and no enemy named since 1624. Furthermore, there had been no account offered for the supply granted then. It was, in any case, a breach of precedent to make a grant so early in proceedings, especially in view of the accumulated violation of the House's privileges and the subject's rights in recent years. The most he would offer was two subsidies, *c.* £140,000, to be accompanied by a petition to Charles to reform his government and to proceed in it 'by a grave and wise counsell'. If the fleet returned successfully, there might then be a better incentive to grant supply.[31] His themes, of reformation in government and the restoration of the King's ordinary revenues, were taken up by Sir Thomas Wentworth and Sir Edward Coke, both of whom supported a grant of two subsidies.[32] Despite the arrival of Court supporters primed to ask for a higher figure, it was on a grant of two subsidies as 'a free guift' that the Commons unanimously agreed.[33]

The tactical significance of Seymour's manoeuvre was clear enough to contemporary observers. Once the House had decided upon a grant, however small, a further request for supply in the same session was fraught with difficulties. The passage of the Subsidy Bill itself could be delayed until the Commons received satisfaction on the toleration of recusants.[34] Charles obviously found the decision to vote him only two subsidies to be paid at the end of October 1625 and of April 1626 unpalatable. He personally gave instructions for a larger grant to be sought and for the House to be divided, if necessary, on the question. If the request was defeated, the House of Commons was then to be asked to specify the times of payment in the Subsidy Bill so that Charles could be sure of the means to repay loans from his subjects. It is significant that members were to have been further informed that, although the King would have been glad of an addition to the subsidies already granted, 'yett he hopeth . . . to preue[n]t the lyke growing necessities by . . a more frugale application of his owne meanes for his owne use'.[35] This would have meant abandoning hope of a further grant from Parliament and relying on the other resources open to the Crown. These instructions must have been formulated before the afternoon of 1 July when drafting of the preamble to the Subsidy Bill was due to begin.[36] But they were never carried into effect: Charles must have altered or been persuaded to alter his mind.[37] The House evidently confirmed the previous day's decision on the size and timing of its grant.[38] A change of course, perhaps under pressure, on the part of the King would help to explain the long-discounted version of the message Lord Keeper Williams delivered to both Houses on Charles's behalf on 4 July that Eliot incorporated in his retrospective analysis of proceedings. His report alone describes the King's satisfaction at the form and manner of the gift before going on, like the others, to record that the House was free to decide when its business had been completed.[39] The deduction he drew from it that Charles had accepted the two subsidies as the most he could get is consistent with the only direct piece of evidence available about Charles's views. Had Eliot actually participated in discussions which led to a change of course, the recurrence of this argument about Williams's message in his subsequent speeches and in *Negotium Posterorum* is more comprehensible.[40] It is important to recognize that this is merely a hypothesis. All that can certainly be said is that Charles's instructions do not appear to have been acted upon.

The King's message apparently left members free to complete their remaining business. They accordingly pressed ahead with the passage of the Subsidy Bill and that for Tonnage and Poundage with an exceptional limitation to a single year. With enquiries into the case of Richard Montague, the divine who had reaffirmed the Arminian views found so offensive by the House in 1624, completed and agreement reached with the House of Lords on the content of a petition on religion to be presented to Charles, many MPs had begun to leave Westminster and the remainder expected an imminent adjournment for some months.[41]

Under these circumstances, the decision of the King and Duke to make another demand for supply was particularly risky. It was apparently taken at a private meeting between them at Hampton

Court on 7 July. The choice of Sir John Coke, Fulke Greville's protégé who was one of the Masters of Requests and Buckingham's subordinate as an Admiralty Commissioner, to explain this demand rather than a Privy Councillor suggests that it did not enjoy full Conciliar approval. Buckingham's 'privados' were briefed at York House that night. Sir John Eliot has left a graphic account of what happened when news of the plan spread the following morning.

> As it came to others, whose qualitie was more knowing and ingenuous, they, as they apprehended it to be fatall & prodigious, soe gave it demonstration to the Duke & with all their power oppos'd it, adding to argumentes, entreaties for the prevention of that evill, which did implie apparantlie dishonor to the King, & danger to him. Of this number (not to deprive anie man of his due) was Sir Humphry May, then Chancelor of the Dutchie, who, having travaild with much industrie in that service, but in vaine, came in great hast to a gentleman whom he thought more powerfull with the Duke & knew to be affectionat to the publicke, & him he importund to a new attempt & triall for staie or diversion of that worke.[42]

While May, the newest member of the Privy Council, went on to the House to delay Sir John Coke's appeal, Eliot himself went to York House. Once admitted to see Buckingham, he warned the Duke that the prevalence of the plague and consequent thin attendance in the Commons was bound to make the manoeuvre appear to be an ambush. It was dishonourable, furthermore, to proceed with it after accepting a grant of two subsidies and the blame would inevitably fall, so he asserted, on Buckingham. The Duke's response was more plausible than Eliot later allowed. He pointed out, quite correctly, that the subsidies voted had been accepted as an accession gift and that absence from the Commons was a matter for members themselves. It was a matter of honour for the King's fleet to be supplied before its departure and that outweighed all personal considerations. Not even Eliot's final warning that the motion was unlikely to succeed could move him.[43] Sir John Coke was thus free to put the case for further supply immediately or at the next session to the Commons. But his description of the King's recent expenditure, his current financial requirements and diplomatic plans proved completely counter-productive. His only recorded supporter in a thin House was Sir William Beecher, one of the Privy Council's clerks. The hostility with which the proposal was received forced Solicitor General Heath to intervene to lay it aside.[44] All the attempt had achieved was to divide the King's supporters and to unite the House.[45]

Buckingham's reaction to this setback was to condemn his confidants for their negligence.[46] Even so, both he and the King were determined to demand further supply. Charles accordingly proposed to the Privy Council at Hampton Court on 10 July that Parliament should be adjourned to meet at Oxford on 1 August. Buckingham supported him by arguing that public necessity was the overriding consideration. Lord Keeper Williams, however, warned that the danger from the plague would make the Commons obdurate and that a second grant in the same session was unprecedented. Privately, he told Charles that Buckingham would certainly be attacked there and advocated postponement to a later date. But his counsel was ignored.[47] To the amazement of many MPs, both Houses learnt on 11 July that they were to adjourn and to reassemble at Oxford on 1 August. They carried with them the news that the war to recover the Palatinate was expected to cost £700,000 p.a. and an assurance that the recusancy laws would be enforced.[48]

The objectives Charles had in mind when he opened Parliament – rapid supply, postponement of debate on domestic affairs and the pre-emption of attacks on his policy towards recusants – had clearly been frustrated at Westminster. The tactical initiative had been seized by the Commons' leaders who moved the attention of the House on to the need for a reply to their outstanding petition of grievances from 1624, the *de facto* toleration of Catholics as a result of the French match, and the continuing dissemination of Montague's doctrines. It is noticeable that no reply was made to the 1624 petition of grievances until 4 July and that its contents did not satisfy the Commons.[49] Charles was even more reserved in dealing with matters of religion: he accepted the joint petition of both Houses on 8 July with a promise merely to study it and then tried to deflect the Commons' attack on Montague by announcing that he was his Chaplain, that he had considered the case already and would satisfy the House on the issue.[50] Where Charles and Buckingham were positive was on the House's engagement to support the war, on the urgent need for supply for the fleet and for the support of the King's continental allies. But with only one Privy Councillor, Sir Humphrey May, admittedly backed by Solicitor General Heath, taking an active part in the House's proceedings, it was impossible to press these priorities on to the Commons. It may be significant that Sir Benjamin Rudyerd, Pembroke's ally, appears to have fallen silent after 30 June. Men like Seymour, Phelips and Sir Edward Coke were much too skilful at articulating the concerns of other members to be diverted by royal messages or the interventions of minor officials. Without able and effective management and a willingness to respond positively to members' anxieties, appeals to respect Charles' contribution to Parliament in 1624 and to help him to achieve the initial foreign policy objectives of his reign carried too little weight. Supply on the scale the King envisaged was not forthcoming and the attempt to win an enlarged grant on 8 July lacked court support. It is clear that there were divisions in the Privy Council over this manoeuvre. May's opposition to the request itself and the absence of speakers to back Sir John Coke and Beecher in the Commons are evidence of that. But, despite Lord Keeper Williams's warnings about the difficulties of seeking further supply and the likelihood of an attack upon Buckingham, the King and the Duke were resolute in pressing ahead.

III

It is naturally tempting to assume that the clarity of the King's intentions over supply united the court and the Privy Council. It is questionable, however, whether this was true. The threat that a more serious attack might be launched on the Duke at Oxford was obvious. There are indications that the idea of using the recusancy issue to divert such an attack had been entertained by Buckingham.[51] In fact, when the Commons met again at Oxford on 1 August, Sir Edward Coke did move successfully for a committee of the whole House to take the accounts of the 1624 subsidies.[52] This would have exposed the Duke to severe criticism over the expenditure of this grant. Sir Edward Coke's motion was followed by an attack by Sir Edward Giles and Sir John Eliot on a pardon granted to a group of Catholic priests the day after the adjournment from Westminster. The complaint was clearly aimed at discrediting the Lord Keeper and was transparently inspired by Buckingham who had attempted to recruit Seymour for the same purpose.[53] But Williams was too well armed to be caught by so obvious a manoeuvre and the Duke himself, as Pembroke and Arundel told Henrietta Maria's Almoner, the Bishop of Mende, was highly vulnerable to an attack of the kind Sir Edward Coke had launched. The demand for the account was intended to encompass his ruin.[54]

There are further grounds, moreover, for thinking that the Privy Council was divided over the terms on which supply should be sought. It had clearly been the intention of Charles and Buckingham at Hampton Court on 10 July that such a request should be directly made to the House of Commons. The instructions, however, given to Sir John Coke on his arrival in Oxford on 2 August envisaged his employment to explain diplomatic developments since 1624 and Charles's pressing need for financial assistance to the Commons but leaving it 'to their judgment whether they would now proceed to a resolution or adjourn till winter in regard of the sickness'. Offering this choice would open the way to a further denial of supply. The Venetian Ambassador actually reported that Lord Keeper Williams and the Chancellor of the Exchequer, Sir Richard Weston, had told the Houses as much.[55] Although his report was mistaken, it is likely that a decision not to press the Commons to a conclusion on the issue of supply against its will had been taken by the time Sir John Coke received his orders. But his instructions are known to have been changed on the evening of 3 August to allow him or Lord Conway, one of the Secretaries of State, to make this statement to both Houses. Williams later stated that he had tried to persuade the Duke that evening and the King on the morning of 4 August to include in Charles's planned speech a promise 'that in Your Actions of Importance, and in the Dispositions of what Sums of Monie your People should bestow upon you, you would take the Advice of a settled, and a constant Council'.[56] On his own testimony, he failed. But the episode does reveal that it was the King and Duke who still sought supply and that neither of them was prepared to accept the Lord Keeper's propitiatory suggestion. Nonetheless, it was not until the morning of the 4th that Charles finally instructed Sir John Coke in Christchurch Hall 'to show the importance of the Fleet, and that it could not proceed without a present supply by money or credit'.[57] These changes in the nature of Sir John Coke's instructions suggest that the Privy Council was divided on its immediate objectives and that it was the King and Duke who ultimately prevailed in its deliberations.

The King's speech to both Houses certainly set out the kernel of the case for supply for the common cause in which they were together engaged. He accepted the initial grant they had made but explained that he could not proceed in 'soe many great affayres as were now in hande without further helpe'. It would be better, he dramatically asserted, to lose half the fleet at sea rather than allow it not to go out at all. As an incentive, he promised a reply to their petition on religion in two days.[58] The detailed account of the alliances sought with France and made with the Danes, Dutch and the German Princes were left to Lord Conway and Sir John

Coke. They revealed that Charles had already spent £400,000 and was committed to paying a further £20,000 a month to Mansfeldt and £30,000 a month to the King of Denmark. Just to dispatch the fleet from Plymouth required another £30–40,000. The King's own revenues and credit were exhausted. It was thus for the House of Commons to decide whether supporting the cause was more important than the immediate danger from the plague.[59]

By stressing his personal commitment to the war in such terms, Charles was taking a considerable gamble. He was, in effect, making another personal appeal for support. The only inducement offered was a reply to the petition on religion he had received on 8 July and on whose key complaint, about the failure to execute the recusancy laws, he had yet to make a final decision.[60] The subsequent debate in the Commons on 5 August showed that the King's official spokesmen – Sir Humphrey May, Sir Thomas Edmondes, Sir Richard Weston and Solicitor General Heath – were ready to argue that the House was, indeed, committed to supporting the war and quite precise about the two subsidies and two-fifteenths, *c* £200,000, now required. Once again, supply was to precede the reformation of grievances.[61] But they were confronted with a much more direct attack from Seymour, Phelips and Sir Edward Coke than any developed at Westminster. Seymour was particularly scathing about the divisive motives of Charles's advisers[62] and Phelips questioned not only the need for immediate supply but also the real benefits of the French and Danish alliances.[63] Both men wanted time to do the business of the commonwealth. Sir Edward Coke went further still in attacking the monopoly of major offices by one man and advanced his own programme for investigating and remedying the Crown's poverty.[64] Their only specific difference was that Seymour was prepared ultimately to consider some supply while Sir Edward Coke was opposed to any such grant.[65] Even so, both were clearly in 'opposition' to the King.

There is no doubt, as Eliot later recalled, that the House was fundamentally divided. Indeed, the King's supporters and his critics were engaged in lobbying the uncommitted members.[66] Nevertheless, an attempt at mediation was made. The intermediaries were found amongst the critics of the Lord Keeper – notably Sir John Eliot and Sir Nathaniel Rich – with whom Buckingham had been in private consultation at Oxford and from their local allies, William Coryton, the Vice Warden of the Stannaries in Cornwall, and Sir Henry Mildmay, the Master of the Jewel House.[67] It is likely that they had the support of Rich's cousin, the 2nd Earl of Warwick, who may already have been Mildmay's step father-in-law, and of Viscount Saye and Sele, who, as Williams noted on 14 August, had nominated the Speaker, Sir Thomas Crew, to replace him as Lord Keeper.[68] Eliot has left an account of the advice which was given to Buckingham by his 'frinds' on the evening of 5 August. The Duke was counselled to seek an accommodation with Parliament by blaming the deficiencies of the fleet upon the responsible officers and by sending it to sea under someone else's command: in addition, he was advised to widen the circle of advisers to whom the Privy Council listened, to leave Montague to his punishment and, above all, to offer members the prospect of escaping from their present exposure to the dangers of the plague. This would dissolve the current difficulties and the successful return of the fleet would pave the way for a future agreement.[69] For the moment, Buckingham was persuaded.

The debate in the Commons on the 6th was conducted in radically different terms. The question of the House's engagement to supply the King was cleverly reformulated by Mildmay to identify the King of Spain as their enemy and to highlight Buckingham's positive role in 1624 in order to excuse any later faults. He went on to suggest that the money necessary to dispatch the fleet might be raised with Parliamentary approval although not through subsidies.[70] Coryton then argued that the plague had prevented the present demand for supply being explained in London: if the necessity existed, he would support a grant to the King. But he also wanted a committee to examine the King's revenues, the issue of impositions and the state of religion.[71] Eliot, too, accepted that there was an engagement but denied that there was a desperate need for supply. He excused Buckingham for the delay in dispatching the fleet and tried, to Sir John Coke's chagrin, to lay the blame on the Admiralty Commissioners. If good cause existed, the King should not be denied supply. He accordingly proposed the further debate of their grievances in the winter.[72] The most important contribution came from Sir Nathaniel Rich in a speech setting out a programme for resolving the House's current difficulties. His first request was for a formal answer from the King to the Commons' petition on religion and then for a declaration on the identity of their enemy. For obvious reasons, he did not wish to discuss the fleet's actual objectives but he nonetheless wanted Charles to take the advice of a 'grave counsell' in the war's conduct. He, too, advocated an examination of the King's estate to see how it might 'subsist of it selfe' and a response from Charles on impositions. It would be possible for a committee (rather than for the full House) to draw these points together and present them to the King as part of the process of bargaining. He ended by citing a grant to Edward III that had been conditional upon a war continuing.[73] The speech was a classic example of the redress of grievances being sought in return for supply. It addressed the fundamental issues about which the House was concerned and proposed a solution that might also offer the credit the King required. It is a measure of Rich's tactical genius and persuasive qualities as an advocate that Phelips was prepared to support his proposals in the House itself.[74]

It had been the clear aim of the intermediaries on 6 August to deflect the growing attack on Buckingham. For a moment, it seemed that they might succeed. But over that weekend (and probably without them being informed[75]) there was a further change of course. The Privy Council finally agreed, despite reservations from Williams, that the recusancy laws would be enforced.[76] Buckingham, in addition, was apparently persuaded by his intimates to make an attempt to remove the suspicions hanging over his conduct.[77] He was accordingly authorized to deliver a message from Charles to both Houses on Monday, 8 August along with a highly favourable reply to the Houses' petition on religion. The content of his speech, with its emphasis on the strict adherence to the priorities agreed in Parliament in 1624 and the meticulous expenditure of the money voted then, was predictable. So, too, was his analysis of the diplomatic situation. He claimed to have followed the advice of the Council of War in preparing the fleet and invited his audience to name the prospective enemy they would attack in a war of diversion. The only drawback, of course, was the parlous state of the royal finances which Lord Treasurer Marlborough had to explain.[78]

This renewal of the demand for supply inevitably dashed the hopes of the intermediaries. Charles and his supporters evidently hoped that satisfaction of the Commons' demand for the enforcement of the recusancy laws would be enough to win consent. The King himself explained in a message delivered by the Chancellor of the Exchequer, Sir Richard Weston, on the 10th that an immediate grant to enable his fleet to be dispatched would ensure a winter session to complete the business in hand.[79] His official spokesmen – Naunton, May and Weston – and the minor office holders who supported them pleaded for money to maintain the King's honour and the reputation of the kingdom: without it, Charles's allies would be lost.[80] A crude attempt was made to blame King James for the impoverished state of royal finances. But the loss of all prospect of grievances being redressed until another session was too much for Phelips, Seymour and Sir Edward Coke to stomach. The breach of precedent entailed in a new grant, the lack of wise counsel, the need for an act of resumption to restore royal finances, all were pressed in rejection of the argument that supply had to be given immediate priority.[81] Worse still from Buckingham's point of view was the allegation from Sir Robert Mansell, a member of the Council of War, that it had not been fully consulted by the Duke.[82] The storm raised on the 5th had been revived with added force.

The danger of outright defeat had grown so great that the Court's position changed yet again. On the morning of the 11th, through Rich's intercession and over the objections of Sir Thomas Wentworth, Weston repeated Charles's message but added that the committee proposed on the 6th might indeed meet to debate the concerns of the House if supply was given.[83] And there were further inducements over the conduct of foreign ambassadors and the objectives of the fleet suggested by Sir Henry Marten and Solicitor General Heath respectively.[84] But the House remained deeply divided on the issue and Heath's efforts to refute Mansell simply led to a claim that the naval expedition could not succeed.[85] Charles's patience was exhausted. That night the Privy Council met and, despite objections, the decision to dissolve Parliament was taken.[86] The Commons debate that took place on the 12th involved another forlorn attempt by Heath to answer Mansell and a last-ditch effort to obtain supply by Buckingham's half-brother, Sir Edward Villiers.[87] Nothing had changed to make this possible. The House's last formal action was to approve a protestation drafted by Glanville declaring members' loyalty to the King and readiness to reform the grievances of the realm as well as to supply him in the proper time in a parliamentary way.[88]

IV

The struggle to bend the House of Commons to the King's will was over. He had been determined to win supply on his terms from the opening at Westminster onwards. That meant the relegation of the subject's grievances to second place behind his immediate financial concerns. The King was willing to propose 'new ways' of raising money through Lord Keeper Williams on 18 June and via Sir John Coke on 8 July.[89] He was insistent on adjournment to Oxford for the purpose of seeking a further grant when the Privy Council met on 10 July and equally adamant in going through with the demand when they got there. It is noticeable that, apart from the reply to the 1624 petition of grievances, very little had been conceded to the Commons at Westminster. The enforcement of the recusancy laws and the fate of Montague were claimed as his responsibility alone.[90] Indeed, it was not until after the attempt to obtain additional supply outlined on 4 August had backfired that there was any sign of flexibility at all. Even so, the efforts of Buckingham's intermediaries on the 6th were nullified by the ill-judged speeches made on the King's behalf on 8 August. The possibility that Charles was unaware of the Duke's backstage manoeuvres has to be borne in mind: the alternative explanation is that he was unwilling to accept the bargain suggested by Rich and Eliot. Either way, the opportunity was lost. Thereafter, it was impossible to revive any potential bargain acceptable to the lower House. It is no surprise that the idea of the Crown relying on its own resources first appears in the King's conversation: if Parliament granted him nothing, he told the French Ambassador, the Comte de Tillières, at Oxford that he had 'other resources'.[91] He had also picked up the idea that his critics were a small group of conspirators whose removal would permit a more amenable Parliament to be called.[92] It is his lack of willingness to bargain in the traditional manner that is so striking. Parliament was useful to him only in so far as it complied with his will: if it did not, there were other means of raising money and of securing obedience.

It is quite evident that claims about Court unity and clear conciliar leadership cannot be sustained. There is contemporary testimony to show that Arundel and Williams, at least, had quarrelled with Buckingham at the opening of the reign and incurred the King's displeasure. And there is *prima facie* evidence to suggest, although not to prove, that the King's intention to demand additional supply from the Commons on 1 July may have been given up. The attempt to win it on 8 July did not enjoy full conciliar approval inside or outside the House. From that point onwards, the evidence that divisions in the Privy Council existed is clearer. Lord Keeper Williams opposed an early reassembly of Parliament in the Council on 10 July and had his advice that the King and the Duke should concede that better counsel would be taken in the future rejected early in August. His subsequent advice to Buckingham to divest himself of one or two of his great offices, to adjourn Parliament and to leave it to him to frustrate any charges subsequently sent up to the House of Lords infuriated the Duke. The contacts he had at Oxford with Phelips and Wentworth and the effect that the revelation of his opposition to the adjournment there had on proceedings after 8 August clearly identify him as an opponent of the course taken by Charles and Buckingham.[93] It is harder to assess the attitudes of Pembroke and Arundel. Both clearly understood the nature of the attack on Buckingham at Oxford. Pembroke advised the Earl of Leicester on 5 August not to think of attending Parliament 'where all Things are in Heate, and, I think, will haue a suddaine and distastefull Conclusion' and left the Venetian Ambassador, who had complained of an affront offered to him at James's funeral, convinced of 'his desire that matters shall not go smoothly, so that the duke, whose fortune is threatened, may have the blame of mismanagement' on the 11th.[94] Arundel's ally, Sir Robert Cotton, certainly prepared a speech listing precedents for attacks on ministers.[95] Both peers were apparently questioned over Mansell's allegation that the Duke had failed to consult the Council of War and their response was the cautious one that the matter had not been raised in the Privy Council while they were present.[96] This was hardly a vigorous repudiation of the charge being made to the Commons. So there is contemporary warrant for the suspicions held by the Duke about them. The views of the other Privy Councillors are more obscure still. Nonetheless, Archbishop Abbot's dissatisfaction at his exclusion from influence is well attested and it is difficult to believe that his remarks at Westminster on the need for unity in religion and his revelation that he had failed to deal with Montague were quite as straightforward as they appear: it is more likely that he appreciated that they would arouse fierce controversy.[97] Abbot and Williams definitely opposed the dissolution of Parliament when the Privy Council met at Woodstock on 11 August: nominally, Buckingham did so as well. With or without the majority of his Councillors, Charles was adamant.[98]

The corollary of these arguments – that members of the House of Commons were motivated predominantly by localist considerations – is equally suspect. It is perfectly true that local complaints were made in the House and that members drew on their local knowledge to illustrate their speeches. The debate on the malpractices of recusants on 23 June is a good example of this.[99] It is also true that regional groupings can be detected on some issues: the complaints about piracy on the coasts of the south-west clearly inflamed local members on 11 August.[100] But there is no sign that these were the grounds on which resistance to royal demands was based. It was on national issues – on the duty of the House of Commons to protect the rights of the subject and to ensure that the supplies granted had been and would be spent for the common good – that Seymour, Phelips and Sir Edward Coke resisted Charles and Buckingham. Their demand for the reform of grievances was a traditional one as G. L. Harriss has pointed out.[101] What they did not appreciate was that Charles's willingness to bargain now that he was King was extremely attenuated. Their tactical skill in controlling the House's debates left them exposed when the King decided to dissolve Parliament. The tragedy was that those like Eliot and Rich who might have secured a compromise were undone by the tergiversations of the King and Duke. It is no surprise that they, like Arundel and Pembroke, played a major role in the attempt to bring Buckingham down in the Parliament of 1626.

The orthodox rather than revisionist interpretation of this Parliament is therefore basically right. The King's high conception of his authority and honour did lead him to view Parliament essentially as a subservient instrument for funding his foreign and war policies. He was insistent, despite the experience of 1624, on supply preceding the redress of grievances and without immediate retribution. This was undoubtedly a breach of constitutional convention. Charles was just as ready to accept a new form of grant. All his concessions, however belated, were directed to gaining supply or credit. This is equally true of his succeeding parliaments. The King was fundamentally unwilling to bargain except in the most pressing circumstances. The Duke of Buckingham, who was at least prepared to manoeuvre behind the scenes, was bound to cleave to the King's line. This rigid approach was not one that united the Privy Council in 1625 or later. It is possible to detect the existence of divisions amongst Charles's Councillors and to recognize their growing resentment at Buckingham's monopoly of favour and influence. The attack on the Duke in the lower House in 1625 was developed by a combination of his court opponents and his former Commons' critics and allies in the Parliament of 1626. This was regarded by Charles as a conspiratorial attempt to undermine the foundations of the monarchy. There was an increasing stress in his pronouncements from the spring of that year onwards on the need to uphold royal authority. The threat of 'new counsels' being adopted in the government of the realm if supply, which had been deliberately delayed in the Commons, was not forthcoming was openly made. But it was all to no avail: to save Buckingham, Parliament had to be dissolved. The King was resolved thereafter, as Dr Cust has shown, not to recall the assembly if it could be avoided. The Privy Council itself was divided between adherents of the old way of accommodation with Parliament and supporters of rule without it.[102] Responsibility for the policies of the next two years was directly accepted by the King. The exercise of royal authority was not to be constrained by the accepted conventions on taxation or, as Dr Guy has demonstrated, by technical legal judgements.[103] The struggle to secure the summoning of Parliament in 1628 and to persuade the King to accept the Petition of Right was one to convince a sovereign who, in the last resort, respected only the law of necessity.

The weakness of the Crown's management of Parliament after Charles's accession in 1625 is certainly comprehensible. The King appears to have thought that the simple notification of his wishes ought to have commanded obedience. It is remarkable that he went on doing so in 1626 and in 1628–29. But the official advocates at his disposal at Westminster in June and July, 1625 were few in number and their efforts were poorly co-ordinated: there was a much more organized 'Court' group at Oxford in August in that year but they (and the Duke's unofficial allies) were undone by the King's tactical maladroitness. The idea of excluding the King and Duke's most vociferous opponents from the next Parliament simply provided an opportunity for new leaders to step forward. What was new was the co-ordination of the attack on Buckingham in both Houses. Charles's supporters in the House of Commons became increasingly isolated and, although they were far more numerous in the House of Lords, there, too, the King partially lost control. That is a measure of the crisis the Caroline régime faced within a year of his accession. Out of it came the ideological alliance between the adherents of royal authoritarianism and the Arminian party in the Church which was to be a permanent feature of English political life up to 1640. Their exploitation of the Crown's prerogative rights and emergency powers in the service of the King's war policy was directly responsible for the Parliamentary attempt to re-establish the subject's liberties and to define his religious beliefs in a strict, Calvinist sense in 1628 and 1629. The political nation was ideologically split and the 'political Court' was isolated. To preserve his authority, the King abandoned the war policy he had embraced so enthusiastically in 1625 and dissolved the last Parliament of the decade. It was his admission that he could not manage both together.

The new model of seventeenth-century Parliamentary history that has recently been advanced – that of monarchs wedded to constitutional convention and handicapped by antiquated means of raising revenue and the resistance of localist backwoodsmen to taxation, of a House of Commons unable to use its control over supply to secure the redress of grievances, without an opposition and with no fundamental court–country divide – has the appeal of novelty. But many of its features, particularly its characterization of James and Charles and its view of the House of Commons, are recognizable as those of the Royalists in the Civil War and of the Tories who succeeded them. It is, in fact, the mirror image of the old Whig view dispelled by S. R. Gardiner. Unfortunately, this new analysis of the Parliamentary politics of the period is just as misleading.

Notes and References

1. D. H. Willson, *The Privy Councillors in the House of Commons 1604–1629* (Minneapolis, 1940), pp. 49, 167–82, 212–13, 220, 257–8, 266, 274, 277, 283, 288–9.
2. Russell, *Parliaments,* pp. 12, 204–59. For a radically different interpretation, see idem., *The Crisis of Parliaments. English History 1509–1660* (Oxford, 1971), pp. 300–2 and idem (ed.), *The Origins of the English Civil War* (London, 1973), pp. 16–18.
3. See K. Sharpe (ed.), *Faction and Parliament. Essays on Early Stuart History* (Oxford, 1978), pp. 139–72, 209–44.
4. R. Lockyer, *The Life and Political Career of George Villiers, First Duke of Buckingham 1592–1628* (London, 1981), pp. 225–6. *CSP Ven. 1625–1626,* pp. 12, 21, 602.
5. *Scrin.Res.* Pt II, pp. 5, 17. Unfortunately, Russell made no real use of Lord Keeper Williams's contemporary correspondence preserved here. It contains invaluable information on differences in the Privy Council.
6. Lord Braybrooke (ed), *The Private Correspondence of Lady Jane Cornwallis 1613–1644* (London, 1842), pp. 125–6.·S. R. Gardiner, *England under the Duke of Buckingham and Charles I. 1624–1628,* 2 vols, London, 1875), vol. 1, p. 172, BL Harleian MS 1581, fos 368r–369r.
7. *Scrin.Res.* Pt II, p. 4.
8. D. H. Willson, op.cit., p. 49.
9. *CD 1625,* p. 1, PRO SP 16/3/88(1). BL Harleian MS 389, fos 465r–465v. For a comment on the impact of this speech, see *Neg. Post.,* vol. 1, pp. 44–5. Eliot's account of this Parliament obscures his role as an intermediary for Buckingham. It does, however, shed light on court divisions not noticed by Russell.
10. *CD 1625,* pp. 1–3. *Neg.Post.,* vol. 1, pp. 45–7.
11. PRO, SP 16/3/84.
12. *CD 1625,* p. 5. Pym's notes intermingle Crew's points and Williams' replies.
13. *Chamberlain,* vol. 2, p. 625.
14. *CD 1625,* p. 7; HMC *Manuscripts of the House of Lords,* vol. XI (henceforward *HoL*), p. 179.
15. *CD 1625,* p. 7; *HoL,* p. 179, Cf. *CJ,* vol. 1, p. 800.

16. *CD 1625*, p. 6. *HoL*, p. 178. *Neg.Post.*, vol. 1, p. 61.
17. *CD 1625*, p. 8. *HoL*, p. 179. *CJ*, vol. 1, p. 800.
18. *CD 1625*, p. 8. *HoL*, p. 179.
19. *CD 1625*, p. 8. *HoL*, p. 179.
20. *HoL*, p. 180.
21. *CD 1625*, pp. 9–11, *Neg.Post.*, vol. 1, pp. 66–9.
22. *CD 1625*, pp. 11–12.
23. *CD 1625*, p. 12, *CJ*, vol. 1, p. 800.
24. *CD 1625*, p. 12 and note b.
25. Ibid., p. 16. *HoL*, p. 185.
26. *Neg.Post.*, vol. 1, pp. 61–3. The hostility of west-country members like Eliot, Glanville, Giles and Rolle towards Sir Thomas Wentworth is particularly marked. *CD 1625*, pp. 6, 37, 44–5. *HoL*, pp. 178, 201. H. Hulme, *The Life of Sir John Eliot 1592 to 1632* (London, 1957), p. 79.
27. *Hol*, p. 192. On Charles' reaction to his failure to obtain supply immediately, see *CSP Ven. 1625–1626*, p. 97.
28. *CD 1625*, p. 30. *HoL*, p. 196. *Neg.Post.*, vol. 1, p. 75.
29. *CD 1625*, p. 30. *HoL*, p. 196. Eliot's comments show that Rudyerd had prepared his speech. *Neg.Post.*, vol. 1, p. 75.
30. *HoL*, pp. 196–7.
31. *Neg.Post.*, vol. 1, pp. 76–8. *CD 1625*, pp. 31–2. *HoL*, p. 197.
32. *CD 1625*, p. 32. *HoL*, p. 197.
33. *CD 1625*, p. 33. *HoL*, p. 198.
34. BL Harleian MS 389 fo. 470r; *CSP Ven. 1625–1626*, pp. 107–8; HMC *Skrine*, pp. 25, 27.
35. PRO SP 16/4/26; D. H. Willson, op.cit., p. 170 n. 17. S. R. Gardiner, op. cit., p. 202 n. 1.
36. *HoL*, p. 198, Cf. *CD 1625*, p. 36.
37. Gardiner, loc. cit. Willson, loc. cit.
38. HMC *Skrine*, p. 27.
39. *Neg.Post.*, vol. 1, p. 91, S. R. Gardiner, op. cit., p. 202 n. 2.
40. e.g. *CD 1625*, p. 137.
41. Framlingham Gawdy was one such member. BL Add. MS 27, 395 fo. 177r. Add. MS. 48, 091 fo. 21r. *Neg.Post.*, vol. 1, p. 93.
42. *Neg.Post.*, vol. 1, pp. 110–11.
43. Ibid., pp. 111–13.
44. *CD 1625*, pp. 56–9, 153. *Neg.Post.*, vol. 1, pp. 113–17.
45. Eliot was quite explicit about the divisions amongst the courtiers. *Neg.Post.*, vol. 1, p. 118.
46. Ibid., vol. 1, pp. 118–19.
47. *Scrin.Res.*, Pt II, pp. 13–14. For Lord Conway's view on the need for supply, see *CSP Ven. 1625–1626*, p. 117.
48. *Neg.Post.*, vol. 1, pp. 119, 123. HMC *Mar and Kellie*, vol. 2, p. 230 *CJ*, vol. 1, p. 808. *LJ*, vol. 3, p. 464. *CD 1625*, p. 67. BL Add. MS 48,091 fo. 25r.
49. *CD 1625*, pp. 37–41. *Neg.Post.*, vol. 1, p. 84.
50. *CD 1625*, pp. 62, 153.
51. PRO 31/3/64 fo. 186r.
52. S. R. Gardiner, op. cit., p. 257.

53. *CD 1625*, p. 68. *Neg.Post.*, vol. 2, pp. 8–10. *Scrin.Res.* Pt II, pp. 14–15, 18.
54. BL Add. MS 30,651 fo. 13r.
55. *CSP Ven. 1625–1626*, p. 142.
56. HMC *Cowper*, vol. 1, pp. 208–9. *Scrin.Res.*, Pt II, pp. 20–1. PRO SP 16/5/14.
57. HMC *Cowper*, vol. 1, p. 208.
58. *CD 1625*, p. 73. *CSP Ven. 1625–1626*, p. 142.
59. *CD 1625*, pp. 73–7. *CSP Ven. 1625–1626*, p. 142.
60. The decision was eventually taken at the Privy Council meeting on 7 August. BL Add. MS 30,651 fo. 21v. Cf. *CSP Ven. 1625–1626*, p. 143. PRO 31/3/64 fos. 186r–186v.
61. *CD 1625*, pp. 78–80, 82–4, 87–8, 133–5.
62. *CD 1625*, p. 78. *Neg.Post.*, vol. 2, p. 24.
63. *CD 1625*, pp. 80–2.
64. *CD 1625*, pp. 84–7, 130–3.
65. *CD 1625*, pp. 78, 84.
66. *Neg.Post.*, vol. 2, p. 48.
67. *Scrin.Res.*, pt II, p. 18. H. Hulme, op. cit., pp. 20, 43.
68. See C. Thompson, 'The origins of the politics of the parliamentary middle group 1625–1629', *TRHS* 5th ser., vol. 22 (1972), pp. 78–9. G. E. Cockayne, *The Complete Peerage*, ed. G. H. White and R. S. Lea (London, 1959), vol. 12, Part 2, pp. 410–11.
69. *Neg.Post.*, vol. 2, pp. 53–4.
70. *CD 1625*, pp. 90, 136–7. For a very different view of this speech, see J. N. Ball, 'Sir John Eliot at the Oxford Parliament 1625', *BIHR*, vol. 28 (1955), p. 118.
71. *CD 1625*, p. 137.
72. Ibid., pp. 90, 137–8.
73. Ibid., pp. 90–1, 138–9.
74. Ibid., p. 140.
75. Fleetwood's speech on the 8th suggests ignorance about the King's immediate intentions on the part of a man who was normally a court supporter. Rich's prolonged queries about whether the Speaker was to go to the Lords or not *may* have been designed to allow time to find out what was going on. *CD 1625*, pp. 92–3, 157–8.
76. *Scrin.Res.*, Pt II, p. 17. *CSP Ven. 1625–1626*, p. 143.
77. *Neg.Post.*, vol. 2, pp. 54–5.
78. *CD 1625*, pp. 93–105, 142–3, 158. It is significant that, despite the advice given by the intermediaries, Buckingham received his patent as Admiral and Captain General of the Fleet on Sunday, 7 August.
79. For the reply to the petition on religion, see PRO SP 16/4/28 (wrongly attributed to 11th July). *CD 1625*, pp. 106–107.
80. *CD 1625*, *pp. 107–8, 110–11, 112–15.*
81. Ibid., pp. 109–10, 111–12, 115.
82. Ibid., pp. 115–16. HLRO Braye MS 96, pp. 132–3.
83. *CD 1625*, p. 143.
84. Ibid., pp. 120–1, 143–5, 146.
85. Ibid., pp. 147–8, 161. HLRO Historical Collection 143 unfoliated.

86. HMC *Buccleuch and Queensberry,* vol. 3, p. 252. *CSP Ven. 1625–1626,*
     p. 147. *Scrin.Res.,* Pt II, p. 16.
87. *CD 1625,* pp. 122–4, 126, 162.
88. Ibid., pp. 125–6, 150.
89. Ibid., p. 2. *Neg.Post.,* vol. 1, pp. 46, 117.
90. *CD 1625,* pp. 62, 153.
91. BL Add. MS 30,651 fo. 23r.
92. PRO SP 84/129/27. I owe this reference to Professor Cogswell's
     generosity.
93. *Scrin.Res.,* Pt II, pp. 17,20. *Neg.Post.,* vol. 2, p. 78.
94. Arthur Collins, *Letters and Memorials of State,* 2 vols, (London, 1776),
     vol. 2, p. 359, *CSP Ven. 1625–1626,* p. 139.
95. K. Sharpe, *Sir Robert Cotton 1586–1631* (Oxford, 1979), pp. 177–9.
     Cf. J. N. Ball, 'Sir John Eliot at the Oxford Parliament 1625', *BIHR*
     vol. 28 (1955), pp. 121–5.
96. *CSP Ven. 1625–1626,* p. 146.
97. BRO, Trumbull MSS vol. XVIII no. 138. PRO SP 14/171/59. I am
     again indebted to Professor Cogswell for these references.
98. *CSP Ven. 1625–1626,* p. 147. *Scrin.Res.,* Pt 11, p. 16.
99. *HoL,* pp. 204–5.
100. PRO SP 16/5/6. *CD 1625,* pp. 117–18, 161.
101. K. Sharpe (ed.), *Faction and Parliament,* pp. 94–5.
102. R. Cust, 'Charles I, the Privy Council, and the Forced Loan', *JBS* vol.
     24 (1985), pp. 208–35.
103. J. Guy, 'The origins of the Petition of Right reconsidered', *HJ vol.
     25 (1982) pp. 289–312.*

7 Church Policies of the 1630s

Andrew Foster

I

It is a theme of this volume that the work of 'revisionist' historians since the 1970s, although sometimes quite salutary, has created confusion about the origins of the English Civil War. In place of long-term perspectives and an emphasis on principles, we are currently offered a confusing array of short-term causes with the emphasis on personalities, faction and accidents.[1] There is always scope for revision, but it is argued here that crude though the all-pervasive 'Whig' tradition was, with regard to religious affairs it provided images which are useful to any full understanding of the origins of the war. This is particularly the case when such images are softened by the sophistication of Nicholas Tyacke's views on Arminianism, themselves currently under attack.[2] From such a perspective we can understand the fears of contemporaries about popery, the close connections between Church and the state in the 1630s, the arbitrary rule of bishops which brought their office into disrepute, and the theological framework which exalted the clergy and the sacraments, making this programme so different from Church policies pursued in the reign of James I.

What follows is a defence of old and comparatively recent images alike, against the vogue of revisionism which has thrown up so many new and conflicting ideas. It was once safe to assume that Archbishop William Laud was one of the 'twin pillars of Stuart despotism'; now we are asked to think of him as a kindly old man whom we have all misunderstood, a man who pursued his goals 'with more moderation than fanaticism'.[3] The theology of this period used to be handled crudely, and chiefly from the perspective of the down-trodden Puritans, as Whig historians stressed the aping of Roman ceremonies, the preaching of 'passive obedience to the worst tyranny', and accused Laud of 'turning religion into a systematic attack on English liberty'.[4] Scarcely has this view been replaced by an analysis of English Arminianism providing more subtle grounds for Puritan complaints and a rationale at last for Laud's actions, than it is claimed Laud was no theologian, and was in any event totally subservient to the king.[5] After years of being regarded as an unsuccessful and unlikeable little martinet, Laud is suddenly the object of sympathy. Even his dreams have recently been analysed, revealing 'no doubt that both asleep and awake Laud was a very troubled man'; hence he should be given 'a little nocturnal colour that illuminates his daily humanity'![6] Historians of the Interregnum point to the popularity of 'Prayer Book Anglicanism', which suggests that some of Laud's policies may have actually met a need.[7] This view has been reinforced from the different perspective of an Elizabethan specialist who suggests that moves which seemed to bring the English Church closer to Rome may indeed have suited a large section of the populace still barely won over to Protestantism.[8] On the other hand, in Laud's defence it used to be argued that Archbishop Abbot was a disastrous appointment, 'simply indifferent, negligent, secular', who left the church in a parlous condition.[9] Now however, far from being seen as a mistake, Abbot's appointment is taken as evidence that James I was more astute than his son in appreciating the need to maintain a balanced, broad Church.[10] So we seem to be back where we started with Laud 'indeed the greatest calamity ever visited upon the Church of England'.[11]

There are many reasons for this historiographical confusion: they relate to sources, approaches, and the way in which some historians have confused matters of theology and also swallowed wholesale the Royalist, Anglican tradition stemming from the writings of Laud's chaplain, Peter Heylin.[12] For too long our knowledge of the Church has been derived chiefly from central sources: the printed works of Heylin and Prynne, letters in the Public Record Office, the annual reports of the bishops, details of the metropolitical visitations carried out for Neile and Laud, and the celebrated trials of Prynne, Burton and Bastwick, not to mention that of Bishop John Williams.[13] Relatively little has been published on the basis of local, diocesan research.[14] Even when a more complete picture has been available, it has been flawed because until comparatively recently we have possessed few detailed studies of the Jacobean church against which to measure events in the 1630s.[15] There are also traps for the unwary in diocesan research. First, there is the danger of assuming that because a set of policies was implemented with some degree of success in one area, they were carried out with equal success elsewhere. Secondly, it is possible to be led astray by the intricacies of local policies, their implementation, and the related problems of enforcement. And here lies an archetypal revisionist trap. Close attention to the minutiae of policy, declared intentions, implementation, and analysis of varying degrees of successful enforcement can lead to cynicism about the real effectiveness of central government. It can lead – and this can be seen in recent work on Laud – to an underestimation of the coherence and damaging effect of the programme he pursued in Church and state in the 1630s. It is a truism that central policies were mediated in the localities, but what is striking about the 1630s is the relentless pressure brought to bear by Laud and his bishops on the community. Although eventually unsuccessful, they caused a degree of disturbance which cannot be accounted for simply by talk of a new Bancroftian efficiency.

Several historians had picked up the importance of Arminianism in an English context, but it was left to Nicholas Tyacke to chart the full history of this movement from controversies at Cambridge in the 1590s to power in the 1630s.[16] In the process, Tyacke finally wrenched attention away from the Puritans and rescued that other contemporary term of abuse, 'Arminian'. From this perspective, the ceremonialism of the 1630s was indeed characteristic of theologians who held radical views on predestination. English and Dutch Arminianism were linked, but for various historical reasons took on different forms. Hence in England, Arminians adopted exalted views about the status of episcopacy and the clergy in general, carefully deferential yet ambitious notions about the relationship between Church and state, and a revaluation of the efficacy of the sacraments.

> English Arminians came to balance their rejection of the arbitrary grace of predestination with a new found source of grace freely available in the sacraments, which Calvinists had belittled. Hence the preoccupation under Archbishop Laud with altars and private confession before receiving communion, as well as belief in the absolute necessity of baptism.[17]

Here is a thesis which explains how a small group of theologians came to enjoy a measure of influence under James I, take control of some university colleges and some dioceses, suppress the writings of opponents, and emerge all-powerful in the reign of Charles I. This process broke the Calvinist consensus amongst the élite and led to a

Puritan backlash. In this saga, the 1630s saw Calvinism slyly rejected and godly ministers forced into exile, while church interiors were refashioned according to new ideas of worship.

Initially, it seemed as if this view would be incorporated within revisionist arguments. Arminianism could be used to explain the heated debates in Parliament in 1629 when the death of Buckingham should have reduced controversy. It could be added to the list of 'coincidences' and 'accidents' which made the 1630s troublesome and it could account for the virulent attacks on the bishops of the 1640s. Just as recent writers on English fears of popery seem to concentrate on the short-term events of the late 1630s (an attitude deemed rather short-sighted by at least two authors in this volume), so for some the real explanatory power of the concept of Arminianism was overlooked.[18]

Most recently, however, the proposition that Arminianism existed and explains Laudianism has been strongly denied by Kevin Sharpe and Peter White. For Sharpe especially, Laud was essentially a mild-mannered, misunderstood bureaucrat in Bancroft's mould, with no novel theological ideas. It is claimed that Tyacke 'crudely identifies doctrinal positions with liturgical and disciplinary preferences' and wrongly 'regards shifts in both as "sweeping changes" brought about by the triumph of Arminianism in the 1630s'.[19] To make matters more confusing, Sharpe has gone one stage further in his general analysis of the 1630s to argue that not only was the policy simply about external beauty and holiness, order and decency, with a modicum of discipline, but it was Charles I, not Laud who gave the orders. Apparently, 'throughout his archiepiscopacy Laud remained very much the King's man', appointed 'for his concern with ceremony and his pertinacity as an administrator'.[20] Laud was the obedient servant and the King, by letters and audiences, marginalia on reports, 'chivvied the archbishop', who in turn harried his bishops and clergy. We are informed that:

> Often Charles proved more intransigent than Laud. It was Charles I, who, after hearing the St. Gregory's case at the Council board, recommended the altar to be set at the East end of the church.[21]

Few would deny the importance of Charles I to the success of the Arminian party in his reign, but the possibility that this particular decision was a carefully manipulated formality is not considered.

What follows is an attempt to clarify some of the issues raised by this controversy by drawing heavily on research based on the career of Archbishop Richard Neile. This has a number of advantages.

It offers concrete evidence of what was happening in the 1630s in the province of York where Neile was archbishop after 1632. It thus provides a good regional base upon which to generalize. Close to Laud throughout his career, Neile's work can be taken as fully representative of Arminian policy in the 1630s; indeed, he was possibly Laud's most successful colleague. Finally, Neile's career spans the Jacobean period and affords opportunities to detect trends stemming from his time as the great patron of 'Durham College'.[22] Yet there are also dangers in this approach. It has already been noted that there are problems in generalizing from one region to another. Neile had a notably easier ride on some issues in the north than did Laud in the south, for example in this dealings with foreign congregations. Nevertheless, the problems which Neile encountered, and the methods he used to overcome them, have already misled some historians into becoming enmeshed in his methods of enforcement and into assumptions of greater success than is likely.[23] In fact, Neile's efforts in the north do indeed highlight problems of policy enforcement, but they reveal that even when deemed to be in power in the 1630s, Neile, Laud, and their associates were still an embattled minority in the church.

It should be conceded at the outset that this perspective offers more on the questions of how, where and when policies were implemented than on the vexed question of why they were implemented, their theological justification. There are several reasons for this. Unlike the second generation of outspoken Arminians like Richard Montague, Eleazor Duncon, and Thomas Jackson, Bishops Neile, Buckeridge, Andrewes, Carey and Laud were all more reticent in public on the deep issues of predestination. They had all witnessed bitter controversy at Cambridge, knew of court intrigues, and had seen what had happened to Arminians in the Netherlands. Moreover, Neile was the least intellectual of this group by far. Lampooned by his enemies as a dunce and court buffoon, he cheerfully owned up to his scholarly shortcomings on several occasions.[24] Nevertheless, he was the great administrator, the man with court contacts, the 'fixer' of embarrassing situations and jobs, the great patron of the Arminian party who was pre-eminent particularly during the period when he was Bishop of Durham between 1617 and 1628. Neile was one of William Laud's early patrons and the latter lived with him for several years at Durham House in the 1620s. Several of Neile's other chaplains went on to serve the Church with distinction in the 1630s, notably John Cosin, Augustine Lindsell, and Thomas Jackson. Neile was closely involved in the affairs of Richard Montague which first brought the issue of Arminianism to the attention of Parliament in 1624.[25] Together, Neile and Laud were appointed to the Privy Council in 1627; together they were cited in Parliament as promoters of Arminianism and enemies of the state in 1629; and together they presided over the provinces of Canterbury and York in the 1630s.

For the convenience of this chapter, discussion of Neile's policies in the north has been split under four rough headings: economic affairs, restoration of churches and the altar campaign, enforcement of conformity, and some broad remarks about relations between Church, laity and the state. It is contended that these formed a coherent programme which stemmed directly from Arminian beliefs and that even where policies seem similar to some pursued earlier in the Jacobean Church, we should look closely at what was required, the changed context and perceptions of the 1630s, and not be misled by the obvious, vastly superior degree of enforcement. Indeed, it would be strange if some of these policies did not seem familiar, for Neile and his colleagues had been actively putting some of their ideas into practice for years, hiding when pressed for justification of new forms of worship behind enigmatic remarks like 'the Lord knoweth who are his'.[26] It is hoped that what follows will extend the analysis of events in the 1630s presented by Tyacke in his recent book, refute the criticisms of writers like Sharpe, and reveal ways in which policies in the 1630s should be seen as a coherent programme relating to Church and state.

II

Thanks chiefly to Felicity Heal good progress has been made with research on the economic front. We know that Laud sought 'to see the bishops decently supplied . . . according to their place and dignity', to stabilize and possibly strengthen the position of the church after years of decline.[27] This was to be effected in various ways, the most publicized being through the royal letters circulated to all bishops in 1629, 1633 and 1634. These commanded prelates to reside in their sees, unless specifically required at court, to live in their own residences, preserve their estates, carry out proper surveys and not to make or renew leases after nomination to a new see.[28] The 1634 orders went a stage further in that leases were to be for twenty-one years and not three lives.[29] Dr Heal has drawn attention to the differing degrees of success which attended this policy in several southern dioceses, pointing out how variously it was interpreted and how invariably it was a point of friction with local gentry.

Well aware that economic policy, if handled inflexibly, could jeopardize relations with local people and hence other aspects of church policy, it appears that Neile disagreed with his friend William Laud over the new lease orders. When John Cosin was faced with a decision over whether to grant leases for years or for lives at Durham in 1670, he recalled that there were benefits in the old way of giving leases for lives and that 'for this mind Bishop Neile ever was, though he displeased Archbishop Laud by it'.[30] Cosin even hinted that the dispute between the two men was partly behind the appearance of the royal letters on the subject in 1634. Whatever the truth of that, it looks as if Neile did not seek energetically to convert leases when opportunities arose, and indeed, he seems to have carried on giving some leases for lives after the order of 1634.[31] Moreover, whereas his suffragan bishops in the north always felt compelled to comment on this aspect of their work in their annual reports, as required by the directions of 1629 and 1633, Neile coyly avoided the topic until a rather bland remark that all was well in his report on 1638.[32]

Before we are drawn into the quagmire of local variations in Arminian policy described earlier, it should be pointed out that the broad thrust of Neile's work was certainly in keeping with Laud's designs. Nobody excelled Neile in what he did for the repair of his residences, his annual reports noting the expenditure of thousands of pounds at Cawood, Bishopthorpe and Southwell.[33] When Cosin was praised for such work after the Restoration, it was noted that he was a mere shadow of his great patron Neile in this respect.[34] Such work was characteristic of Neile even as a Jacobean bishop at the outset of his career at Rochester in 1608.[35] He was one of three outstanding bishops of that period who showed real care for their palaces, the other two being Lancelot Andrewes and James Montagu.[36] It is noteworthy that care which was deemed exceptional in the Jacobean period was expected in the 1630s and that most bishops seem to have responded to the challenge.

Evidence of Neile's concern over appropriate leasing policy is revealed in his annual report on 1633, when he criticized a former bishop of Sodor and Man for holding the island archdeaconry *in commendam* and for leasing property at virtually half its real value.[37] Shrewd business acumen was certainly required to cope with the economic problems of York diocese in the seventeenth century. A series of forced exchanges of property, well catalogued by Claire

Cross, had stripped the see of land in return for impropriations, which placed the archbishops of the seventeenth century in the embarrassing position of deriving between a third and a half of their income at the expense of their own clergy.[38] The majority of these impropriations were leased out for three lives and all Neile could do was to ensure that clauses were present concerning chancel responsibilities, payments to vicars, occasionally sums for the poor, and that rights of presentation to the livings were clear and preferably still with the archbishop.[39]

Other exchanges, including the celebrated York House deal which required an Act of Parliament in 1624, usually involved trading good property for bad.[40] It is noteworthy that Neile sided with Abbot against Laud and Buckingham to express doubts about that Bill in 1624.[41] He may have wished he had fought harder when he later got to York, for certainly he was forced to play the entrepreneur to make something of the land he inherited. In May 1636 he petitioned the Privy Council for permission to drain some Nottinghamshire fenland gained in one of these supposedly fair exchanges. He offered to bear all the costs involved and to compensate neighbours affected by the scheme; naturally he hoped to recoup the money later through increased rents. Talks took place with the Commissioners of Sewers at Bawtry in July 1637 and the whole project was eventually ratified by the Privy Council in October.[42]

Surveys of property and of cathedrals were carried out meticulously. Neile acted personally in the purchase of new plate for York Minster in 1633, where in addition the choir was instructed to raise its standards and provided with the incentive of a new organ.[43] Neile's interest in church music was of long standing, for he had brought about changes at Westminster Abbey in 1606 and had been instrumental in the provision of a new organ at Durham Cathedral.[44] When William Prynne dared to attack 'the thundring of the bellows, the roaring of the base, the squeaking of the treble', it moved Neile to remark indignantly that 'your sect was grown soe stiff, that it was faine to be stiffled at Tiburne & Cheapside with a halter'.[45] At Southwell Minster in 1636, Neile ordered that rents were to be trebled when leases were next renewed and the money to be used for fabric. Rent increases of five- and six-fold were attached to certain leases to provide money for this choir, possibly because Neile often resided just next door.[46]

It looks as if we ought to talk of surveys and reports being enforced at parish as well as diocesan level during the 1630s. A glance at material derived from southern dioceses reveals that at Laud's metropolitical visitation held at Gloucester in June 1635, the parish clergy and churchwardens were ordered to make annual glebe terriers for their bishop.[47] Over half the churchwardens for the parishes for which we possess evidence were reprimanded during the visitation for failure to comply with this demand.[48] The survival of glebe terriers for approximately 70 per cent of parishes in Chichester diocese in the 1630s indicates a similar concern which brought the effects of Laudian policy right down to local farmers and gentry who rented the odd acre of glebe, as well as those who rented episcopal property.[49] As with the matter of episcopal palaces, there is evidence of concern over glebe terriers in the Jacobean period, but again what is impressive about the 1630s is the degree of concern which seems to have been expressed and the possible side-effects which such a policy may have had on clerical/lay relationships. What was possibly seen as an acceptable concern in order to provide a better-paid preaching ministry under Abbot, was seen in a far more sinister light in the 1630s.[50]

Evidence of concern over glebe terriers is less clear at York, but what is noteworthy is the small, but significant, number of clergy and churchwardens cited for not perambulating parish boundaries in rogation week.[51] Court cases reveal that people were exceeding their boundaries, neglecting to walk for fear of disputes, and were generally negligent about the church property in their care. This may appear to be a minute point of Arminian policy, but it clearly irritated some in the 1630s, when, for example, one Alice Metcalf of St Cuthbert's, York was arrested in 1632 while switching boundary marks with the neighbouring parish of St Saviour's.[52] Indeed, the issue of perambulations provides a microcosm of Arminian policy: at one and the same time, we have concern for property, with the matter of boundaries obviously affecting issues like payment of tithes and church rates, while we also have the issue of church attendance should movement to another parish be seen by the authorities as 'gadding' to sermons. Keith Thomas has noted that for Puritans perambulations represented another form of regrettable idolatry, while for the Arminians it was a revival of a ceremony which blessed crops and was a means of intercession at times of threatened scarcity.[53]

Under the general heading of restoration of churches, Laud's concern is exemplified by the care he took over St Paul's Cathedral, while the ideological nature of the campaign, if we can put it that way, is caught by the St Gregory's case concerning the position of the communion table in November 1633.[54] Research confirms that this was indeed a major plank of policy in the north, if not the major issue for Neile. However, it should be stressed that this matter did not arrive out of the blue in 1633. Maintenance of churches had been a matter of concern long before Laud. Whitgift had ordered a thorough survey of churches in 1602, aware of widespread neglect since the Reformation.[55] A committee of the House of Lords was set up to look into the problem in February 1629, and included people like Neile and Laud, together with strange company like Viscount Saye and Sele and the Earl of Dorset.[56]

We know very little about this committee, but the opportunity for bipartisan action was lost with the rapid closure of this parliamentary session. What did emerge was a proclamation in December 1629 calling for better care of all churches and chapels and for regular inspections.[57] The decision over St Gregory's in 1633 needs to be placed in this context, and indeed in the context of work which Neile and Laud were carrying out in the Court of High Commission in 1632, of which more later. It was the proclamation of 1629 which Neile seems to have taken as his authorization for a campaign for church restoration in York province. And it was to that proclamation that Neile referred when he made his annual reports to the King. Hence in 1637 he wrote:

> in pursuance of your Majesties Proclamation for the repairing of churches, I have received certificates of very large sumes of money expended in the repairing and adorning of churches and chapels and making decent and uniform seats.[58]

By 1640 approximately 355 churches in York diocese, 309 in Chester, and 200 in the archdeaconry of Nottingham had been ordered to make repairs of some kind, roughly 65 per cent of the churches and chapels in the area.[59] And they are only the ones for which we have information, for certainly the campaign extended to the dioceses of Carlisle and Durham. Indeed, it is interesting that Neile's suffragan bishops felt compelled to comment on their work in this regard, for they were under no royal command to do so, and reports from the southern province never contained such comments. Yet Barnabas Potter of Carlisle declared in 1637 that 'by your godly care we have gotten all our churches (almost) newly seated and made very fine and uniform'. And Bishop Bridgeman of Chester also praised Neile, for in 'your Metropolitical Visitation you began an excellent work, namely to repair and uniform the churches of your province', in which cause Bridgeman claimed also to have laboured, 'wherein the laity have most cheerfully bestowed many thousands of pounds, but the theme of cost and 'cheerful' payment will be returned to shortly.[60]

Again comparisons with the Jacobean period are fruitful, for although evidence of church surveys survives, nothing matches the scale of operations in the 1630s when bishops took charge of a matter previously in the hands of the archdeacons. Church cases arising out of Neile's metropolitical visitation of the dioceses of York and Chester quadrupled those discovered by his immediate predecessors.[61] The critical point is that Samuel Gardiner and Nicholas Tyacke were correct to see that church restoration, and more particularly, the placing of the communion table within churches, was an ideological issue in the 1630s.[62] Although he most frequently defended his demands over the placing of the communion table on practical grounds and with reference to Elizabethan injunctions (until he passed the new canon seven of the seventeen in 1640), Laud is also known to have said:

> The altar is the greatest place of God's residence upon earth, greater than the pulpit; for there 'tis *Hoc est corpus meum*, This is my body; but in the other it is at most *Hoc est verbum meum*, This is my word.[63]

The point about a clear division of opinion need not be laboured if one refers to William Prynne:

> Christians have no other altars but Christ alone, who hath abolished all other altars, which are either heathenish, Jewish, or Popish, and not tolerable among Christians.[64]

Altar policy was clearly seen as innovatory by contemporaries and when the churchwardens of Beckington presented their arguments at the time of St Gregory's case they claimed that the orders had not been sanctioned by the King, a parliamentary statute, or a canon. They urged that 'we expect no change of religion – blessed be God', and added an interesting argument that 'if we should be hereafter questioned in a parliament, we know not how we would answer it'.[65] Here were people who had listened when they had been warned that Arminians were enemies of the state in 1629.

Evidence of widespread resistance in the localities corroborates the impression that this was one of the most hated aspects of Church policy in the 1630s. In his annual report for 1633, Neile offered a bleak picture of his province in which he concluded:

> It was scarcely found in any place that the communion table was placed in such sort as that it might appear it was any whit respected.[66]

It was not even in the correct place at Carlisle cathedral![67] Yet Neile did not trust even this gloomy report. Over the next few years he employed roving commissioners to check particularly the Puritan towns of the West Riding, commissioners who reported directly to his Chancery Court. Thanks to this action we know that he was issuing orders over communion tables before the St Gregory's case of November 1633.[68] Moreover, we know that of 100 churches which received repair orders from the Chancery Court between 1633 and 1640, 45 had evaded detection at Neile's visitations in 1632–33 and again in 1636.[69] Temporary blindness must have afflicted the churchwardens of Sheffield, for example, for although nothing was reported in 1632, it was discovered later that the communion table stood in the centre, seats cluttered the east end, there was no font cover, no royal arms, the organ was out of tune, various stalls and alleys were unpaved, and certain lofts and bell closets needed to be removed.[70] The same churchwardens conveniently forgot to mention that their minister, Thomas Toller never wore a surplice, never bowed at the name of Jesus, never stood for the Creed, never knelt for public prayers, and never used the sign of the cross in baptism! Needless to say, they were encouraged to do their duty in future.[71]

In all, over 70 of the 100 churches cited before the Chancery Court coincide with known Puritan areas, chiefly in the West Riding and also around Hull; a very different picture from that which was initially revealed by Neile's visitation in 1632–33.[72] It is an interesting warning to the local historian about taking sources at face value, for if we did not possess the records of the Chancery Court and indeed, had not bothered to cross-check the findings of one set of courts with another, a simple correlation between the poverty of the East Riding churches and the need for repairs would have been an attractive line of argument, and the ideological nature of this campaign would have been missed. As it is, the bulk of the Chancery Court cases were found to involve orders over the communion table and/or seating, where seats were behind the altar or obscured the view.

The point about seating is important because it is arguable that the altar campaign owed a lot to an earlier series of cases which the High Commission dealt with in 1632. The series culminated in a case over St Leonard's, Foster Lane, London in June 1632, where apparently the churchwardens wished to erect seats at the east end of the church. Laud protested angrily that three or four churches were at that game and demanded an end to the suits.

Neile fired the revealing question: 'Do you think you are worthy to sit above the Lord's board in his house?'[73] When the decision was given over a similar case involving St Austin's, London on 21 June 1632, the churchwardens were ordered to submit to the authority of their bishop, and Archbishop Abbot, no less, was prevailed upon to issue a general statement declaring his dislike for seats above the communion table.[74] It was the seating issue which exposed what few cases concerning the communion table were detected in Neile's primary visitation of 1632–33.

Some examples of what these changes to church fabric entailed are revealing. At St Mary's, Kingston-upon-Hull in October 1633, seats were changed to allow people to 'conveniently kneel in time of divine prayers and perform such other comely gestures as at so holy an exercise are to be performed'.[75] The seats of the Mayor and Aldermen of Doncaster were turned to face east in 1637,[76] while at Batley, the minister's reading pew was cut back because it presently blocked part of the aisle and was 'an hindrance and blemish to the sight of the communion table there'.[77] Changes did not come overnight, and some of the delaying tactics employed by the churchwardens are as revealing as the initial cases of evasion. In December 1633 it was claimed at St Mary's, Hull that they had sent for special wood from Amsterdam, and the repairing and beautifying of their church could not be achieved for six months.[78] The commissioners had to pay several visits to some churches and the number of orders given by the Chancery Court did not peak until 1637.[79]

The pressure for clerical and lay conformity should need little illustration because it is reasonably well covered by the pioneering work of Ronald Marchant. Neile described himself as a 'great adversary of the Puritan faction' and his time at York was marked by a sharp increase in church court activity. Marchant has drawn up an impressive catalogue of 115 ministers who appeared before Neile's courts in the 1630s, but even this figure does not do justice to the numbers who allowed themselves to be silenced, or those who emigrated, and to the number who felt harassed and spied upon.[80] Even though he followed the relatively zealous Samuel Harsnett at York, Neile's visitation records of 1633 still record a vast increase in the number of cases involving clergy and churchwardens, thanks largely to improved cross-questioning at the visitation through the use of three commissioners.[81]

Many of the cases were simply for non-use of surplice, but Neile's concern about catechism classes came through strongly in special orders on the topic given to York ministers in December 1632 and in references in his annual reports.[82] His report of 1633 discussed common abuses in the use of the Prayer Book, but he went on to add 'as in the public prayers so likewise in the administration of the sacraments, the forms, rites, and ceremonies prescribed very much neglected'.[83] It is clear that Neile felt strongly about this and blamed ministers for setting the laity a bad example:

> The disrespect that the ministers have shewed to the public prayers of the church hath bred such irreverence in the people that it is a rare thing in many places to see any upon their knees at the reading of the prayers, or (almost) at the receiving of the Sacraments: and some stick not to say, that sitting was the fittest gesture both at the prayers, and at the sacrament.[84]

It should be remembered that some of the 'crimes' which Thomas Toller committed at Sheffield, such as not bowing at the name of Jesus, were new in the 1630s. Moreover, that the policy of enhancing the role of the clergy stemmed from Arminian principles which required a more seemly attention to ceremonial, in return for which Laud and Neile were intent upon improving their economic status.

Yet again there are caveats to be made about methods of enforcement. Although he had a tough image, Neile was fairly flexible in his treatment of ministers and laity. While he treated John Shaw, a clergyman whom he suspected had been brought to York to lead Puritans against him, to 'very terrible threatening language',[85] he had earlier allowed the suspended Ezekiel Rogers of Rowley to receive a salary for several years while they talked things over.[86] In his annual report of 1635 Neile noted that various ministers had not conformed over reading the Book of Sports, but he had given them time to read the Bishop of Ely's excellent work on the subject and to repent.[87] Nobody was actually deprived, but a large number of unlicensed ministers found themselves out of work, many were suspended, and others somehow felt obliged to emigrate. Such a one was Ezekiel Rogers in 1638 when he could evidently stand his private conversations with the archbishop no longer.[88]

Examples of apparent tolerance are deceptive, for as Marchant spotted, Neile's régime in the north was characterized by the 'iron hand in the velvet glove'.[89] In York diocese alone 115 ministers found themselves in trouble with the church courts at some time between 1632 and 1640. 55 of those ministers appeared before the Chancery Court, the same court that was backing up the visitation over churches.[90] Amongst that number was William Brearcliffe,

Vicar of North Cave near Hull, charged with various offences including simply being a supporter of William Prynne.[91] A sign of the paranoia which the name of Prynne induced in people like Neile and Laud is superbly captured by the story that when Prynne was transported north via Chester in 1637, his portrait was painted for admirers. Unfortunately, Neile got to hear of the affair and not only were the paintings publicly destroyed, but by separate orders given later, so too were the frames.[92]

Religious innovations coupled with a tougher attitude towards uniformity had the noticeable effect of making some people emigrate. Joseph Lister, the Bradford Puritan, wrote later of the years 1639–41 when it was generally thought:

> That Popery was likely to be set up and the light of the gospel put out. Many ministers were silenced, and great numbers for three or four years past were posting away to New England.[93]

Such reports were confirmed by Brent and the bishops in their annual reports and Neile seemed to be lamenting the fact when he wrote in 1639 'that too many of your Majesties subjects inhabiting in these east parts of Yorkshire are gone into New England'.[94] Yet on other occasions it is clear that emigration suited the authorities. When Yeldard Alvey, Neile's spy set to watch over Bishop Morton in Durham, reported to the archbishop in 1640, he concluded that with Dr Jenison preparing to leave for Holland and Mr Lapthorne silenced, 'there is great hope that now the work of the puritanical faction is broken, if my Lord of Durham will but have a vigilant eye and keep a strict hand over them'.[95] The language is revealing, as too is the fact that Neile and Laud were quite prepared to keep the pressure on their episcopal colleagues by use of spies and informers. A recurring problem in the historiography of the Church in the early seventeenth century has been how to strike the right balance between describing elements of consensus and conflict, coupled with the placing of undue stress on either the Puritans or the Arminians. What comes through here is the sense of a constant struggle between warring factions, even when the odds had shifted dramatically in favour of the Arminians.

Reference was made earlier to the Book of Sports. It seems that whereas Laud and his colleagues felt inclined to enforce altar policy with vigour, particularly after the order of November 1633, they proceeded with far more caution in implementing the other famous order of October 1633, that which reissued the Book of Sports. Ironically, it is possible that they felt even more vulnerable to charges of innovation here, for what began as an assertion of episcopal authority in Somerset ended in a theological dispute with Heylin, White and Pocklington drawn in to defend the measure and brand sabbatarians as judaizers.[96] To the godly it seemed to presage a return to Rome and was the occasion of many leaving the country. For Arminians it reflected an awareness of Catholic criticisms of their Church and was a relaxation of discipline on non-essential matters of religion. Both Neile in the north and Laud in the south seem to have pursued a policy of giving people time to reflect and conform. Apparently, 'it was thought fit that the Bishops should first deal with the refusers in a fatherly and gentle way, but adding menaces sometimes to their persuasions if they saw cause for it'.[97] That was certainly Neile's way.

It remains to broaden this discussion to consider relations between church, laity and the state. One issue which highlights relationships between episcopal and lay authority concerns the attempt made by the bishops to gain greater control over town corporations in their cathedral towns. The policies can be dated back to the early 1620s, but during the 1630s great pressure was brought to bear on cathedral town corporations. First, they were called upon to alter town charters to give clergy more places as justices of the peace, in other words to allow a clear extension of clerical power.[98] Secondly, town corporations were ordered to attend cathedral services in full regalia on Sunday mornings to set a good example to the local populace and reduce competition between pulpits in the towns.[99] Royal orders on the latter subject were sent to York in 1637 and relayed by Neile to Bridgeman for use at Chester.[100] Charter disputes of various kinds involving rights of clergy occurred at Winchester, Chichester, Exeter, Salisbury and York; one is tempted to argue for a mini *quo warranto* campaign in the late 1630s.[101] This would fit with the king's known suspicions of godly town corporations and his support for the clerical estate. It also adds an hitherto neglected urban dimension to the policies of the 1630s which were in this case just gathering momentum when the Scots war erupted.

Neile was in the forefront of these unpopular endeavours. He had experienced trouble in Parliament in 1621, when it was discovered that he had extended clerical representation on the Durham commission of the peace and was automatically claiming places for prebendaries.[102] When he left Winchester for York diocese in 1632, he warned Laud that Farnham's attempt to gain a charter of incorporation should be watched closely for it might 'prove prejudicial to the inheritance of the bishopric'.[103] He was still pushing this policy in a letter to Laud in January 1638, when he claimed that Laud already knew and supported his ideas, but that the opportunity was now ripe for a campaign 'for bishops and their chancellors to be made justices of the peace in their cities and corporations of their dioceses'.[104] This was a reference to what was by that time a rather prolonged dispute over the renewal of York's charter. Neile's efforts at York came to nought with the events of the 1640s, but the policy was significant. Although there are many examples of disputes between town corporations and bishops and the cathedral chapters in the Jacobean period, most were initiated by the corporations concerned, and most related to problems of jurisdiction in the close or to matters of precedence in cathedral ceremonial and seating.[105] What is intriguing about the 1630s is that it was largely the bishops who were on the offensive and that the disputes contained this vital ingredient of enlarged claims for secular power for the clergy.

These remarks would fit easily into the frameworks adopted by historians of the left like Christopher Hill and Mary Fulbrook.[106] For them there is no doubt that the Arminians in the 1630s sought to undermine the power of local gentry élites and thus contributed to the later breakdown of government. For such historians, the rise of Arminiansm is seen as no coincidence, it seemed rather:

> . . . the culmination of long-standing government policies aimed at
> reducing the hard won authority of the new ruling elites. It gave
> these policies ideological form and coherence as well as offering the
> government in the machinery of the church the nearest it ever got to a
> bureaucracy.[107]

And there is much to be said for this line of argument. With the stress on residence and regular reports, the bishops could be likened to the Intendants in France in their service to the state. From the Arminian point of view, the reports also served as a way of isolating the king from alternative points of view of what was going on in the dioceses. They thus represent a part of the change from the openness of the court of James I to the isolation of his son, and a clear victory to the Arminians in their fight against populist traditions within the Church of England.[108] The importance of these reports and the way in which they were used by the Arminians is reflected in the fact that Laud had to defend their existence at this trial.[109] A clear and particular framework was laid down for the reports which were carefully processed by Neile and Laud before they were passed to the king.

On several occasions Neile can be seen using his reports to gain a royal reprimand for his bishops. A casual statement of regret that he had no reports on time for Durham and Sodor and Man in 1636, earned the royal comment: 'I like your diligence, but they must be checked for their slackness.'[110] On another occasion he reported that Durham lecturers were conformable 'so far as I could be informed . . . yet I must confess to your majesty I have reason to suspect some of them'.[111] In 1634 Neile apologized to the king for having previously simply relayed certificates from the bishops of Chester and Carlisle 'giving credit to them; but, having this last summer visited those dioceses, I find things much differing from the said certificates'.[112] However, nothing matches the way in which Laud humiliated Bishop Wright for a late account on Lichfield and Coventry in March 1638. He intimated that the king was unhappy over such 'slips' and demanded answers concerning poor estate management at Wright's previous see of Bristol.[113]

III

It is one thing to sketch a confusing debate and to hazard some remarks about certain policies, but now is the time to start drawing some conclusions. First, who was behind the policies pursued in the 1630s? This could be said to be something of a red herring. In some senses it does not matter what the truth was, as discerned by historians, but rather what people felt at the time. Likewise, even if we can show that intentions were sincere, we still have to analyse consequences, intended or otherwise, and to comment on how those intentions were put into practice. Kevin Sharpe seems to feel that marginalia on reports indicate that Charles I was in control, likewise his public stance over St Gregory's in 1633.[114] Certainly Charles signed a lot of critical documents during this period, but this debate has all the hallmarks of that about signatures denoting literacy. It has already been revealed that St Gregory's case needs to be set in context and was not the signal of the start of the campaign in the north; and marginalia are open to varying interpretations. Most of the comments which the King made on Neile's reports suggest a king dutifully reading dispatches, as one imagines Philip II did closeted in the Escorial, but just as woefully out of touch and responding to tactfully phrased suggestions from his ministers. If Charles was really the man behind the altar campaign, why did Laud get himself into so much trouble on that issue when dean of

Gloucester in 1617? Likewise, why should Neile bother to beautify the altar at Westminster in 1606 and permit a controversial stone altar at Durham in the 1620s?[115] When Neile, Andrewes, and Laud grilled Wren about Charles on his return from Spain in 1623, they received the assurance that the Prince was not as learned as his father, but that he would be steadfast to their vision of the Church of England. The significance of that story cannot be overstated: it reveals both the existence of an Arminian party and the fact that they sought to manipulate the Crown.[116]

A larger problem, considering the amount of research still needed, concerns who actually implemented the policies, where, when, and how? In other words, who were the good 'Laudians'? A glance at a diocesan map with thoughts of obvious dissidents like Bishops Williams, Davenant, and Goodman, suggests problems which are usually confirmed by analysis of the annual reports. Bishops Juxon, Wren, Montague, Piers and Neile emerge as the heroes from Laud's point of view.[117] However, there are surprises, for no doubt under the supervision of Lambe and Newell, there are quite good reports for Lincoln, whereas others counted as 'Laudian', like Robert Wright, were in fact poor correspondents.[118] The witty poet, Richard Corbett, turns out to have been a tough character at Norwich where he informed his clergy that 'if to repair churches be to innovate, I am of that Religion', adding that from what he had seen of some pews, 'there want nothing but beds to hear the word of God on'.[119]

Just as the metropolitical visitation was a vital instrument in Laud's attempt to galvanize his southern bishops into action, so was Neile's in the north. Bishops Bridgeman and Potter paid a backhanded compliment to its success when they complained to Neile that his commissioners had extracted more in fees than their officials had achieved in sixteen years.[120] Yet the visitation revealed tremendous problems within Neile's own diocese and indeed his own cathedral city, let alone the province as a whole. Repairs were carried out on 21 York city churches in the 1630s; at 10 it was necessary to move the communion table; the churchwardens of 15 were prosecuted for making false or inadequate presentments.[121] The appointment of Edward Mottershed as Advocate-General in the north, and the extension of powers of York High Commission pursuivants to operate in Chester diocese after 1632 strengthened Neile's hand, but he knew how little he could trust his suffragan bishops.[122] Bridgeman and Potter at Chester and Carlisle, he bullied, but to what real effect it is difficult to assess. On Morton he set spies; of

Sodor and Man he must have despaired.

No doubt the picture that will eventually emerge will be one of very different sets of priorities in various parts of the country, slightly different rates of change, differing problems of enforcement and personnel leading to apparent contrasts over matters of dating and general effectiveness. If Neile was even partly successful in the north over some issues like the church restoration campaign, it owed a lot to his loyal team of civil lawyers, William Easdall, Edward Mottershed and Edward Liveley, and to clergymen like Henry Wickham and his own nephew, John Neile.[123] We need to look carefully at the methods employed by the 'sucessful' bishops like Wren, Piers and Neile, but perhaps the true test will be to look at precisely those dioceses like Salisbury and Durham, which one would imagine to be under least control. Morton could prevaricate for a while, and keep emphasizing his feelings about recusancy in the annual reports, but even he had to bow to Neile's pressure in the end, and silence people like Jenison, Lapthorne, and frail old Peter Smart.

Mention of methods of enforcement brings us to a disturbing feature of recent research on the 1630s. Current work on Laud has produced the image of a misunderstood, kindly old man. Now we have seen that both Neile and Laud could be flexible in their methods, but to claim that they were just mild-mannered bureaucrats flies in the face of the experience of contemporaries. It is necessary to reinvoke some of the old Whig images of tyranny in the 1630s lest we forget Messrs Prynne, Burton, and Bastwick and their ears. The Arminians in the 1630s never lost the defensive, factional outlook which characterized their rise in the 1620s. When Juxon was placed as Clerk of the Closet in 1632, it was because Laud was adamant that he needed someone he could trust near the King.[124] Their attitude after the 1629 session of Parliament was to seek revenge on their enemies, hence Cotton's study was ransacked and several people, including ex-Member of Parliament Walter Long, arrested. When the latter was tried for election irregularities, 'My Lord of Winchester (Neile) was the first man that fined him at £2,000.' It had been Long who had first named Neile in earlier parliamentary attacks.[125]

It was even worse for clergy who got in the way of this faction. Peter Smart, the Durham prebendary who had called the attention of Parliament to ceremonial changes under Neile in 1628, found himself stripped of his office, degraded and imprisoned until 1632.[126] Although a broken man in his seventies, he was arrested again on trumped-up charges of dealing with the Scots in 1638, and only the kindness of Bishop Morton ensured that he reached

London alive for another spell in prison.[127] It was hardly surprising that the Arminians arrested Smart and kept such a sharp eye on the activities of Puritans in Newcastle for they were convinced that they were the victims of a Puritan conspiracy against them, and retained the attitudes of an embattled minority in the decade of their triumph. Events in Scotland only served to convince each side of the evil-doings of the other: for Puritans it was the Bishops' war, for the Arminians it was a Puritan conspiracy.[128]

Mention has already been made of Prynne's portraits. Equally revealing of the attitude of the times was the plotting between Neile and Bridgeman to send pursuivants to raid the house of a Puritan lawyer named Bostock while he was away in London in 1637.[129] There was nothing conciliatory about Neile's tone when directing that town corporations or foreign congregations should be brought to heel; his zeal over the latter on Hatfield Chase was doubled by his xenophobic belief that they were 'as vipers nourished in our bosoms that take the bread out of the mouths of English subjects'.[130] This same old man was very chary of granting preaching licences, giving only 14 for the diocese and province between 1632 and 1640.[131] It was also his claim that he could not ordain for the ministry because he saw few graduates of sufficient worth.[132] In 1640 he was only too ready to recommend another public execution for heresy for it would do a 'great deal of good in this church' and 'the present times do require like exemplary punishment'.[133] Concern over problems of enforcement should not distract us from noticing the tough and ideologically committed nature of this régime.

The critical question concerns why these policies were implemented? Was this just a case of ecclesiastical conservatism as suggested by Ronald Marchant and latterly by Kevin Sharpe, a tight interpretation of the 1604 canons in Bancroftian style; or did this reflect a new theology as Nicholas Tyacke maintains? It might be useful to approach this from the angle of the charges brought against Neile and Laud in 1629 and the 1640s. The broad thrust of those charges was that the Arminians were introducing innovations in matters of religion. To this the answer must surely be guilty. The first canon to authorize the placing of the communion table solely at the east end of the church, and condone bowing in that direction, was passed in 1640.[134] And not until the 1630s was it a serious crime if a minister failed to bow at the name of Jesus, or failed to administer communion at the altar rails, or failed to read the Book of Sports, or to place emphasis on sermons at the expense of catechism classes and the homilies. Nor were those who entertained doubts about parts of the Prayer Book, or who happened to appreciate sermons, labelled with 'factious people' and 'sectaries' as they were under canon five in 1640.[135]

Yes, new life was being breathed into the canons of 1604. But I agree with Nicholas Tyacke that this was because the people in charge held religious beliefs which questioned old assurances about predestinarian theology and hence placed greater emphasis on the sacraments and the ministry. This view is controversial largely because of the differences between English and Dutch Arminianism, and the fact that the leaders of the group in England were practical men who rarely expressed themselves clearly on the theological issues at stake. Certainly, Neile was always carefully ambiguous on the subject. In his draft defence speech which was never given in 1629, he gave the classic reply: 'I do not know that I ever read 3 lines of Arminius's writings.' Yet curiously enough, he felt bold enough to add that, apart from the questions of predestination and reprobation, Arminius was held in all other points to be a rigid Calvinist. Like his friend Laud, Neile claimed to be unable to master deep points of theology, but again made the ambiguous aside that:

> I will not take upon me to open the mouth of the clay to dispute with the potter, why hast thou made me thus, or to enter into the secrets of God's unrevealed counsels.[136]

As one who had witnessed constant sniping against himself and friends for their religious beliefs over many years, what more would Neile say in the circumstances? It was always his way to leave people like Cosin, Montague, Lindsell, Jackson, Duncon and White to do the talking and writing.[137] The outspoken Richard Montague wrote the most partisan visitation articles in the 1630s and appreciated that Laud and Neile were more moderate in their tactics, but when he gave Laud power to alter his writings in 1638, as he had once done with Neile in 1624, he noted that 'we are I know, of the same religion, drive to the same end, though not the same way'.[138]

In the end, it is through guilt by association that we pin Neile down. For there is no denying that he was a leader of the group known to a wide number of contemporaries in the 1620s as Arminians, even if they preferred to go under the label of 'Durham College'.[139] An anonymous libel pinned to the door of Durham House on the occasion of Francis White's consecration in 1626 expressed what most people thought with shrewd questions:

> Is an Arminian now made Bishop? And is a consecration translated from Lambeth to Durham House?[140]

This group was a tight-knit faction which mobilized rapidly in defence of its members, like Montague and Cosin in the 1620s, which placed its followers in strategic positions in church and universities, and which cultivated like-minded civil lawyers ready to emerge and take power in the 1630s. It is widely accepted that the 1626 declaration for peace and quiet in the Church was used to suppress Calvinist works, something feared by Bishop Davenant at the time as he watched the Calvinist consensus collapse.[141]

Thanks largely to Ken Fincham, we now know that Abbot was less conciliatory and more of a confessional politician than was hitherto supposed, yet his coalition of allies was never as compact or as ruthless as the Durham House set.[142] Nor was Abbot's tenure of office marked by such rigorous purges of opponents and such tight control of the episcopal bench. If one only allows the term 'Laudian', and that word is useful for some later appointments like Skinner, we are in danger of employing a label which concentrates on the effects, but which says little about the rationale of policies which were formulated in the 1590s.

Even if one accepts that doctrinal issues lay at the root of problems in the 1630s, it is not necessary or desirable to limit so closely the definition of what Arminianism entailed. The church restoration campaign, and the drive to get ministers to raise and maintain new standards of worship, can be squared with Arminian theology, while the attempt to recover some degree of economic independence for the Church and to assert the role of the clergy in the state also makes sense in the light of greater stress on the ministry. Moreover, that might have seemed doubly attractive, as Tyacke suggests, to a clergyman like Neile who was the son of a tallow chandler.[143] Yet this is not to argue that people who were disturbed by events in the 1630s necessarily saw things in this integrated fashion.

A certain number of people do seem to have left for New England, convinced they were living in the godless land. For those who stayed many different things could have caused resentment: championship of the Book of Sports, changes in ceremonial order, and controls on preaching obviously affected the godly. Simple financial costs would have affected many more. Apparently, in 1635 alone, over £1,300 was spent on churches in the East Riding; a further £1,200 in the archdeaconry of Nottingham, while for the most populous areas of York and the West Riding, the figure stood at £4,000.[144]

The cost becomes even clearer when seen at parish level. One or two examples from York city should suffice: the average rate for church maintenance at St Martin's, Micklegate in the 1620s seems to have been about £11 per annum. This trebled in the 1630s.[145] The churchwardens were stung for £53 in 1633 and a further £77 in 1635, notably after a visit from Neile's roving commissioners.[146] Likewise, at St John's, Ousebridge the average expenditure in the 1620s was roughly £17 per annum; in the 1630s, £37 per annum.[147] Few parishes provide decent runs of churchwardens' accounts, but a sample of four York deaneries reveals that cases of non-payment of church cessments virtually trebled between the visitations of 1632–33 and 1636.[148] Such cases are crude indicators but the trend is undeniable. Ronald Marchant calculated that between 1635 and 1639 about £50 was spent on each church in the archdeaconry of Nottingham, a large figure for such a short period of time. Anthony Fletcher discovered similar increases for Sussex.[149]

Church repairs could arouse bitterness for social and political reasons. A fair number of cases involved the destruction of family pews of the gentry, who had often erected elaborate box pews to the east end of the chancel. Hence the churchwardens of Holy Trinity, Micklegate, York were ordered 'to cut Sir Henry Goodriche's stall and likewise Mr Alderman Micklethwaite's and make them uniform to the rest of the stalls' in October 1633.[150] Ministers and churchwardens were harassed over the altar and its implications for worship; gentry patrons were ordered to look to the chancels, church property and to the poor.[151] Parishioners, high- and low-born, with the conspicuous attendance of mayors and aldermen required, paid more in their rates and were urged to comply with more services. So the church restoration campaign, which was probably the centrepiece of Neile's work in the north, serves as a microcosm of how Church policies could disturb people on a variety of levels in the 1630s.

What made this a coherent programme rather than just a collection of policies was an Arminian outlook which stressed different attitudes towards God, to the nature of worship and to the sacraments. Arminians likewise adopted a more relaxed attitude towards what was permissible on the Sabbath and were even prepared to scoff at Puritan claims for sermons. They reacted angrily when church music was abused and saw ceremony as essential to true worship. With such attitudes went greater respect for the clerical estate – intellectual, spiritual and economic. Most of all, the clergy sat at the hand of secular power, which they exalted, and which in turn gave them increased – ultimately unacceptable – levels of control both at court and in the country. With this understanding of the ways in which Arminianism integrated theology, church organization and the power of the state, it is possible to see some substance in Anthony Fletcher's 'competing myths' which fed into the civil war.[152] It makes sense of the virulent abuse directed at the bench of bishops in the Long Parliament in 1640–41.[153] Most important of all, the heady events of the 1640s are placed within a context which encompasses intellectual disputes at Cambridge in the 1590s and court and diocesan faction- fighting in the early 1600s.

Notes and References

In its long gestation, versions of this article have been read at postgraduate seminars at the Universities of Sussex and Birmingham and at the Institute of Historical Research. I am grateful to all present on those occasions for helpful comments in debate. I owe more particular debts for assistance to David Smith and his staff at the Borthwick Institute of Historical Research, Ken Fincham, Peter Lake, Richard Cust, Ann Hughes, Sears McGee, Nicholas Tyacke, Conrad Russell, John Fielding, George Bernard, John Fines, my old mentor John Hadwin, present and past students of my special subject group, my father, and my wife Liz. I would also like to acknowledge a small measure of financial assistance towards research costs from the Research Committee of the West Sussex Institute of Higher Education.

1. See introduction for a full discussion of 'Revisionism'.
2. N. Tyacke, 'Puritanism, Arminianism and Counter-Revolution', in C. Russell (ed.), *The Origins of the English Civil War*, (London, 1973), pp. 119–43; N. Tyacke's, *Anti-Calvinists: The Rise of English Arminianism c. 1590–1640*, (London, 1987), has just been published and I am grateful to him for allowing me to see material from that book in draft. Tyacke's views have been attacked by P. White, 'The rise of Arminianism reconsidered', *P&P*, 101 (1983), 34–54 and also by K. Sharpe, 'Archbishop Laud', *History Today*, 33 (Aug. 1983), 26–30. For the latest rounds see: W. Lamont, 'Comment: the rise of Arminianism reconsidered', *P&P*, 107 (1985), 227–31; P. G. Lake, 'Calvinism and the English Church 1570–1635', *P&P*, 114 (1987), 32–76; and N. Tyacke and P. White, 'Debate: the rise of Arminianism reconsidered', *P&P*, 115 (1987), 201–29.
3. Sharpe, 'Laud', 29.
4. J. R. Green, *A Short History of the English People*, 4 vols, (1893), III, 1040–1.
5. See material cited for Tyacke, White and Sharpe above plus K. Sharpe, 'The personal rule of Charles I', in H. Tomlinson, (ed.) *Before the English Civil War*, (1983), pp. 53–78.
6. C. Carlton, 'The dream life of Archbishop Laud', *History Today*, 36 (Dec. 1986), 9–14 (C. Carlton, *Archbishop William Laud* (London, 1987) appeared too late to be used in this Chapter).

7. J. Morrill, 'The Church in England, 1642–9', in J. Morrill (ed.), *Reactions to the English Civil War 1642–1649* (London, 1982), 89–114; see also Morrill's important, 'The Religious Context of the English Civil War', *TRHS*, 5th ser., 34 (1984), 155–78, in which he stresses that it would be impossible to overestimate the damage which Laud's rule did to the Church.

8. C. Haigh, 'The Church of England, the Catholics and the people', in C. Haigh (ed.), *The Reign of Elizabeth I* (London, 1984), pp. 195–219.

9. H. Trevor-Roper, 'King James and his Bishops', *History Today*, 5 (Sept. 1955), 571–81.

10. K. Fincham and P. Lake, 'The ecclesiastical policy of King James I', *JBS*, 24 (Apr. 1985), 169–207; see also K. Fincham, 'Prelacy and politics: Archbishop Abbot's defence of Protestant Orthodoxy', *HR*, 61 (1988), 36–64.

11. P. Collinson, *The Religion of Protestants* (London, 1982), p. 90.

12. See particularly P. Heylin, *Cyprianus Anglicus* (1671) and I apply this criticism to the work of White and Sharpe.

13. H. Trevor-Roper, *Archbishop Laud 1573–1645*, 2nd edn (1965); C. Cross, *Church and People 1450–1660*, (London, 1976), pp. 175–198.

14. What research has been carried out has remained unpublished: see J. Macauley, 'Richard Mountague Caroline Bishop, 1575–1641' (Cambridge Ph.D thesis, 1965); A. Foster, 'A biography of Archbishop Richard Neile, 1562–1640', (Oxford D.Phil. thesis, 1978); and H. Hajzyk, 'The Church in Lincolnshire, c.1595–c.1640' (Cambridge Ph.D thesis, 1980). The most impressive recent work is by Ken Fincham, 'Pastoral Roles of the Jacobean Episcopate in Canterbury Province' (London Ph.D thesis, 1985), which is shortly to be published as *Prelate as Pastor? The Episcopate of James I*, by OUP.

15. This has been remedied by the appearance of Patrick Collinson's magisterial *The Religion of Protestants* (London, 1982), and the recent work of Ken Fincham.

16. A. W. Harrison, *Arminianism* (London, 1937); H. Porter, *Reformation and Reaction in Tudor Cambridge* (London, 1958); T. Parker 'Arminianism and Laudianism in seventeenth century England', C. Dugmore and C. Duggan (ed.), *Studies in Church History*, I, (London, 1964), pp. 20–34 raised important questions but concluded in contradictory terms that although there were common doctrinal assumptions, it was 'not so much doctrine as discipline which was the distinguishing mark of the Laudian'. Tyacke, article and book cited above.

17. Tyacke 'Puritanism, Arminianism', p. 130.

18. C. Russell, 'Parliamentary history in perspective, 1604–1629', *History* (Feb. 1976), 22, suggests that Arminianism did not really become a divisive issue until the death of Buckingham; C. Hibbard, *Charles I and the Popish Plot* (Chapel Hill, 1983); A Fletcher, *The Outbreak of the English Civil War* (London, 1981); and chapters 3 and 4 in this volume by Peter Lake and Tom Cogswell.

19. K. Sharpe correspondence with N. Tyacke in *History Today*, 34 (Jan. 1984), 56–7.

20. Sharpe, 'Laud', p. 29.

21. Ibid., pp. 29–30.

22. Foster thesis; A. Foster, 'The function of a bishop: the career of Richard Neile, 1562–1640', R. O'Day and F. Heal (ed.), *Continuity and Change* (Leicester, 1976), pp. 33–54.

23. R. Marchant, *The Puritans and the Church Courts in the Diocese of York, 1560–1642* (London, 1960) not only praises Neile's work in revitalizing the church courts but also feels that essentially conservative and non- doctrinal policies were pursued in the north.

24. Foster, 'The function of a bishop', p. 41; Foster, thesis, ch. 7, pp. 192–229 addresses the question of his Arminian beliefs in detail.

25. Foster, 'The function of a bishop', p. 42.

26. This was a common defence used by both Laud and Neile when questioned about Arminianism: *The Works of William Laud*, ed. W. Scott and J. Bliss, 7 vols (Oxford, 1847–60), I, pp. 130–1; Prior's Kitchen Durham (hereafter PKDurham), Hunter MS. 67, Item 14 contains Neile's draft speech which was never given to Parliament in 1629 which contains this remark amongst others discussed later in the article.

27. F. Heal, 'Archbishop Laud revisited: leases and estate management at Canterbury and Winchester before the Civil War', R. O'Day and F. Heal (ed.), *Princes and Paupers in the English Church 1500–1800* (1981), pp. 129–51.

28. Heylin, *Cyprianus Anglicus*, pp. 188–9.

29. York Minster Library (hereafter cited as YML), Wd. f.121.

30. 'The Correspondence of John Cosin', ed. G. Ornsby, *Surtees Society*, 54 (1871), 240.

31. Evidence deduced from analysis of Neile's lease register held at the Borthwick Institute of Historical Research, York (hereafter cited as Borthwick), CC, AB 5/1 (1632–39).

32. PRO, SP 16/412/45.

33. Ibid.

34. Foster, 'The function of a bishop', p. 48.

35. Heylin, *Cyprianus Anglicus*, p. 67.

36. I owe this information to the kindness of Ken Fincham.

37. PRO, SP 16/259/78.

38. C. Cross, 'The Economic Problems of the See of York: Decline and Recovery in the Sixteenth Century', *AHR*, 18 (1970) Supplement; Impropriations were cases where the benefice had been annexed to a layman, or a senior cleric, and the person who served the living therefore did not receive the larger rectorial tithes; impropriators for their part took on obligations to maintain the church chancel which could lead to difficulties when the churchwardens obeyed orders to carry out repairs in the nave, but the impropriator would not co-operate.

39. Borthwick: CC, AB 5/1, 253–8 gives a good example of such practice concerning the rectory of Doncaster in Oct. 1635.

40. The York House exchange required an Act of Parliament because it violated the Act passed in 1604 to prevent further exchanges for property even when they benefited the Crown. It has always been held as a mark of James I's respect for his Church that he passed this Act and allowed few cases like that of York House to destroy

the principle established. C. Hill, *Economic Problems of the Church* (London, 1956).

41. S. R. Gardiner (ed.), 'Notes of the Debates in the House of Lords, 1624 & 1626', *Camden Society*, new series, 24 (1879), 95.
42. PRO, PC/2/46, 184; PC/2/48, fo. 138.
43. J. Raine Jnr. (ed.), 'The Fabric Rolls of York Minster', *Surtees Society*, 35 (1858), 319–25; YML/Wd, fos 112v–114v.
44. Foster, thesis, 28, 209.
45. Bodl. L.: Tanner MS. 299, fo. 133.
46. Borthwick: Neile's Episcopal Register, 32, fos.76–9.
47. Gloucester Record Office (hereafter GRO): GDR 189, fo.9. Glebe land belonged to the Church and could be leased out but not alienated; terriers were land surveys of such property.
48. GRO: GDR 189 (Liber Cleri) and analysis of GDR 174, 175, 190 and 191 (Detection Books) which all contain material relating to Laud's metropolitical visitation missed when I. Kirby produced her catalogue of the diocesan records.
49. F. Steer and I. Kirby (eds), *Diocese of Chichester: A Catalogue of the Records of the Bishop Archdeacons and former Exempt Jurisdictions* (Chichester, 1966), p. 46.
50. Apparently, Archbishop Abbot showed great concern over glebe property in his metropolitical visitations and several dioceses, including Chichester, reveal a high survival of terriers for the period 1612–26. *Diocese of Chichester Catalogue*, 46. I am grateful to Ken Fincham for this point.
51. Borthwick: V1633/CBI. York Visitation Book.
52. Ibid., fo. 502.
53. K. Thomas, *Religion and the Decline of Magic* (Penguin edn, 1973), pp. 71–4.
54. S. R. Gardiner, *History of England from the Accession of James I to the Outbreak of the Civil War 1603–42*, 10 vols (London, 1896), VII, 313.
55. C. W. Foster, 'The State of the Church', Vol. I, *Lincoln Record Society*, 23 (Horncastle, 1926), 220.
56. *LJ*, III, 31.
57. PRO, SP 45/10.
58. PRO, SP 16/345/85.
59. Foster, thesis, 303,306,307.
60. PRO, SP 16/345/85.
61. Foster, thesis, 303.
62. S. Gardiner, *History of England*, VII, p. 313 noted that the 'position of the communion table could never be a question of mere decency', while in Vol. VIII, pp. 114–15 he remarked 'it would be impossible to choose a better symbol of the victory of one set of ideas over another'; Tyacke, 'Puritanism, Arminianism', pp. 130, 138.
63. As quoted in Tyacke, 'Puritanism, Arminianism', p. 130.
64. W. Prynne, *A Quench-Coale or a Briefe Disquisition and Inquirie, in what place of the Church or Chancell the Lords Table ought to be situated, especially when the sacrament is administered?* (1637), Title-page.
65. Lambeth Palace Library: Ms. fos 943, 481.

66. PRO SP 16/259/78.
67. Ibid.
68. Borthwick: York Chancery Act Book 25, fos.9v–10, 125–9, 130v–31.
69. Foster, thesis, 306–7.
70. Borthwick: York Chanc. AB 26, fo. 36.
71. Borthwick: Cause Papers H 2087.
72. Foster, thesis, 306.
73. S. R. Gardiner (ed.), 'Reports of Cases in the Courts of Star Chamber and High Commission', *Camden Society*, New ser., 39 (1886), 302.
74. Ibid., 312–13.
75. Borthwick: York Chanc. AB.25, fos. 130v–31.
76. Borthwick: York Chanc. AB.26, fo. 243.
77. Ibid., fo. 49.
78. Borthwick: York Chanc. AB.25, fo. 158v.
79. Foster, thesis, 307.
80. Marchant, *Puritans and the Church Courts*, pp. 222–318.
81. Foster, thesis, 303; R. Marchant, *The Church under the Law*, (London, 1969), pp. 115, 121, remarks on the use of more visitors and cross-examinations of churchwardens.
82. Borthwick: York Chanc. AB 24, fos. 321v–322v; PRO, SP 16/259/78. Another matter on which Neile acted in advance of royal orders.
83. PRO, SP 16/259/78.
84. Ibid.
85. J. Shaw, 'The Life of Master John Shaw', *Surtees Society*, 65 (1875), 129.
86. C. Mather, *Magnalia Christi Americana* (1702), 102.
87. PRO, SP 16/312/84.
88. Neile actually boasted that he had never deprived a minister in 1637: PRO, SP 16/345/85; PRO SP 16/412/45 notes the departure of Rogers.
89. Marchant, *Puritans and the Church Courts* p. 56.
90. Ibid., pp. 222–318; Foster, thesis, 304.
91. Borthwick: Cause papers H 2046.
92. W. Prynne, *A New Discovery of the Prelates Tyranny* (1641), pp. 103–5, 218–226.
93. J. Lister, *Historical Narrative* as quoted by J. Miall, *Congregationalism in Yorkshire* (1868), p. 36.
94. PRO, SP 16/412/45.
95. PRO, SP 16/442/136.
96. T. G. Barnes, 'County politics and a Puritan *cause célèbre*: Somerset church ales, 1633', *TRHS*, 5th ser., 9 (1959), 103–22; I am grateful to Ken Parker for ideas on this complex matter which are now presented in his book, *English Sabbatarianism* (Cambridge, 1987).
97. Heylin, *Cyprianus Anglicus*, p. 279.
98. York city Archives: Corporation House Book, Class B,36, fos. 40v–41v.
99. YML/Wd, fo. 135.
100. G. Bridgeman, 'The history of the church and manor of Wigan', *Chetham Society*, New ser., part II, Vol. 16 (1889), 301–3.

101. PRO, SP 16/357/3 (Winchester); SP 16/325/60 & 74 (Chichester); SP 16/326/7, 389/54 (Exeter); SP 16/325/59, 354/11, 356/50, 323/ pp. 337–8 (Salisbury); SP 16/325/64 (York).
102. *LJ*, III, 143–4; *Commons Debates 1621*, ed. W. Notestein, F. Relf, and H. Simpson, 7 vols (New Haven, 1935), II, pp. 368–9. VI, pp. 396; M. James, *Family, Lineage and Civil Society* (London, 1974), p. 163.
103. *H. M. C. Cowper MSS.*, 3 vols (1888), I, 466, Neile to Laud, 28 July 1632. In the same letter Neile remarked that Taunton had recently received a charter prejudicial to the bishop and that 'his Majesty's public services are little beholden to the headiness of such corporations'.
104. Lambeth Palace Library: MS. 943, 562; Foster, thesis, 130, 269–70.
105. I am grateful to Ken Fincham for advice on this matter.
106. C. Hill, 'Parliament and people in seventeenth-century England', *P&P* 92 (1981), 100–24; M. Fulbrook, 'The English Revolution and the revisionist revolt', *Social History*, 7, 3 (1982), 249–64; M. Fulbrook, *Piety and Politics: Religion and the Rise of Absolutism in England, Württemberg and Prussia* (1983).
107. Hill, 'Parliament and People', 122.
108. See article in this volume by Peter Lake.
109. W. Laud, *The History of the Troubles and Tryal of the Most Reverend Father in God, and Blessed Martyr, William Laud, Lord Archbishop of Canterbury* (1695), 356.
110. PRO, SP 16/312/84.
111. PRO, Sp 16/259/78.
112. Ibid.
113. PRO, SP 16/386/2.
114. Sharpe, 'The Personal Rule of Charles I', 62–3; Sharpe, 'Laud', pp. 29–30.
115. Tyacke, 'Puritanism, Arminianism', p. 130; Foster, thesis, 208–11.
116. Foster, thesis, 222–3; C. and S. Wren (eds), *Parentalia* (1750), p. 45.
117. Analysis of annual reports found in *Laud's Works*, Vol. V, Part II, pp. 317–70.
118. There are seven reports for Lincoln diocese, a total only equalled by Canterbury and London, while only three are printed for Lichfield and Coventry.
119. PRO, SP 16/266/58.
120. Bridgeman, 'History of the Church', p. 377.
121. Foster, thesis, 249–50, 307.
122. Ibid., 236, 240.
123. Ibid., 236–42; Foster, 'The function of a bishop', pp. 47–8.
124. *Laud's Works*, III, pp. 215–16.
125. T. Birch, *The Court and Times of Charles I*, 2 vols (1848), II, 38–40, 55; BL; Stowe MS. 366, fo. 248v.
126. W. Longstaffe (ed.), 'The Acts of the Court of High Commission at Durham', *Surtees Society*, 34 (1858), Appendix A, pp. 197–242.
127. PRO, SP 16/412/58.
128. P. Heylin, *Aerius Redivivus or The History of the Presbyterians*, (1670), pp. 433–46; W. Prynne, *The Antipathy of the English Lordly Prelacie*, (1641), pp. 305–6 provide good examples of these opposite viewpoints.

129. Prynne, *New Discovery of the Prelates Tyranny*, p. 225.
130. PRO, SP 16/327/47.
131. Borthwick: Sub.Book 2.
132. PRO, SP 16/345/85.
133. PRO, SP 16/427/78.
134. F. Cardwell, *Synodalia*, 2 vols (Oxford, 1842), Canons of 1640, 380–415, Canon 7, 404–6.
135. Ibid., 400–2.
136. PKDurham: Hunter MS 67, Item 14, 12.
137. Foster, 'The function of a bishop', p. 42; for a fuller discussion of Neile's theology and his connections with this group see Foster, thesis, 192–229 or N. Tyacke, *Anti-Calvinists*, pp. 106–24. It is intriguing that whereas Abbot in his annual report noted that 'of Arminian points there is no dispute', Neile used the coy formula 'of matters of doctrine there is no dispute'.
138. PRO, SP 16/386/63.
139. Heylin, *Cyprianus Anglicus*, p. 75.
140. Birch, *Court of Charles I*, I, pp. 179–80.
141. Foster, thesis, 219; at the time of the proclamation Bishop Davenant asked prophetically 'How far those of Durham House will stretch the meaning thereof I know not.' Bodl. L.: Tanner MS. 72, fo. 135.
142. Fincham, 'Prelacy and Politics', 36–64; I am grateful to Ken Fincham for permitting me to see this in draft.
143. Tyacke, 'Puritanism, Arminianism', p. 140.
144. PRO, SP 16/312/84.
145. Borthwick: Y/MG19, accounts 1560–1669.
146. Ibid, pp. 194–5, 211; Borthwick: Chanc. AB 25, ff.138v, 173, 220; Chanc. AB 26, fos 34, 52–3, 156.
147. Borthwick: Y/J/17, accounts 1585–1668.
148. Borthwick: analysis of V1633/CBI.
149. R. Marchant, 'The restoration of Nottinghamshire churches, 1635–40', *Trans. Thoroton Society*, 65 (1961), 57–93; A. Fletcher, *A County Community in Peace and War: Sussex 1600–1660* (1975), 76–93.
150. Borthwick: Chanc. AB 25, fo. 139.
151. Over 100 parishes in the dioceses of York and Chester were ordered to provide their churches with alms boxes in 1633 which must have grated with many; Borthwick: V1633/CBI, CBIIA & B.
152. Fletcher, *Outbreak of the English Civil War*, p. 415.
153. Morrill, 'Religious context of the English Civil War'.

8 Local History and the Origins of the Civil War

Ann Hughes

I

In the introduction to his *Parliaments and English Politics*, Conrad Russell wrote:[1]

> The object of this book is to reconstruct the Parliamentary history of the 1620s using a set of analytical tools which owe more to local studies than to previous Parliamentary Studies.

A particular approach to local studies, especially county studies, has made a major contribution to the ways of understanding the Civil War which have, perhaps unfairly, come to be comprehended under the label of revisionism. This chapter seeks to unravel some of the connections between local approaches to early seventeenth-century English history and interpretations of the Civil War. Its first sections are critical and rather negative but I later argue that local history can help to create a more satisfying general account of the origins of the war than has hitherto been provided. The focus is mainly on county history but a broader range of local studies are also considered.

The most obvious and important thrust of county studies has been to discredit general theories explaining the origins of the Civil War. The idea of the war as a social conflict has been undermined by two rather different kinds of county studies. Some works are in part attempts to use the county as a laboratory in which the various theories put forward by the 'gentry controversy' could be tested. It has already been shown in the introduction that studies of the gentry in Yorkshire, Lancashire and other counties gave little support to any of the attempts to link social and economic change with political conflict and Civil War allegiance.[2] A rather different approach was pioneered by Alan Everitt in his study of

224

Kent. Here the county is not simply a means by which a convenient sample and a set of sources can be generated, it is a 'community' – a social reality for seventeenth- century men and women and a crucial theoretical concept for historians. Everitt's work undermines any notion of the Civil War as a social conflict simply because in seventeenth-century Kent as he described it, social conflict hardly occurs. The gentry of Kent, long established in the shire and bound together by elaborate kinship ties, formed one harmonious society. They were 'one great cousinage', 'unusually deeply rooted in their native soil, temperamentally conservative and excessively inbred'. There was little tension between the gentry and the 'lower orders' who were instead united by vertical social links forged by local loyalties. A benevolent patriarchal rule made the gentry's 'organic conception of their community, as a single united family' into a reality.[3]

Whereas Blackwood and Cliffe found a clear ideological division (based on religion) between royalist and parliamentarian gentry, Everitt's account eliminated ideological as well as social explanations. Everitt wrote that local and national awareness were both increasing in this period but this point has not really been developed: his main emphasis is on the cleavage between local and central concerns, and the gentry's ignorance of the antipathy towards national politics: 'for most of the people, most of the time, political matters scarcely existed'. The provincial gentry's non-political suspicious and obstructionist resentment of central interference underlies the major developments in mid-seventeenth-century England. It was this stubborn localism that paralysed Charles I by 1640 but also defeated the attempts of successive parliamentarian régimes to establish an alternative system. The cleavage of 1642 cannot be, and is not, explained in the same way and indeed on the Everitt approach, the Civil War is irrational, inexplicable.

As David Sacks has suggested,[4] Everitt assimilates seventeenth-century English counties to the small, face-to-face, 'traditional', pre-political communities of classical sociology. In such communities politics does not exist as a distinct realm of human activity, power struggles depend instead on personal matters: links of kinship, patronage and neighbourliness, not ties of principle, are what count. Everitt's county community of Kent is a natural phenomenon which is almost personified in his account: the chapter headings of *The Community of Kent* include 'The Community in Opposition', 'The Community at War'. Political division in this natural, harmonious society could only be produced by unnatural artificial factors.

> By 1640, the local loyalties and the conservatism of the community of Kent had united the county, like most others, in opposition to the political autocracy and religious novelties (as most people regarded them) of Strafford and Laud. This unity of outlook lasted, despite a good deal of family rivalry, until 1642, when, under the pressure of national political events two small cliques of genuine royalists and ultra-parliamentarians emerged on either wing of the Kentish community, which at heart wished to remain neutral.

[Again the county is seen as a person.] The members of these two small cliques were a very unpleasant lot:

> The genuine parliamentarians were mainly men of strong and indeed violent personality.

The cavaliers were courtiers, officials, recusants, 'a few of them were drunken debauchees'.

> The one characteristic which the cavaliers held in common with the parliamentarians and which distinguished them from the moderates, was that they were often relative newcomers to the shire and derived part of their income from some other source than the land. In other words, neither parliamentarians nor cavaliers represented the deepest interests of the county.

The 'distinguishing characteristics' of the moderates on the other hand included, 'their more or less complete identity with the ancient Kentish gentry' and 'their incapacity to adhere firmly to either king or parliament'.

In Everitt's account there is a sliding between, an identification of, the natural, the local, the moderate and the conservative – which may be valid but which needs an elaboration or justification which it does not get. Few commentators would agree completely with Everitt on the insularity of the county communities or on the lack of provincial awareness of national politics but the general tone of his interpretation has been very influential. This is in great contrast to an earlier account of the Kentish gentry, by Peter Laslett.[5] For Laslett the county community mediated between the individual and Engand as a whole; it was 'a medium of political consciousness' through which constitutional ideas were developed; and the forum for a sophisticated, even cosmopolitan, cultural life. Laslett's work is frequently referred to as part of the pre-history of county studies but its insights have not been pursued. Everitt's view of 1642 as an unnatural division is echoed by Ronald Hutton who writes of 'an artificial insemination of violence into the local community', while John Morrill in *The Revolt of the Provinces* regards provincial gentry as 'sub-political' – they 'responded to the effects of royal policies rather than to their origins or purpose which remained concealed'.[6] Morrill distinguishes between the backwoodsmen who made up the 'pure country' opposition to Charles and the 'official' 'country' of Bedford, Warwick, Saye, Pym and Hampden. The former simply wanted to stop central government interference or pressure whilst the latter wanted to reform or change the direction of that government and formed, 'an alternative court, a shadow cabinet'. Morrill also shares with Everitt the view that the war was created by a minority of extremists:

> In 1642 men desperately wished to avoid a conflict or, at least, to let it pass them by . . . [but] while the moderates, as always, talked and agonised extremists seized the initiative.

As Peter Lake discusses in this volume (Ch. 3), these extremists, particularly on the Parliament's side, are now usually seen as motivated by an irrational religious impulse.

The county history inspired by Everitt has had some salutary effects on Civil War studies. We are now well aware that politics or ideological commitment were not all-important in the lives of the gentry and others, and it is no longer possible to believe (if anyone ever did) that the English divided neatly and easily into royalists and parliamentarians in 1642. The hesitation and anguish with which people approached civil war are now appreciated. The study of local activities and loyalties and the recognition of England's regional diversity and complexity are crucial to a full understanding of the war. However we are left with a fundamentally unsatisfactory account of the Civil War as an irrational, unnatural, accidental conflict brought about by a few religious extremists. The understandable reluctance of many to take an active part in the Civil War is assumed to come from a localist 'non-political' stance on the divisions between King and Parliament. Allegiance is seen as determined largely by contingent factors: the relative proximity of the King's army or of London; or the comparative strengths and energy of the small groups of local zealots.[7]

However, a rather more coherent and elaborate interpretation of the Civil War is based, in part at least, on a similar view of local politics and society. This view sets the English Civil War in a European context, as one of many clashes between aggressive, centralizing 'absolute' monarchs and their subjects.[8]

The ambitions of rulers, developments in the nature and extent of warfare, the inflation of the sixteenth century all contributed to an intensification of the state's pressure on the population. Monarchs raised taxes, conscripted and billeted an increasing number of soldiers and in the process infringed on local rights and liberties and bypassed obstructive representative assemblies. In this framework the English Civil War is one of the conservative 'revolts of the provinces' which sought to defend local customs and traditions and to hold back the extension of state power. Here again, though, doubts immediately arise, for a comparison of the English Civil War with the almost contemporaneous revolt of the Catalans or with the Fronde highlights differences more significant than the similarities. (As we discuss in the introduction, a 'European' analysis may have more relevance to the 'British' conflict between Charles and his three kingdoms of England, Scotland and Ireland.)

The autonomy and isolation of English counties are clearly minimal compared to the provinces or sub-kingdoms of the larger and more complex western European kingdoms of France and Spain. On the other hand, a comparison highlights the centralized, or better, the integrated nature of the English political system and England's high degree of cultural, legal and administrative uniformity. A crucial difference is that in France and Spain provinces negotiated in an individual and piecemeal fashion with the central authority while at key points in seventeenth-century English history – 1628, 1640–2 – the English localities could combine together through Parliament in a general presentation of common grievances to the Crown. An examination of the Civil War itself in isolation tends to emphasize the well-known reluctance to co-operate in a national struggle: the refusal of Cornish royalists to cross the Tamar into Devon or of Stockport parliamentarians to aid besieged Manchester in 1642. In a European context, however, what is remarkable is the degree to which local susceptibilities were overcome to establish a co-ordinated national struggle of two parties quarrelling over the direction of the central government. It was not a provincial attempt to defeat central government interference. Again in a European context the English Civil War is remarkable for its ideological sophistication, for the existence of widespread divisions over abstract principles.

II

If the 'localist' model and the interpretation of the Civil War based on it are unsatisfactory, what alternatives can be proposed? In the next sections of this essay I will make more positive suggestions about the nature of local politics and about the contributions local studies can make to our understanding of the Civil War.

Record-keeping arrangements in England make the county a very convenient generator of sources for many kinds of studies. But historians have thereby been seduced into an overestimation of the county's importance in the lives of the seventeenth-century gentry and others. There were no unitary local communities in seventeenth-century England whether these are sought in counties, parishes or villages. Rather local communities were elaborate overlapping entities, 'an incredibly complex set of "planes" which may or may not overlap' in Macfarlane's phrase.[9] For some aspects of life the county clearly was a crucial 'community': it was the major legal and administrative unit and with the breakup of the regional power bases dominated by great territorial magnates, it was the most important arena for political debate and conflict after the kingdom as a whole. Even in these areas, however, some qualifications need to be made. Corporate towns and cities had a jealously guarded administrative independence from the rural counties they were sited in; relationships were often very tense as the frequent conflicts between Chester and Cheshire, Gloucester and Gloucestershire, Coventry and Warwickshire reveal. County administration itself often reflected geographical divisions within counties. Even where a single commission of the peace met constantly in one town as in Warwickshire or Norfolk, quarter sessions tended to be dominated by magistrates living near that town. Where meetings of quarter sessions rotated between different towns, as in Somerset, Lancashire and Wiltshire, the JPs attending and the business dealt with, tended to rotate also. Finally, some counties, like Sussex or Lincolnshire, had what were in effect separate benches operating in different divisions of the county. Units of ecclesiastical administration, and so the focus for the many important aspects of life covered by the church courts, rarely coincided with county boundaries. Even as a political unit, the role of the county was not necessarily clear-cut: all but one of the knights of the shire for Warwickshire from 1604 until the Short Parliament came from the southern 'sheep-corn' areas of the county and a similar phenomenon has been identified in Norfolk, Suffolk, Wiltshire and Somerset in the same period by Hassell Smith.[10]

Geographically, few counties were homogeneous while patterns of settlement or economic activity and marketing areas did not respect county boundaries. Great variations are found in Durham, Sussex, Norfolk and Wiltshire amongst many other counties; a distinction is usually made between 'wood-pasture' and 'sheep-corn' areas although agricultural historians are now insisting on subtler distinctions. A brief sketch of Warwickshire suggests some of the basic contrasts, however. South of the Avon the county was a fielden, mixed-farming area which included the great sheep pastures bordering on Northamptonshire and fertile corn-growing lands running into Oxfordshire. Here the typical community was a highly manorialized nucleated village with a resident lord; it tended to be closely knit and hierarchial. North of the Avon lay the Arden region; an old forest area with a pastoral economy in the sixteenth century, it was by the mid-seventeenth the site of a more complex, labour-intensive agriculture based on dairying and a fast-expanding metal-working industry. Parishes were larger than in the south and only a minority contained a single manor with a resident lord; much of the land had never been farmed through communal open-field agriculture and the hamlet rather than the village was the typical community. Society was more diffuse and broader based than in south Warwickshire: there were fewer great gentry and more poor while yeoman and freeholders of more modest wealth were able to flourish through independent enterprise in an expanding economy. Economic change had been more marked in the north than in the south of the county; population change had been more dramatic, industrial development and a more productive agriculture being both a response to and a cause of the population increase.

These differences of environment have been discussed chiefly in relation to the social and religious behaviour of the ranks below the gentry. Only recently, in the work of David Underdown has their importance to the gentry been suggested.[11] Underdown's contribution will be addressed directly below but here it is worth mentioning that the friendships of the Warwickshire gentry tended to be concentrated in particular areas of the county (and beyond it) rather than stretching over the county as a whole and the contrasts in social environment between the southern gentry and those of the Arden must be one explanation for this. Similar regionalization was found by Fletcher in his account of Sussex.[12] The minority of the greater Warwickshire gentry who lived in the Arden faced most clearly the problems of rapid economic change, large numbers of landless labourers and independent freeholders while the southern gentry lived in a more settled, securely hierarchical society.

Loyalties based on social status or on co-residence of a particular county were therefore cut across by differences in social environment, contrasts in relationships between the gentry and lower social groups. Loyalties were disrupted also by factional and ideological divisions. Early-seventeenth-century Somerset was riven by the long struggle between the 'protagonists' Sir Robert Phelips and Lord Poulett who made county institutions a prey to their ambitious struggle for pre-eminence.[13] In such struggles there are elements of divisions between 'court' and 'country' while most counties, after the Reformation, experienced religious divisions amongst élite families and indeed all social ranks. Lancashire and Warwickshire are examples of counties which had both important closely knit Catholic gentry networks and an influential Puritan presence. In Essex, Wiltshire and elsewhere Puritans were opposed by adherents of a more ceremonial, communal and perhaps more easy-going Protestantism.[14]

I am not suggesting that England was simply divided into sub-units, communities smaller than the county. Rather, the fact that there were several, overlapping local communities on which people based their social, economic, religious or political affairs makes it harder to discern any coherent local entity that could be opposed to the nation state. More important are the possibilities for comparison and generalization created by an emphasis on the diversity *within* counties. A continuing problem with case studies in the humanities and social sciences is that of comparability. Many, however, would not accept this as a problem – the predominant conclusion drawn from county studies of the English Civil War is that each county is unique (as it must be if the crucial determinant of the behaviour of the gentry and of other ranks is mere co-residence of a particular county) and so no generalization is possible. This fragmentation of analysis of 1642 is often coupled, though, with a covert generalization, designating the overall provincial response to the cleavage between King and Parliament as localist and neutralist. This could be described in Clifford Geertz's phrase as the 'lowest common denominator' method of drawing conclusions from local studies and it ignores the complex and distinct patterns of allegiance within counties. A more fruitful approach is to see a local 'community', in this case a county, as a unique combination or configuration of various elements or components, the elements being present in all counties.[15] Each county may experience 1642 differently but its reactions were a product of a set of factors common to all counties of which the most important were the geographical, economic and social divisions within them; the degree of cohesion amongst the social élite; and the nature of ideological, especially religious divisions. An analysis of the ways in which these factors interrelated in 1642 will be presented at the end of this chapter.

A recognition of factional or political conflict within counties does not of course detract from the importance of the county as one of the local communities to which people owed allegiance. The county was the arena of conflict and so its importance was emphasized: in his 1942 Ford lectures Sir John Neale compared intra-county rivalries to the house system in public schools which did not detract from 'the unity of the whole'.[16] Internal conflicts do undermine any notion of the county as an isolated unit, however, for local rivals frequently appealed to outside, central authorities and so it is necessary to examine the nature of local–central relationships. Studies focused on a specific geographical area (the county) have not been as illuminating as work based on the networks and attitudes of individuals or on examination of dynamic events or situations. Recent examples include discussions of the world view of the Cheshire gentleman Sir Richard Grosvenor; of the networks of Thomas Dugard, a Warwick schoolmaster and protégé of Lord Brooke; and analyses of the Forced Loan, ship-money and the coming of the Civil War.[17] Such work has drastically undermined notions of a split between local and central concerns.

It is clear that, whatever the response in specific situations, no general distinction was drawn between the centre and the localities. At the funeral in 1640 of Sir Thomas Lucy, a leading Warwickshire gentleman who had been knight of the shire for all parliaments from 1614 until the Short Parliament, the preacher declared:[18]

A noble lady hath lost, not an husband (as she saith) but a father.
Many children have lost, not a father but a counsellor.
A houseful of servants have lost, not a master but a physician . . .
Towns full of tenants have lost a landlord that could both protect and direct them in their own way.
The whole neighbourhood have lost a light.
The county a leader:
The country a patriot, to whom he was not wanting, till he was wanting to himself in his former vigour and health.

A prominent gentleman thus operated in overlapping and ever widening arenas from the family, through neighbourhood and county to the nation, with no sign of conflict or contradiction. Sacks has shown that the two frameworks within which the role and nature of towns were discussed – the 'liberties and franchises' model of Thomas Wilson and the 'commonwealth' view of John Stow – both presented towns as part of a whole. The same approach is found in works making up the burgeoning genre of county surveys and histories. Richard Carew dealt with Cornish government as 'a double consideration: the one as an entire state of itself; the other as part of the realm' and he credited Cornwall's special privileges to the 'reverend regard' the national Parliament had for their preservation.[20] William Dugdale regarded county history as part of a general endeavour; writing of his 'diligently searching into the vast treasures of public records . . . therein imitating Polybius, Livy, Suetonius and Tacitus, who made special use of the public records of Rome'. His *Antiquities of Warwickshire* was dedicated to the county's gentry, to whom it had a special relevance, but Dugdale saw it also as generally important because history has 'given us life in our understanding since the world itself had life and beginning'.[21] The new county atlases show a similar interweaving of the local, the national and the general: they showed England as a whole divided into its constituent parts, the counties; their production was stimulated both by the desire of central government to be better informed, and by the espousal by local men of the Renaissance humanist ideal of the educated, cultivated, active public man.[22] A rare distinction between local and central was made in 1608, significantly, by the Earl of Northampton, a man with a reputation as an authoritarian royalist, who used the distinction to limit the scope of the House of Commons. The Commons, Northampton claimed, represented a 'private and local wisdom' only; they should therefore not 'examine or determine secrets of estate'.[23] But most disagreed and in the light of the more common theoretical framework it is localist responses that need explaining, not national awareness. It seems probable that 'localism', far from being 'natural' was a constructed and specific response to particular circumstances, especially the levying of heavy taxation.

It is thus perhaps a misnomer to talk of the interrelationship of the centre and the localities because even this suggests too sharp a polarity; but as yet, no alternative presents itself. England was an integrated but not bureaucratized polity; consequently the

Crown was dependent on the involvement and consent of some at least amongst local élites. Conversely, because local offices were appointed by the Crown and the English legal system was basically uniform, local élites needed central support. Sir Robert Phelips was usually careful enough not to offend the central government sufficiently to risk losing his vital local offices. Jill Dias has shown how even the Talbots, Earls of Shrewsbury found their influence in Nottinghamshire and Derbyshire affected by the vagaries of their standing at court in the last years of Elizabeth and at the beginning of James' reign.[24] In pre-Civil War Warwickshire people sought the intervention of the Privy Council on a wide range of issues from the personal – Sir Thomas Lucy's attempt to get Privy Council intervention in his daughter's troubled marriage – to the generally significant: the complex and bitter dispute between Coventry and Warwickshire over the city's ship money assessment.[25]

Recent studies have indicated how King and Council could benefit from acting as the 'honest broker' in local struggles. The collection of the Forced Loan or of ship-money could be facilitated as men exhibited an enthusiasm for the Crown's business in the hope of obtaining central backing in some local dispute. Local conflicts also reveal a capacity for efficient and sophisticated lobbying, suggesting a political culture far removed from a 'sub-political' localism. Coventry aldermen addressed the Privy Council, mobilized London contacts and headed off influential men who might favour Warwickshire; similar examples are found in Bristol. Provincial people from outside the landed and mercantile élites knew the type of approach that would appeal to central authority. Clive Holmes has shown how the fenmen protesting against drainage projects varied their appeal with the changes in national authority: before 1642 the fenmen were poor, humble people in need of royal protection; between 1649 and 1653 they had a more aggressive stance, demanding the legal rights they had fought for in the Civil War.[26]

This skilled and knowledgeable lobbying derived from information about and experience acquired within a national legal–administrative–political system. As discussed by Cogswell and Cust in this volume (Chs 4 and 5), a vast amount of news about local, national and international affairs circulated in a variety of media amongst a large literate and semi-literate public. A broad section of the male property-holders of England participated in administration and politics as electors or MPs, as jurors or litigants, constables or justices. They thus acquired a more or less sophisticated familiarity with legal rights, the role and functions of a Parliament, factions or divisions in the council and the court. It was not just that those with most experience of 'central' politics – MPs for instance – took back a more sophisticated awareness to the gentry and freeholders of their counties; or that central emissaries, such as assize judges, were sent out to educate local governors on the finer points of the law or on central administrative priorities. Local experience and attitudes could have an influence on central policy and politics. The Elizabethan Poor Law was a summation of local initiatives while the supposedly 'centralizing' Book of Orders was based in part on practice in Northamptonshire. The petitioning campaigns in the early years of the Long Parliament for and against episcopacy, in favour of the Grand Remonstrance, and in favour of accommodation in 1642 reveal a two-way set of influences. These initiatives were both responses to national developments and attempts to influence central affairs.[27] The House of Commons frequently played a crucial role in integrating local experiences into a generally influential position: the Petition of Right was in part the result of such a process.

A range of evidence suggests that their information and their experience led provincial people to view the political process as characterized by conflict and divisions rather than as the harmonious and consensual system depicted in recent studies. Particularly important to provincial opinion were the interlocking sets of attitudes and ideologies which were summed up as a 'court and country' polarity. The ambiguity of the term 'country' in particular has caused much historiographical debate but it was precisely the ability of the concept to conjure up various shades of meaning that gave it its seventeenth-century resonance. Topographically, its meaning was imprecise: my 'country' could mean the most immediate neighbourhood, one's farming region or 'pays', occasionally the county (but by no means exclusively or even often), and finally, as in the quotation from Lucy's funeral sermon it could mean the whole kingdom or realm and thus was very similar to the term 'commonwealth'. Like the 'commonwealth', the 'country' carried ideological connotations: ultimately 'court' and 'country' were not places at all, but sets of contrasting attitudes, ideal types which stood for vice and virtue, corruption and purity. Hence members of the court like Archbishop Abbot or even Buckingham, when he resisted the Spanish match in

1624, could hold or adopt 'country' attitudes and thus appeal to a broad constituency. This ideological polarity between court and country did not of course rule out practical links between the centre and the provinces which, as we have seen, were taken for granted. The range of positions comprised within 'country' ideology is discussed in the introduction so we can be brief here. The 'country' attitudes of a gentleman like Sir Richard Grosvenor of Cheshire included a commitment to the rule of law, and to regular parliaments with the active involvement of freeholders in elections which were seen as necessary precautions against the tendency towards corruption and popery at court. A zealous commitment to Protestantism and to the struggle against popery were also involved. Finally the court-v.-country polarity shaded into rival conspiracy theories, alternative explanations of why the harmony and co-operation which all believed essential to the political system had broken down. The 'country' view tended to a belief in a popish plot to undermine the laws, and liberties of England, to attack Parliament and true religion while Charles I and the court became convinced of a popular Puritan plot, centred on Parliament, committed to depriving the monarch of his just powers.[28]

There was a wide awareness of such polarities in the localities. Local governors like Sir Thomas Lucy who dutifully collected subsidies and organized the levy and billeting of troops in the 1620s, were conspicuously absent from activity to collect the Forced Loan. Those who opposed the loan outright like Sir Francis Barrington of Essex or Sir Nathaniel Barnadiston of Suffolk, 'standing up for his country and the defence of the just rights and liberties thereof', were praised as patriots while the biographer of Lord Montague of Northamptonshire considered twenty years later that 'his paying the loan lost him the love of the country'. Men like the Earl of Newcastle who leaned towards the court also recognized the popularity of 'country' ideals. The Earl lamented to Wentworth his lack of promotion at court after he had zealously organized the collection of knighthood fines in Nottinghamshire: 'if your lordship and I lose our countries and have but little thanks above neither, we have taken a great deal of pains in vain'.[29] The general acceptance of a court–country division, and the sophistication of English (and Welsh) political culture is revealed in the cynical manipulation of the ideology. In November 1626 Sir William Thomas of Caernarvonshire wrote to Sir John Wynne, his neighbour, on ways of dealing with an unpopular patentee:

> it behoveth us carefully to hearken after it, either as good country
> and commonwealthsmen, to withstand the patent by informing my
> Lord Keeper of the general grievance and poverty of the country; or
> otherwise by letting Wood [the patentee] to understand of our intended
> opposition, to bring him rather thereby to yield us an easy composition
> as you do write . . . If I might escape for a small matter I would not
> stand in opposition.[30]

Finally, as Richard Cust has also demonstrated, it is clear that
an understanding of court–country divisions went far beyond the
gentry but was shared also by that imprecisely defined group,
the 'middling sort': the local yeomen, substantial craftsmen and
husbandmen who were the parish officers and the parliamentary
electorate. The struggles in the fens revealed a commitment to
Parliament's authority on the part of the leaders of the fenmen –
who were from the 'middling sort'. There was most resistance to
fen drainage in Lincolnshire where the fenmen had the greatest
confidence in their legal rights while conversely the most successful
drainage schemes were those which had the backing of parliamentary statutes. Similarly, after the 1624 Parliament failed to pass a
Bill to abolish the tithes on Derbyshire lead, the miners began to
pay this levy which they had been challenging through the law and
through direct action for the previous ten years.[31]

III

The preceding account of the nature of local politics in the earlier
seventeenth century makes a localist-neutralist response to the 1642
cleavage implausible. Indeed, much recent work, most notably
Anthony Fletcher's thorough study of the outbreak, suggests a more
complex picture. Fletcher concluded that very few were neutral in
their opinions although many were understandably reluctant to
engage in armed conflict. As significant is Fletcher's unpicking of
localism and neutralism, as *distinct* elements in provincial responses
whereas earlier studies too often conflated them. Neutrality moves
were occasionally mere stratagems by one side to gain time, not
truly pacific in their intention: pacts in Yorkshire, Lancashire and
Cornwall are examples. More genuine peacekeeping initiatives such
as that in Staffordshire were very complex affairs combining a
general desire for peace with some inclination towards one side in
the struggle and a particular set of local circumstances.[32] Petitions

for accommodation such as those from Yorkshire in June 1642 usually blamed one side more than the other for the breakdown echoing the conspiracy theories discussed above. All petitions from Yorkshire swore allegiance to the King, the privileges of Parliament and the liberties of the subject; all regretted the spread of divisions and the separation of King and Parliament. Those inclining to the King, however, believed the solution lay in Parliament giving Charles guarantees that would make it possible for him to return to London, especially reparation for the slight to his honour through the defiance of Hull which had caused great wrong and scandal to all well-affected persons. A rival petition blamed divisions on the King's absenting himself from the Parliament and his raising of troops – especially recusant forces. The solutions therefore were for Charles to consent to Parliament's proposals, to dismiss his guard of foreigners and cavaliers, and return to London.[33]

There were however differences between 1642 and the 1620s or even between 1642 and 1640. The great expansion in Parliament's responsibilities between 1640 and 1642, the close involvement of MPs with Privy Councillors, and the mere fact of Parliament's sitting for so long gave MPs insights into Charles' attitudes and an understanding of political divisions which took some time to spread to the provinces. Inevitably, by the summer of 1642, there was something of a gulf in understanding between the provinces and central politicians although this was more a time-lag than a distinctive view of politics. Attempts to secure peace thus continued in the counties for some weeks or months after men in London had given up hope and were preparing for war. The seriousness of the crisis of 1642 meant that there was no necessary continuity between 'country' attitudes before 1640 and parliamentarianism in 1642, as Johann Sommerville has also shown. A fear of disorder, a simple loyalty, a bedrock devotion to a non-Laudian episcopal church, or alarm at the extension of Parliament's powers all brought many 'country' gentlemen to the royalist side. For some the horrors of civil war prompted the 'construction' of a localist response, a separation of local loyalties from national allegiance.[34]

Nonetheless there were continuities and counties' responses in 1642 reflected the complexity of local communities discussed above. There were sharp ideological divisions in almost all counties: even in Puritan Essex, 'the first-born of parliament', a royalist element, with much Catholic support, promoted neutralist petitions while some actively fought for the King. These divisions were expressed most often in a religious form, or, following Underdown, as a cultural cleavage, rather than in the constitutional terms analysed by Sommerville. Brilliana Harley complained in June 1642 'at Ludlow they set up a maypole, and a thing like a head upon it, and so they did at Croft, and gathered a great many about it and shot at it in derision of roundheads'. The Herefordshire opponents of her parliamentarian husband called for the establishing of the 'uniformity of common prayer and the bringing of sectaries, separatists and all such recusants' to obedience to the King.[35] However, it is artificial to distinguish too sharply between religious and secular political attitudes. Parliamentarian adherents of godly reformation attacked the profane and the papists but amongst the crimes of the papists was a conspiracy to undermine the laws and liberties of England and to overthrow Parliament. Supporters of episcopacy and of a more settled, ritualized and ceremonial parochial worship attacked divisive, hypocritical, Puritans. But they regarded such a church and such worship as essential to order, hierarchy, authority and stability while seeing Puritans as subversives bent on the overthrow of monarchy.

In most counties there were patterns to allegiance which reflected their geographical diversity discussed above. In Norfolk, royalism was strongest in the north-west of the county around King's Lynn; in Lancashire parliamentarianism was strongest in Salford Hundred in the south-east; in Derbyshire an iron and coal belt on the eastern and southern edges of the shire was predominantly royalist; the lead areas to the north enthusiastic for the Parliament; the most committed parliamentarian areas in the West Country were the dairying and clothmaking regions in north Wiltshire and northern Somerset.[36]

How are we then to draw general conclusions from these fragmented provincial responses in 1642 which incorporate the geographical patterns and emphasize the importance of ideological divisions? One valuable approach is to focus not on social categories – not on how many rising or declining peers, gentlemen or yeomen can be found on each side – but to examine instead the social relationships and alliances revealed in local patterns of allegiance. Crucial here are the variety of ways in which the landed élite and lower-born social groups reacted to, or coped with, the tensions arising from the economic and social changes of the previous century and the conflicts over authority and belief which derived ultimately from the Reformation. In the Introduction we suggested that divisions over religion and politics on the one hand, and the problems of social change on the other, came together in a mutually reinforcing way. Religious and political crisis intensified the fears which arose from social restructuring, while political and religious disputes can themselves be linked to social change: court fears of 'popularity' against country desires for wider political participation; godly attempts at moral reform versus communal solidarity expressed in ceremonial worship and parish festivities have obvious social contexts.

A variety of local evidence and local studies have helped to develop this basic framework. The small-scale village studies of Margaret Spufford and Wrightson and Levine have highlighted the complex processes of social differentiation and connected them particularly to religious divisions. These studies have not addressed the origins of the Civil War directly although Wrightson and Levine's Terling, in particular, is often used to support general views of seventeenth-century social and political change.[37] More directly relevant are the works of Brian Manning, William Hunt and David Underdown which all emphasize the importance of social relationships to an understanding of the coming of civil war, and all use local evidence. Brian Manning has argued that the Civil War arose out of conflict within a feudal society between the 'people' and an aggressive landed and commercial élite. The 'people' usually include that ambiguous, and for Manning, unstable, group the 'middling sort' who are motivated by a Puritanism which provides them with an embryonic class-consciousness, a way of distinguishing themselves as the 'godly' from both rich and poor. Parliament acquired in 1640–42 a brief and precarious role as the focus of popular support against the king, the greatest and most aggressive of landlords. The royalist party of 1642 was a 'party of order' terrified by popular demonstrations in support of Parliament, particularly by the artisans and small merchants of London. Manning's emphasis on class conflict and his reliance on printed sources have been criticized although his information on the popularity of Parliament amongst the people in several industrial areas is used by Fletcher, for example.[38] Manning's characterization of the royalists as a party of order is convincing; it is less clear, however, why anyone from the élite should have supported Parliament and indeed Manning has an extremely attenuated explanation of élite parliamentarianism. Parliament's leaders are mainly disgruntled would-be courtiers, uneasy at the radicalism of the London crowd on whom they were partly dependent.[39]

In Hunt's account of Essex the opposite problem arises: here it is difficult to understand why anyone from the middle or upper ranks of society should be a royalist. In an account that echoes Wrightson's, Hunt locates the appeal of Calvinist Puritanism in its providing for the middling sort of parish élites, and to a lesser extent, the landed gentry and peers, a way to distinguish themselves from the 'rude' ungodly multitude and a means of subjecting the culture of the unruly poor to godly reformation, a 'culture of discipline'. Calvinist doctrines of election made sense to parish élites who felt they were an isolated minority in a dangerous world; Puritan sobriety and conscientiousness were necessary to their survival in hard times. Activist Puritanism could also offer upper ranks a solution to social problems through a rousing anti-popish crusade against the ungodly at home and an imperialist crusade against papists abroad. Shocked by Charles' espousal of non-Calvinist religious tenets and his support for 'traditional' or popular culture in the Book of Sports, a broad social alliance supported Parliament in Essex in 1642.[40] Again, much of this is convincing but there remains the problem of explaining élite royalism. Hunt himself mentions in passing anti-Puritan and royalist elements in Essex, while courtier, royalist and Catholic groupings have been discussed in greater depth by Cust and Holmes.[41]

The value of David Underdown's account is that it does allow for divisions of culture and political principle amongst élites, and suggests that there were a variety of responses, at all social levels, to the problems of social change and ideological conflict. On the basis of research in Dorset, Somerset and Wiltshire, Underdown presents the Civil War as a cultural conflict, connecting cultural divisions to the geographical and social diversity within his region. The war was fought between parliamentarians who were pressing for godly reformation of popery and profanity and royalists who supported the traditional social order, believed that parochial rituals and festivities were a guarantee of social harmony, and feared Puritan disruption more than any popish conspiracy. The 'wood-pasture' and clothing areas of north Wiltshire and north Somerset were identified with the parliamentarian stance: these areas contained large socially polarized parishes which had great numbers of unruly poor and had undergone rapid economic change. Like Hunt, Underdown emphasizes the appeal of Puritanism to the middling and upper ranks in these areas as a means to reform traditional culture and to discipline the poor; Underdown also sees a link here between Puritanism and market-orientated individualism. In the mixed farming downland areas, on the other hand, communal solidarity survived in deferential, hierarchical nucleated villages and was reflected in widespread support for parochial festivities; here economic change had been less rapid and royalism had most appeal.[42]

Underdown's work shows how local history can contribute more fruitfully to general interpretations of the Civil War. The social and ideological elements he has identified are surely crucial to allegiance in the localities; one may doubt, however, if the elements should be slotted together as neatly as they are in Underdown's account. We can return to the suggestion made earlier that general conclusions are better derived from examining the many ways in which a constant set of factors can combine rather than searching for total similarities. It is clear from the recent work of agrarian historians that the wood-pasture/sheep-corn dichotomy adopted by Underdown (and most local historians) is itself too crude and that the social characteristics associated with such farming practices are more complex.[43] Economic change could be dramatic in sheep-corn areas, through enclosure for instance; the degree of social polariz-ation, of deference, or independence on the part of middling and poorer groups varied more widely than Underdown allows. The connections between economic activity and political attitudes are rarely automatic. Parliamentarianism seems to have attracted small men who were sufficiently prosperous to be independent as in the Derbyshire lead areas where wealth was widely dispersed; in the iron and coal belt enterprises were larger and the great men could carry their tenants and labourers with them into support for the king.[44]

Furthermore the view of Puritanism as an ideology of 'social control' is open to question. Puritanism is also seen as divisive and disruptive, while it could also be a rousing, socially subversive even liberating creed; as such its social appeal was wide.[45] A disruptive and liberating Puritanism is often associated with industrial or wood pasture areas (in Derbyshire, Durham and Warwickshire for example) but these are seen as relatively egalitarian rather than the polarized communities described by Underdown. On the other hand a disciplinary Puritanism has been found in East Anglian arable communities by Hunt and Wrightson but these are polarized, market-orientated and 'capitalist', not relatively homogeneous as in Underdown's West Country.

Finally it is not clear why all social groups within an area should react in a particular way. Among the possibilities not considered by Underdown there is space to mention only two. The first is that the support for Parliament and Puritanism apparent amongst middling and lower ranks in some industrial and wood-pasture regions encouraged the greater gentry of those areas into support for the King as the guarantor of social and political order. This process – a 'Manning model' – can be seen in north Warwickshire, in Derbyshire, and in the West Riding of Yorkshire where royalist gentry outnumbered parliamentarians by more than two to one; a proportion greater than in the rest of the county.[46] On the other hand it is possible that in some mixed farming, 'traditional', deferential areas the gentry's own sense of security made them more willing to risk opposing the King, again Warwickshire is an example. When looking at the ranks below the gentry in such areas it seems to be an open question as to whom deference was due when authority was divided: to lord of the manor, minister, bishop or king. There was less popular support for Parliament in south Warwickshire than in the Arden and a similar pattern can sometimes be found in the nature of resistance to the Forced Loan. In the far north-east of Essex, a deferential area dominated by great landlords (but not a 'sheep-corn' area) Earl Rivers efficiently oversaw an enthusiastic co-operation with the loan while the Puritan loan resister Sir Harbottle Grimston who also lived in this part of Essex, failed to carry most of his own parish with him.[47]

IV

These points can be illustrated through an examination of Lord Brooke's leadership of the parliamentarian cause in Warwickshire. Parliament had secured Warwickshire by August 1642 despite the royalism or neutrality of most of the leading gentry. Indeed by background and belief, Brooke was ill-equipped to rally the county gentry. Robert Greville, second lord, was something of a parvenu; the adopted son of the first lord he was himself from a minor gentry family, and his succession was resented by relatives who felt they had a better claim, including members of a senior Warwickshire family the Verneys. More significant was the radical and uncompromising nature of Brooke's opposition to Charles I. In 1619 Brooke's adoptive father Fulke Greville had lavishly entertained James I at Warwick Castle. In contrast when Charles visited the town on 20 August 1636 Robert Greville was conspicuous by his absence. In a departure from his normal practice of spending July and August in the country, Brooke returned to London on 15 August. In the Scots crisis which ended the personal rule, Brooke's position was clear. Brooke and Saye were imprisoned at York in April 1639 for refusing the oath of loyalty required by Charles as he raised forces for the first Bishops' War. Brooke encouraged the spread of Scots propaganda in the provinces. The Warwick schoolmaster Thomas Dugard heard 'Dr Rutterford, a Scot', preach three sermons in Warwick, in the castle and in St Mary's church, between 29 December 1639 and 1 January 1640. It is just possible that this was Samuel Rutherford, the eminent Presbyterian and resistance theorist. In published work Brooke openly welcomed the Scots victory:

> blessed be God that hath delivered that Church and State from tyrannical prelates and will ere long deliver us also.

While many English people showed little enthusiasm for Charles' war against the Scots, committed support for them was much rarer. Brooke's religious beliefs were equally distinctive. By 1640 there were many calls for reform of the national Church and much opposition to Laudian bishops. Brooke, however, praised the religious toleration practised in the United Provinces; presented the arguments of poor 'unordained' preachers as he had heard them delivered at ecclesiastical trials, refusing to condemn or condone lay preaching himself; and suggested that 'anabaptists', hated bogeymen in most seventeenth-century opinion, were less of a danger to religion than supporters of 'lordly prelacy'. As might be expected, Brooke gave practical support to a wide variety of ministers. His chaplains in the 1630s were Simeon Ashe who had been ejected from a Staffordshire living for opposition to the Book of Sports and who was to become a leading Presbyterian in the 1640s and 1650s; and the very different Peter Sterry, a Platonist like Brooke himself, who became an Independent after 1642 and was a chaplain to Oliver Cromwell during the Protectorate. Ministers harassed by the ecclesiastical authorities were welcome at Warwick Castle in the 1630s as were local godly ministers and schoolmasters. This local circle of Brooke's clerical associates and protégés included both conformists like Thomas Spencer of Budbrooke or Thomas Dugard and those whose alienation led them to emigrate to New England, like Ephraim Huitt of Wroxall.[48]

Brooke's contempt for the low birth of English bishops is well known and he clearly advocated a prominent political role for the peerage. But his political practice is marked also by support for broad participation and like Cromwell he chose his allies for their zeal to the cause, not for their social status. Locally, his influence was as a leader of the godly not as a major landowner who was a focus for the county élite. Very few leading Warwickshire gentry seemed to have been close to Brooke although the staunch Puritan Sir Thomas Lucy was a friend. Rather Brooke relied on godly clerics and middle-ranking or lesser gentry who shared his views, putting them in touch with the national 'opposition' figures who visited Warwick, like Pym, Knightley, Saye and Bedford. This pattern survived in 1642 when Brooke made little effort to work with the moderate parliamentarians who were clearly to be found amongst the Warwickshire gentry preferring more militant figures, even if their social status was lower.

Almost twice as many royalists as parliamentarians can be identified amongst the Warwickshire gentry with an even greater royalist preponderance amongst senior families: 13 of the county's 21 resident JPs sided with the king, only 5 including Brooke himself, and 3 who were not of the quorum, gave support to Parliament. Nonetheless it was the parliamentarians who won the struggle to control the county and Brooke's success can be attributed to three main factors. In the first place, the lack of a cohesive, county-wide gentry 'community' encouraged, or at least permitted, the emergence of an 'extreme' and determined parliamentarianism. Secondly, Brooke obtained more effective outside help than the royalists could muster: an army of some 6,000 men sent from London entered Warwickshire on 22 August, prompting the royalists to abandon their sieges of Warwick Castle and the city of Coventry. Most important of all, Brooke received the more significant 'popular' support particularly in Coventry and amongst the lesser gentry, independent freeholders and metalworkers of the Arden region ('sectaries and schismatics' from Birmingham, as the historian Dugdale called them). In August 1642, as the King and his army approached Coventry, the city corporation prepared to receive him, arranging gifts and entertainment. But, when the army arrived the city gates were closed against it, and volunteers swore to resist the royal forces. Hence a vital breathing space was gained during which the relieving army could be dispatched from London. If Charles' forces had occupied the crucial stronghold of Coventry, the course of the Civil War in Warwickshire and the midlands as a whole might have been very different.[49]

Brooke was a skilled popular leader: volunteers were rallied with music and feasting; peals of church bells rang out when Brooke seized the county arms magazine at Coventry to take it to safety at Warwick Castle. The rank and file were involved in the struggle through the election of the officers for their troops and companies and through their assent to petitions to Parliament. Through anti-papist rhetoric Brooke linked personal concerns to a wider, indeed international cause: papists and malignants had undermined true religion and the subject's liberties – their machinations were revealed in the Armada and the Gunpowder Plot but also, by 1643, in their plundering the towns and lands of local people. Above all, Brooke portrayed the war as God's war with Parliament's soldiers as the zealous agents of a godly cause; praying:

> that God almighty will arise and maintain his own cause, scattering and confounding the devices of his enemies, not suffering the ungodly to prevail over his poor innocent flock. Lord we are but a handful in consideration of Thine and our enemies, therefore O Lord fight Thou our battles, go out as Thou didst in the time of King David before the hosts of the servants, and strengthen and give us hearts that we show ourselves men for the defence of Thy true religion and our own and the kingdom's safety.[50]

Ideological and social change had produced a situation where aristocratic leadership could not be based on landed power alone. Brooke's influence, like that of the Earl of Lincoln in Lincolnshire during the Forced Loan or the Earl of Warwick's position in Essex from the 1620s to the 1640s, reveals how effective an appeal based on ideology could be. These peers were patrons and leaders of the 'godly' and the 'country', and supported as 'patriots' not just as landlords. In fact Brooke's appeal was best supported not near his own estates which were mostly in the more settled parts of south Warwickshire (where indeed there are hints of popular royalism – including in Warwick itself) but in the industrial and urban areas of north Warwickshire where men of middling wealth had a greater degree of independence and control over their own lives. Here Parliament's call to the defence of liberties, law and true religion seems to have had a particular attraction and early musters of Parliament's Warwickshire forces reveal much more successful recruiting in the north than the south. I do not want to suggest that this type of aristocratic leadership simply manipulated lower social groups. On the contrary, the existence of the broad, well-informed political nation, committed to Parliament and to Protestantism (discussed extensively by Richard Cust in Ch. 5) had a vital influence on the kinds of aristocratic leadership that were possible in the first half of the seventeenth century.

A further significant aspect of Brooke's leadership is that it was not based on 'traditional' or paternalist attitudes to economic and social relationships. He was an efficient and improving landowner who had zealously defended his inheritance against legal suits by aggrieved relations and had attacked his adopted father's executors' handling of his property before he came of age. One function of Brooke's rousing Protestantism (though of course one cannot reduce it to this, or explain it only in these terms) was that it enabled him to combine apparently contradictory responses to the problems of social change. He could be an economically 'advanced' landowner while side-stepping possible problems in his role as a social leader by building a dynamic social alliance working for godly rule and the creation of a new Jerusalem.

Besides the popular support for Brooke, the other 'pattern' in civil war allegiance in Warwickshire is the committed royalism of most of the greater northern gentry. This suggests another possible combination of social and political attitudes. Most of these gentry were also improving landlords who had taken advantage of the insecure tenures on their mainly copyhold manors so as to profit from inflation; as discussed earlier they lived in an area which had seen much economic change and were 'threatened' by a large landless population and independent middling groups who had given enthusiastic support to Parliament. Their royalism is surely, in part, a reaction to this insecurity, an aggressive adherence to a strict conception of hierarchy and order. In another area, a parallel case must be Sir Thomas Aston of Cheshire, the zealous defender of episcopacy, who has been described by Anthony Fletcher as 'an improving landlord . . . obsessively preoccupied with the preservation of social order'.[51] In the terms of Underdown's discussion, it is difficult to find evidence of the attitudes of the north Warwickshire gentry to festivities or 'traditional' culture while Underdown does not discuss the farming or estate policies of his royalist gentry. I suspect, however, that many of those gentry who deliberately promoted or 'revived' supposedly 'traditional' festivities were also improving landlords, using a 'cakes and ale' policy as a means of defusing the socially disruptive consequences of their actions. Certainly the celebrated Cotswold games revived and promoted by Robert Dover early in James' reign were not the preserve of 'traditional' gentlemen. Dover himself was an attorney and a newcomer to the west Midlands; the courtier Endymion Porter was heavily involved and amongst those poets who praised the games were Captain John Mennes, a sea-captain who became a royalist commander in the Civil War and Ben Jonson, a conscious social authoritarian. Jonson saw the function of the games very clearly:

> I can tell thee Dover how thy games . . .
> How they advance true love and neighbourhood
> And do both church and commonwealth the good.

while for Dover they were a deliberate response to the 'fine refined clergy' who attacked games and sports:

> I was bold, for better recreation,
> T'invent these sports, to counter check that fashion.[52]

In a sense, the preceding discussion has focused on extreme though significant cases. Many other combinations existed: there were paternalist landowners who were Puritans and Parliamentarians, usually moderate in their views; one example is Sir Thomas Lucy of Warwickshire. In other circumstances gentry who were 'traditional' in their economic attitudes were easy-going (rather than deliberate) promoters of parish festivities and episcopalian Protestantism, and royalists in 1642. There is great, not infinite variety, but this does not suggest that contingent or accidental explanations are appropriate. To return to the framework discussed earlier in the chapter, the way localities divided in 1642 was produced by a multitude of *different* combinations of *constant* factors. We do not yet have a sufficiently subtle explanation of how and why these factors are connected but a crucial element in explanations of the division of 1642 can be elucidated through analysis of the ways in which the landed élite and other social groups reacted economically, socially, politically and culturally to the tensions in social relationships produced over the previous century.

I will conclude by clarifying the nature of the contribution local approaches can make. It is possible that the analysis sketched out above has more relevance to the cleavage of 1642 than to the 1639–40 crisis of Charles' personal rule. Charles' difficulties in mobilizing English strength against the Scots may be due in part to a simple localist reflex – a reluctance to provide enough men and money for the task. This sort of response was clearly more important in 1640 than in 1642, but also vital were the issues of what Charles wanted revenue and an army for and the unparliamentary and dubiously Protestant nature of his régime. A chronological distortion of a rather different kind has done more to produce misconceptions about 1640 and especially 1642: that is a reading back of attitudes which were a response to the war itself, to the time of its outbreak. By 1644–46 the massive demands for men and money, the plunder, billeting and troop movements, the attempts at militant Puritan reform and the general ecclesiastical disruption had indeed produced a conservative and localist response in many areas. This conservatism and localism was not natural, or pre-existing, but was created, called into being by the strains of war. Too often local historians forget that people develop new ideas, change their minds under the pressure of events, and argue for similar responses in 1642. Thus the conservatism and localism of provincial responses to the outbreak of war are greatly overestimated.

It is currently being argued that the most convincing explanations of the outbreak of the Civil War are to be found through studying central politics and particularly through looking at the policies of Charles himself. The approach I have adopted has an obvious relevance to explanations of how local people *reacted* to a conflict that was not entirely, or mainly, of their making. I want to suggest much more than this however. In the first place studies of local politics show how difficult it would have been for Charles to establish permanently the sort of monarchy and Church he wished for. Furthermore, as discussed earlier in this chapter and elsewhere in this volume, much recent work stresses the importance of rival conspiracy theories in the division of 1642 (and in earlier conflicts): Parliament's popish plot versus the King's Puritan plot. Peter Lake has stressed particularly the explanatory power of the popish-plot; the analysis here helps us understand Charles' fear of 'popularity' – of a Puritan-led subversive conspiracy focused on Parliament and aiming at the undermining or overthrow of monarchy. The roots of the King's fears lay in his understanding of local politics, indeed fear about the nature of local responses spurred Charles into devices like the forced loan in an attempt to avoid Parliament, and into the great reluctance to summon Parliament after 1629. Finally, an examination of the way local gentlemen like Sir Richard Grosvenor encouraged broad participation in politics, or of the broad social alliances of the godly, on which Brooke, Warwick or Lincoln based their local leadership suggests that the King may have been justified in his fears of popularity.

Notes and References

1. Conrad Russell, *Parliaments and English Politics*, p. 8.
2. J. T. Cliffe, *The Yorkshire Gentry From the Reformation to the Civil War*, (London, 1969). B. G. Blackwood, *The Lancashire Gentry and the Great Rebellion 1640–1660* (Chetham Society 3rd Series XXV, 1978). See the introduction, pp. 34–5.
3. The discussion of Everitt is based especially on Alan Everitt, *The Community of Kent and the Great Rebellion* (Leicester, 1966) see esp. pp. 14–15, 117–19; See also Everitt, *Change in the Provinces: the Seventeenth Century* (Department of English Local History, Occasional Papers, 1, Leicester 1972), esp. p. 9. Everitt, 'Kent and its gentry 1640–1660: a political study' (University of London, Ph.D, 1957), esp. p. 52.
4. David Sacks, 'The corporate town and the English State: Bristol's 'Little Businesses' 1625–1641', *P&P*, 110 (Feb. 1986).
5. Peter Laslett, 'The gentry of Kent in 1640', *Cambridge Historical Journal*, IX (1947–49), pp. 148–64.
6. Ronald Hutton, *The Royalist War Effort* (London, 1982), p. 201; John Morrill, *The Revolt of the Provinces* (London, 1976), esp. pp. 14–22, 34, 42–51.
7. See for example, Hutton, *The Royalist War Effort*; Morrill, *Revolt of the Provinces*; John Morrill (ed.), *Reactions to the English Civil War* (London, 1982).
8. Russell, *Parliament and English Politics*, e.g. pp. 64, 81; *idem*, 'Monarchies, wars and estates in England, France and Spain, c. 1580–c.1640', *Legislative Studies Quarterly*, VII (May 1982); Geoffrey Parker and Lesley M. Smith (ed.), *The General Crisis of the Seventeenth Century* (London, 1978) esp. article by Steensgaard. Richard Bonney, 'The English and French Civil Wars', *History*, 65 (1980) examines similarities and contrasts.
9. Alan Macfarlane, *Reconstructing Historical Communities* (London, 1977), pp. 12–13.
10. For Warwickshire in this and the following paragraphs see Ann L. Hughes, 'Warwickshire on the eve of the Civil War: a county community?', *Midland History*, VII (1982), 42–72. Hassell Smith, 'Electoral geography 1585–1629', paper presented to the 'Coral Conference' on Relationships between Local Communities and the Nation, Norwich (Sept. 1986).
11. See, for example. Margaret Spufford, *Contrasting Communities: English Villagers in the Sixteenth and Seventeenth Centuries* (Cambridge, 1974); Alan Everitt, 'Nonconformity in county parishes', in Joan Thirsk (ed.), *Land, Church and People: Essays Presented to Professor H. P. R. Finberg* (Reading, 1970).
12. Anthony Fletcher, *A County Community in Peace and War: Sussex 1600–1660* (London, 1975), pp. 46–8.
13. T G. Barnes, *Somerset 1625–1640: A County's Government under the 'Personal Rule'* (Oxford, 1961), esp. pp. 282–97.
14. Hughes, 'A county community'; Blackwood, *The Lancashire Gentry*, pp. 26–8; Martin Ingram, 'Religion, communities and moral discipline in late sixteenth and early seventeenth century England: case studies', in

Kaspar von Greyerz (ed.), *Religion and Society in Early Modern Europe 1500–1800* (London, 1984) for Wiltshire; R. P. Cust, *The Forced Loan and English Politics* (Oxford, 1987), pp. 260–84; and Clive Holmes, *The Eastern Association in the English Civil War* (Cambridge, 1974), pp. 34–48, for Essex.

15. This argument is based on Clifford Geertz, 'Form and variation in Balinese village structure', *American Anthropologist*, 61 (1959).

16. J. E. Neale, *The Elizabethan House of Commons* (Ford Lectures for 1942), published in 1949, p. 22. Neale is usually credited with the first discussion of county communities.

17. Richard Cust and Peter Lake, 'Sir Richard Grosvenor and the rhetoric of magistracy', *BIHR*, 54 (1981); Ann Hughes, 'Thomas Dugard and his circle in the 1630s: a parliamentary–Puritan connection?', *HJ*, 29 (1986); Cust, *The Forced Loan*; Lake, 'The collection of ship money in Cheshire: a case study of the relations between central and local government', *NH*, 17 (1981); Anthony Fletcher, *The Outbreak of the English Civil War* (London, 1981).

18. Robert Harris, *Abner's Funeral* (London, 1641) pp. 25–6.

19. Sacks, 'The corporate town'.

20. Richard Carew, *The Survey of Cornwall* (London, 1602), fos 76v, 79v.

21. William Dugdale, *The Antiquities of Warwickshire* (1656). Preface.

22. Victor Morgan, 'The cartographic image of the country in early modern England', *TRHS*, 5th ser., vol. 29 (1979).

23. Linda Levy Peck, 'The Earl of Northampton, merchant grievances and the addled Parliament of 1614'. *HJ*, 24 (1981).

24. Jill R. Dias, 'Politics and administration in Nottinghamshire and Derbyshire 1590–1640' (Oxford, D.Phil. thesis, 1973), pp. 172–282.

25. Hughes, 'Warwickshire on the eve of the Civil War', p. 56.

26. Clive Holmes, 'Drainers and fenmen: the problem of popular political consciousness in the seventeenth century', in Anthony Fletcher and John Stevenson (eds), *Order and Disorder in Early Modern England* (Cambridge, 1985).

27. Brian Quintrell, 'The making of Charles I's Book of Orders', *EHR*, XCV (1980); Fletcher, *Outbreak of the English Civil War*, ch. 6.

28. Peter Lake, 'Constitutional consensus and Puritan opposition in the 1620s: Thomas Scott and the Spanish Match', *HJ* 25 (1982); see also the Introduction and Cust (Ch. 5) in this volume.

29. Hughes, 'A county community', p. 57; Cust, *The Forced Loan*, pp. 224–6; Dias, 'Politics and administration', p. 356.

30. NLW, Wynn of Gwydir Papers, 1257.

31. Holmes, 'Drainers and fenmen'; Dias, 'Politics and administration', p. 417.

32. Fletcher, *Outbreak of the English Civil War*, pp. 380–404.

33. *To the Right Honourable The Lords and Commons in Parliament Assembled* . . . (BL 105 f17 (11) York, 1642); *Two Petitions of the County of York* (BL E149 (28), London, 1642).

34. Perez Zagorin, *The Court and the Country: The Beginning of the English Revolution* (New York, 1970) pp. 305–14; Fletcher, *Outbreak of the English Civil War*, pp. 264–80 is more dubious about a central-provincial gulf in 1642.

35. Holmes, *The Eastern Association*, pp. 40–7; David Underdown, *Revel, Riot and Rebellion: Popular Politics and Culture in England 1603–1660* (Oxford, 1685) which is discussed more fully below; *Letters of Lady Brilliana Harley* (Camden Society, 1854), p. 167; *Royal Commission on Historical Manuscripts, Report Portland Mss*, III, p. 85; J. Levy, 'Perceptions and Beliefs: The Harleys of Brampton Bryan and the Origins and Outbreak of the First Civil War', Ph.D. thesis, London University, 1983, pp. 237–45 and 269–72.

36. R. W. Ketton-Cremer, *Norfolk in the Civil War: A Portrait of a Society in Conflict* (London, 1969) p. 156; Blackwood, *The Lancashire Gentry* pp. 46–7. Dias, 'Politics and administration', 473–5; Underdown, *Revel, Riot and Rebellion, passim* but esp. pp. 164–76.

37. K. Wrightson and D. Levine, *Poverty and Piety in an English Village: Terling 1525–1700* (New York, 1979); Margaret Spufford, *Contrasting Communities: English Villagers in the Sixteenth and Seventeenth Centuries* (Cambridge, 1974).

38. Brian Manning, *The English People and the English Revolution* (London, 1976); John Morrill, 'Provincial Squires and 'Middling Sorts' in the Great Rebellion', *HJ*, 20 (1977); Fletcher, *Outbreak of the English Civil War*, p. 417.

39. Cf. Manning, 'The aristocracy and the downfall of Charles I', in Manning (ed.), *Politics, Religion and the English Civil War* (London, 1973), an account that revisionists can largely agree with.

40. William Hunt, *The Puritan Moment: The Coming of Revolution in an English County* (Cambridge, Massachusetts, 1983).

41. Hunt, *Puritan Moment*, pp. 281, 295; Cust, *The Forced Loan*; Holmes, *The Eastern Association*, pp. 34–47.

42. Underdown, *Revel, Riot and Rebellion* esp. pp. 40, 73–105, 164–81.

43. Mark Overton, 'Depression or revolution?, English agriculture 1640–1750', *JBS*, 25 (1986) and references there cited.

44. Dias, 'Politics and administration', pp. 33–40, 446–8, 473–5. See Derek Hirst, *Authority and Conflict: England 1603–1658* (London, 1986), pp. 228–30 for a sensitive general discussion.

45. Among many challenges to the 'social control' view of Puritanism see Ingram, 'Religion, communities and moral discipline'; Peter Lake, 'William Bradshaw, Anti-Christ and the community of the godly', *JEH*, 36 (1985); M. E. James, *Family, Lineage and Civil Society* (Oxford, 1974) pp. 195–6.

46. Dias, 'Politics and administration', pp. 446–8; Cliffe, *The Yorkshire Gentry*, p. 338.

47. For Warwickshire see below; Cust, *The Forced Loan*.

48. For Brooke and Warwickshire in general see Ann Hughes, *Politics, Society and Civil War in Warwickshire* (Cambridge, 1987) esp. ch. 4; Hughes, 'Thomas Dugard'; the quotations are from Brooke's *A Discourse Opening the Nature of that Episcopacy which is exercised in England* (London, 1641), repr. in William Haller (ed.), *Tracts on Liberty in the Puritan Revolution 1638–1647* (New York, 1965), vol. 2.

49. Hughes, 'Warwickshire on the eve of the Civil War', pp. 59–64.

50. *A Worthy Speech Made by the Right Honourable the Lord Brooke at the election of his Captaines and Commanders at Warwick Castle* (26 Feb. 1643).

51.   Fletcher, *Outbreak of the English Civil War*, p. 107.
52.   *Annalia Dubrensia or Celebration of Captain Robert Dover's Cotswold Games*, ed, A. B. Grosart (Manchester, 1877), introduction and pp. 23, 67.

Suggestions for Further Reading

Ideology, property and the constitution.

Many of the points discussed in this chapter can be followed up in my *Politics and Ideology in England, 1603–1640* (Longman, 1986). A forthcoming volume on the history of freedom in England in this period by J. H. Hexter, Derek Hirst, Tom Cogswell and others contains very interesting discussions of various aspects of the subject. Margaret Judson's *The Crisis of the Constitution: an Essay in Constitutional and Political Thought 1603–1645* (New Brunswick 1949) remains essential reading for anyone interested in the details of early Stuart political debate. It is very rich in quotations from contemporary sources, and surveys the whole period. The fundamental study of political history is still S. R. Gardiner, *History of England 1603–1642*, 10 vols (Longman 1883–84). Richard Cust's valuable *The Forced Loan and English Politics 1626–1628* (Oxford, 1987) is a sensitive, nuanced and very readable discussion of an exceptionally important period in English politics. It demonstrates the fundamental significance of divisions on points of constitutional principle. The best attempts to place constitutional and ideological conflicts in their social and economic contexts are the works of Christopher Hill. Perhaps the most important from the perspective of questions discussed in this chapter is his *Economic Problems of the Church from Archbishop Whitgift to the Long Parliament* (Oxford, 1956).

In view of recent works on early-modern England, all the authors mentioned above may now be regarded as traditionalists – though not all would be happy with that title. Traditions can, however, be based on truth, and it is likely that when the dust of battle has settled the traditional account of sixteenth-, seventeenth- and eighteenth-century politics will turn out to be largely accurate. Nevertheless, the writings of recent anti-traditionalists have certainly led to significant reappraisals on a number of points. Moreover, their questioning attitude has encouraged greater precision in the formulation of old ideas. Some anti-traditionalist works are, indeed, extravagantly wrong-headed and misleading. Others are intelligent, interesting and provocative. Perhaps the best of the latter group are the writings of G. R. Elton (mainly on the sixteenth century, but with occasional forays into the seventeenth) and of Conrad Russell. These two writers do, indeed, adopt very different approaches, but they agree in rejecting older accounts of the period. Elton's *Studies in Tudor and Stuart Politics and Government*, 3 vols (Cambridge 1974–83), and Russell's *Parliaments and English Politics 1621–1629* (Oxford, 1979) are particularly valuable.

Anti-popery: the structure of a prejudice

Still of use is William Haller, *Foxe's Book of Martyrs and the Elect Nation* (London, 1963), but now see J. Facey, 'John Foxe and the defence of the English church', in P. Lake and M. Dowling (eds) *Protestantism and the National Church*, (London, 1987). The best account of the theological and eschatological background to anti-popery is R. J. Bauckham, *Tudor Apocalypse* (Abingdon, 1978). Less sophisticated but useful for the political consequences of apocalyptic thought is P. Christianson, *Reformers and Babylon* (Toronto, 1978). Also see C. Hill, *Antichrist in the Seventeenth Century* (Oxford, 1971). On popular anti-popery see R. Clifton, 'Fear of popery', in C. Russell (ed.), *The Origins of the English Civil War* (London, 1973), and R. Clifton, 'The popular fear of Catholics during the English revolution', in *P&P*, 51 (1971). Also see W. Hunt, *The Puritan Moment* (Cambridge, Mass., 1983) and B. Manning, *The English People and the English Revolution* (London, 1976). For a case study of popular belief in the politics of the popish plot see P. Seaver, *Wallington's World* (London, 1985). See also W. Lamont, *Marginal Prynne* (London, 1963). Also relevant are P. Lake, 'The significance of the Elizabethan identification of the pope as Antichrist', *JEH*, 31, (1980); 'William Bradshaw, Antichrist and the community of the godly', *JEH*, 36 (1985); 'Constitutional consensus and puritan opposition; Thomas Scott and the Spanish match', *HJ*, 25 (1982). Two forthcoming articles also significantly advance our knowledge of the political role of anti- popery. See

K. C. Fincham 'Archbishop Abbot and the defence of protestant orthodoxy' *HR*, 61 (1988); and J. Fielding, 'Opposition to the "personal rule" of Charles I: the diary of Robert Woodford 1637–1641', forthcoming, *HJ*.

England and the Spanish Match

The best general account of English foreign policy in the early seventeenth century remains S. R. Gardiner, *History of England 1603–1642*, 10 vols (1883–84). G. Parker, *The Thirty Years War* (1984) provides a good discussion of the European context and A. W. White, 'Suspension of arms: Anglo-Spanish mediation in the Thirty Years War, 1621–1625' (Tulane University, Ph.D, 1978) is an excellent detailed account of diplomacy in the period of the Spanish Match. The themes and priorities of English foreign policy in the early Stuart period are clearly delineated in S. Adams, 'Spain or the Netherlands? the dilemmas of early Stuart foreign policy', in H. Tomlinson (ed.), *Before the English Civil War* (1983).

The relationship between foreign policy and domestic and parliamentary politics, in the aftermath of the Spanish Match, is discussed at length in T. Cogswell, *The Blessed Revolution* (Cambridge, 1989). For opinions about foreign affairs at this time see: C. S. R. Russell, 'The foreign policy debate in the House of Commons in 1621', *HJ*, XX (1977); S. L. Adams, 'Foreign policy and the Parliaments of 1621 and 1624', in K. Sharpe (ed.), *Faction and Parliament* (Oxford, 1978); P. G. Lake, 'Constitutional consensus and Puritan opposition in the 1620s: Thomas Scott and the Spanish Match', *HJ*, XXV (1982); T. Cogswell, 'Thomas Middleton and the court, 1624: *A Game at Chesse* in context', *HLQ*, 47 (1984).

Politics and the electorate in the 1620s

Recent studies of early Stuart elections have been much influenced by the seminal article by J. H. Plumb, 'The growth of the electorate in England from 1600 to 1715', *P&P*, 45 (1969). His work has been refined and developed in D. Hirst, *The Representative of the People?* (Cambridge, 1975). However the emphasis of these two works on contested elections and conflict has been challenged in an important book by M. Kishlansky, *Parliamentary Selection* (Cambridge, 1986).

For an excellent discussion of the political concerns of electors and the background to elections in the 1620s see D. Hirst, 'Court, country and politics to 1629', in K. Sharpe (ed.), *Faction and Parliament* (Oxford, 1978). The conclusions offered here are to be preferred to some of Hirst's remarks on the same subject in the *Representative of the People?* R. P. Cust, 'News and politics in early seventeenth century England', *P&P*, 112 (1986) and R. P. Cust, *The Forced Loan and English Politics 1626–1628* (Oxford, 1987) are also helpful, particularly for assessing the elections of 1628.

C. S. R. Russell, *Parliaments and English Politics 1621–1629* (Oxford, 1979) discusses ways in which the electorate influenced the behaviour of MPs in Parliament and P. Salt, 'Sir Thomas Wentworth and the parliamentary representation of Yorkshire, 1614–1628', *NH*, XVI (1980) investigates the relationship between a leading MP and his constituents. Both emphasize the 'localism' of the electorate. By contrast R. P. Cust and P. G. Lake, 'Sir Richard Grosvenor and the rhetoric of magistracy', *BIHR*, LIV (1981), and P. Clark, 'Thomas Scott and the growth of urban opposition to the early Stuart régime', *HJ*, XXI (1978) suggest that the electorate was concerned with broader political issues. Hill and Fletcher discuss the political awareness of electors while debating how far ordinary freeholders could act independently of their social superiors: C. Hill, 'Parliament and people in seventeenth century England', *P&P*, 92 (1981) and A. Fletcher and C. Hill, 'Debate: parliament and people in seventeenth century England', *P&P*, 98 (1983).

The influence of the Crown over elections is discussed in D. H. Willson, *The Privy Councillors in the House of Commons 1604–1629* (Minneapolis, 1940) and J. K. Gruenfelder, *Influence in Early Stuart Elections 1604–1640* (Columbus, Ohio, 1981).

Court politics and parliamentary conflict in 1625

Modern studies of the parliaments of the early Stuart period rest on the foundations laid in S. R. Gardiner, *History of England 1603–1642*, 10 vols (1883–84) and Wallace Notestein, 'The winning of the initiative by the House of Commons', *Proceedings of the British Academy*, xi (1924–25). The best general account of the relations between court politics and Parliament is still D. H. Willson, *The Privy Councillors in the House of Commons 1621–1629* (Minneapolis, 1940). The traditional approach has been challenged in a crucial revisionist article by Conrad Russell: 'Parliamentary history in perspective 1604–1629', *Hist.*, 61 (1976). He has developed his argument further in the most important modern work on parliaments: *Parliaments and English Politics 1621–1629* (Oxford, 1979). A critical view of the revisionist approach can be found in Christopher Thompson, *Parliamentary History in the 1620s: in or out of perspective?* (Wivenhoe, 1986).

Useful studies of individual parliaments are provided by: R. Zaller, *The Parliament of 1621* (1971) and R. E. Ruigh, *The Parliament of 1624* (Cambridge, Mass., 1971). The Parliament of 1625 has not attracted much scholarly attention hitherto. There are, however, two articles which bear directly on it: J. N. Ball, 'Sir John Eliot at the Oxford Parliament, 1625', *BIHR*, 28 (1955) and G. A. Harrison, 'Innovation and precedent: a procedural reappraisal of the 1625 Parliament', *EHR*, 102 (1987), For the activities of an important group of MPs in the mid-1620s see Christopher Thompson, 'The origins of the politics of the parliamentary middle group', *TRHS* (5th ser., 22, 1972).

Since this essay was composed, the sources for the 1625 Parliament have been published in *Proceedings in Parliament 1625*, edited by Maija Jansson and William B. Bidwell (New Haven and London, 1987). I have also learnt of the existence of R. E. Shimp, 'The Parliament of 1625' (Ohio State University Ph.D, 1970) which I have not seen.

Church policies in the 1630s

Most works of importance on this topic are referred to in the notes which accompany the article. H. Trevor-Roper's *Archbishop Laud*, (1940, 2nd edn 1962), remains the standard biography and we await C. Carlton's study with interest. In the meantime, the article by J. Sears McGee, 'William Laud and the outward face of religion', in R. DeMolen, (ed.) *Leaders of the Reformation* (London and Toronto, 1984), 318–44 deserves to be widely read, Patrick Collinson, *The Religion of Protestants*, (Oxford, 1982) is essential background reading even though it does not explicitly cover this period. Dewey Wallace Jnr, *Puritans and Predestination: Grace in English Protestant Theology, 1525–1695* (Chapel Hill, 1982) is an interesting survey, but it has probably now been largely superseded by the appearance of Nicholas Tyacke's *magnum opus, Anti-Calvinists: The Rise of English Arminianism c. 1590–1640* (Oxford, 1987). Much can be gained from chapters in local studies like: A. Fletcher, *A County Community in Peace and War: Sussex 1600–1660* (1975); J. Evans, *Seventeenth-Century Norwich* (Oxford, 1979); J. Morrill, *Cheshire 1630–1660* (Oxford, 1974); Clive Holmes, *Seventeenth Century Lincolnshire*, (Lincoln, 1980); and P. Clark, *English Provincial Society from the Reformation to the Revolution* (Hassocks, 1977). Although my article stresses the contribution of the Arminians to the Civil War, it is important not to neglect the other side, on which W. Hunt, *The Puritan Moment: the Coming of Revolution in an English County* (Cambridge, Mass., 1983) is useful, if flawed. Likewise, we have the excellent *Wallington's World: a Puritan Artisan in Seventeenth Century London*, by P. Seaver (Stanford, 1985). For those who want to find out more about Arminius see: C. Bangs, *Arminius: A Study in the Dutch Reformation* (Nashville, 1971). For excellent material on English Arminians at Cambridge in the 1590s see: H. Porter, *Reformation and Reaction in Tudor Cambridge* (Cambridge, 1958) and P. Lake, *Moderate Puritans and the Elizabethan Church* (Cambridge, 1982). R. Richardson, *Puritanism in North-West England: a Regional Study of the Diocese of Chester to 1642* (Manchester, 1972) remains a sound diocesan study, but great care must be exercised with the useful sounding, M. Stieg, *Laud's Laboratory: the Diocese of Bath and Wells in the Early Seventeenth Century*, (Lewisburg, 1982).

Local history and the origins of the Civil War

The most influential work on the 'county community' and the Civil War has been by Alan Everitt: his arguments are stated briefly in *The Local Community and the Great Rebellion* (Historical Association Pamphlet, 1969), and elaborated in his full-length study, *The Community of Kent and the Great Rebellion* (Leicester, 1966). John Morrill, *Cheshire 1630–1660: County Government and Society During the English Revolution* (Oxford, 1974), and Anthony Fletcher, *A County Community in Peace and War: Sussex 1600–1660* (1975) are the most wide-ranging and important county studies for this period. They draw on Everitt's approach without accepting it completely. Clive Holmes, 'The County Community in Stuart Historiography', *JBS*, vol. 19, (1980) is a general critique of Everitt; Ann Hughes, *Politics, Society and Civil War in Warwickshire 1620–1660* (Cambridge, 1987) presents some of the arguments of this essay in more detail.

John Morrill *The Revolt of the Provinces* (1976) is an account of the personal rule and the parliamentarian war effort in the 1640s, which emphasizes the 'localism' of the provinces; Ronald Hutton,

The Royalist War Effort (1982) is a parallel study of the relationship between the King's forces and the localities; Clive Holmes, *The Eastern Association in the English Civil War* (Cambridge, 1974) and Ann Hughes, 'The King, the Parliament and the localities', *JBS*, vol. 24 (1985) draw different conclusions about the balance between local and national concerns.

Imaginative attempts to analyse the complex inter-relationships between the English provinces and the kingdom as a whole include Victor Morgan, 'The cartographic image of the country in early modern England', *TRHS*, 5th ser., vol. 29 (1979) and Richard Cust and Peter Lake, 'Sir Richard Grosvenor and the Rhetoric of Magistracy', *BIHR*, 54 (1981).

Finally, David Underdown's book *Revel, Riot and Rebellion: Popular Politics and Culture in England 1603–1660* (Oxford, 1985) should have a profound influence on the ways local and regional historians think about politics in the seventeenth century, and the connections between politics and other aspects of life. We may not agree with Underdown's conclusions (see the debate between Underdown and Morrill in 'The ecology of allegiance', *JBS*, 26 (1987), 451–79, for some matters in dispute) but further exploration of the issues he raises should lead to more sophisticated and satisfying analyses of the Civil War, firmly rooted in local realities.

Notes on Contributors

Thomas Cogswell: Assistant Professor at the University of Kentucky, Dr Cogswell is the author of *The Blessed Revolution: English Politics and the Coming of War, 1621–1624* (Cambridge, forthcoming) and several articles on diplomacy and domestic politics. He is presently working on a study of war and Parliament in early Stuart England.

Richard Cust: Lecturer in Modern History at the University of Birmingham, Dr Cust's publications include *The Forced Loan and English Politics 1626–1628* (Oxford, 1987). He is currently working on the political culture of the Jacobean gentry.

Andrew Foster: Senior Lecturer in History at West Sussex Institute of Higher Education, Dr Foster has published several articles on early modern ecclesiastical and regional history. He studied history at The University of Kent before moving to Balliol College, Oxford where he undertook research on Archbishop Richard Neile and the Arminians.

Ann Hughes: Lecturer in History at the University of Manchester (previously a research assistant at the Open University), Dr Hughes' publications include *Politics, Society and Civil War in Warwickshire 1620–1660* (Cambridge, 1987). She is currently working on religious disputes during the interregnum.

Peter Lake: Lecturer in History at Royal Holloway and Bedford New College, Dr Lake's publications include *Moderate Puritans and the Elizabethan Church* (Cambridge, 1982) and *Anglicans and Puritans?* (London, 1988). He is currently working on different visions of the ministry from 1560 to 1660, and conformist thought from Hooker to Laud.

Johann Sommerville: currently a Research Associate at Sheffield University, working on the Hartlib project, Dr Sommerville has recently been appointed Visiting Assistant Professor at the University of Wisconsin-Madison. His publications include *Politics and Ideology in England, 1603–1640* (London, 1986).

Christopher Thompson: Now a Research Consultant, Christopher Thompson studied and taught Modern History at Oxford University. His most recent publication is *Walter Yonge's Diary of Proceedings in the House of Commons 1642–1645*.

Index